INTRODUCTION TO

MUSICOLOGY

INTRODUCTION TO
MUSICOLOGY

A SURVEY of the FIELDS, SYSTEM-ATIC & HISTORICAL, of MUSICAL KNOWLEDGE & RESEARCH

by

GLEN HAYDON

PROFESSOR OF MUSIC
UNIVERSITY OF NORTH CAROLINA

Chapel Hill
THE UNIVERSITY OF NORTH CAROLINA PRESS

Chapel Hill

Printed in the United States of America

The University of North Carolina Press

To
OTTO KINKELDEY

PREFACE

T O THOSE WHO WISH TO BROADEN THEIR UNDERSTANDING of music by surveying the fields, both systematic and historical, of musical knowledge and research, the present work offers information not usually covered in the musician's technical training [1] and presents a survey of these fields as a whole.

Inevitably, the greater the area surveyed, the more superficial the treatment. But loss in depth is in some measure compensated; the synoptic view avoids the errors arising from "not being able to see the woods for the trees." It may not be possible to see both at once. Particular experience is a matter of immediate awareness; generic concepts result from later reflection and interpretation. Yet musicians may attain some happy balance between immediate awareness, rich in content but without depth, and abstract concepts, full of depth but without content. Some such balance is necessary for a well-rounded philosophy of music.

As a research subject, *musicology* properly belongs in the graduate field; but, as the broad systematization of musical knowledge, an introductory course in musicology belongs among the undergraduate studies of every music student. Many reasons support this conclusion. First, every musician should have some fundamental knowledge of acoustics, psy-

---

[1] This refers particularly to the chapters on *acoustics, physiology* and *psychology,* and *aesthetics.*

chophysiology, and aesthetics in relation to music; and, second, he should have some insight into the principles underlying his practical and theoretical courses in music. Musicology may enable the student to synthesize the knowledge acquired in his other courses in music and to lay the foundations for a broad philosophy of music. Furthermore, it may give him orientation in the extensive literature of music that should be invaluable for his future development regardless of what particular career in music he follows.

*   *   *

For his first acquaintance with the term *musicology*, the author is indebted to a music teacher of his high school days, James D. Murphy, who presented him a little book entitled *Musicology*, by Maurice S. Logan.[2] For his first formal course in musicology and for the stimulation of an enduring interest in the subject, he is under obligation to Charles Louis Seeger, formerly Professor of Music at the University of California.[3]

The present book is the outgrowth of the author's "special studies" seminar in musicology at the University of California and of his course "Introduction to Musicology" given during the past seven years at the University of North Carolina. The author is indebted to those students and colleagues, too numerous to be mentioned here by name, who have encour-

---

[2] New York: Hinds, Noble & Eldredge, 1909. The object of this work, as stated in the preface, is "to furnish a practical and comprehensive textbook on the theory and philosophy of music, for schools and for general use." It deals chiefly with the theory of music in a narrow sense — the *rudiments of music, harmony, counterpoint,* and *form* — and has sections devoted to *acoustics* and the *history of the scale.*

[3] To the author's knowledge, the first formal course in musicology offered in an American university was a course, "Introduction to Musicology," given by Professor Charles Seeger at the University of California in the academic year 1917–18. The author was a member of that class and still has his lecture notes. Professor Seeger left the University at the end of the year and the course was not repeated. *Cf. University of California Register 1916–17,* Part II, *Announcement of Courses for 1917–18,* page 200.

aged and aided him in preparing the manuscript — many no doubt unaware of any influence on the writer.

Among European musicologists and musicians who have been directly helpful are Edward Dent, Donald Francis Tovey, Reverend Edmund Horace Fellowes, C. H. Kitson, R. O. Morris, and Dom Anselm Hughes, in England; Knud Jeppesen, in Copenhagen; Robert Lach, Robert Haas, Alfred Orel, Egon Wellesz, and Guido Adler, in Vienna; and André Pirro and Eugène Cools, in Paris.

The author, of course, is responsible for the views expressed; but he feels that some passages, obscure in their original form, have been improved as a result of the criticisms, and that certain inaccuracies have been avoided through the kindness of those who have read portions of the manuscript. An expression of deep appreciation is accordingly extended to each of the following: Professor Paul E. Shearin, of the Department of Physics; Professor John F. Dashiell, of the Department of Psychology; Professor Helmut Kuhn, of the Department of Philosophy; Professor Arthur M. Jordan, of the Department of Education; and Professor Jan Philip Schinhan, of the Department of Music. The author is also indebted to Professor J. O. Bailey, of the Department of English, for stylistic suggestions; to Mrs. J. Arthur Branch, for technical assistance in preparing the manuscript; and to his wife and family for their continual encouragement and help.

The author, finally, is grateful to the following publishers and authors for permission to quote from their publications, each of which is duly cited in the course of the text:

Thomas Y. Crowell Company, New York: David W. Prall, *Aesthetic Analysis.*

Henry Holt & Company, Inc., New York: Robert S. Woodworth, *Experimental Psychology.*

Houghton Mifflin Company, Boston: John F. Dashiell, *Fundamentals of General Psychology.*

PREFACE

Liveright Publishing Corporation, New York: Maurice Mandelbaum, *The Problem of Historical Knowledge.*

The Macmillan Company, New York: John Dewey, *Democracy and Education.*

W. W. Norton & Company, Inc., New York: James L. Mursell, *The Psychology of Music.*
Paul Bekker, *The Story of Music.*

Prentice-Hall, Inc., New York: Harold N. Lee, *Perception and Aesthetic Value.*

Princeton University Press, Princeton: Theodore M. Greene, *The Arts and the Art of Criticism.*
Theodore M. Greene (Editor), *The Meaning of the Humanities.*

Charles Scribner's Sons, New York: Stephen C. Pepper, *Aesthetic Quality.*

GLEN HAYDON

Chapel Hill, North Carolina

CONTENTS

CONTENTS

INTRODUCTION TO
MUSICOLOGY

Chapter I

INTRODUCTION

MUSICOLOGY IS THAT BRANCH OF LEARNING WHICH concerns the discovery and systematization of knowledge concerning music. But, as all knowledge depends on direct awareness, intuition (or, as the philosopher might say, perceptual intuition), and reflection, so musicology depends on direct musical experience or an immediate sensitivity to musical values, and the application of scientific methods in the discovery and organization of whatever we may think we can know about music. Every trained musician knows a good deal about music, has a more or less well-organized, systematic knowledge of music; but we do not ordinarily regard him as a musicologist unless he devotes himself particularly, through the application of scientific methods, to the advancement of our knowledge concerning music. Musicology is, then, the field of musical research, the careful or critical inquiry or examination in seeking facts or principles concerning music.[1] Thus, by no means everything written about music qualifies as musicological literature, but only that which exhibits an acceptable quality of scholarship.

In a sense, then, musicology is the science of music. But the application of the word *science* to an art has given rise

---

[1] Since the 1934 edition *Webster's New International Dictionary* has the definition of musicology: "Music as a branch of knowledge or field of investigation; . . ."

to many misunderstandings; hence it seems necessary to consider, briefly, the relation of art and science.

ART AND SCIENCE

If we accept the classic dictum of Jevons, "A science teaches us to know and an art to do," [2] there seem to be no very real grounds for confusion about the relation of musicology to music. The art of music concerns the activities of composition, performance, and listening to music; and the science of music concerns musical knowledge. Emphatically, this distinction entails a complementary, not an opposed, relationship between art and science. It is well to remember that the art of musical composition is based upon the scientific knowledge of music; and conversely, that the successful prosecution of a research project not only usually demands sensitivity to the art of music, but is also an art in itself.

That the art and science of music are complementary may be made clearer by means of an example. Suppose we consider the work of the conductor of a symphony orchestra. The performance of music is primarily an art, but it is based upon, and supported by, a great deal of systematized technical knowledge which is scientific in character. This systematized knowledge, to be exact, depends upon and implies the careful investigation which is ordinarily called research. And, in a narrow sense, as science means research in any given field, so musicology means research in the field of music.

If, in a rehearsal, the conductor stops the orchestra and says, "The oboe A in bar seventeen is flat," he is calling attention to an element in the performance that tends to destroy the work of art. His sensing that something is wrong in bar seventeen involves his artistic judgment; but, in correcting the flaw, he draws upon his scientific knowledge of acoustics,

---

[2] W. Stanley Jevons, *Elementary Lessons in Logic*, page 7. New Edition. New York: The Macmillan Company, 1914.

orchestration, and the like. And, again, an apparently wrong note in the score may lead to an extended search through first editions and original manuscripts — an investigation that is essentially scientific in character, that requires the safeguards of scientific methodology to insure the accuracy and dependability of the results.

If the general distinction between art and science is kept in mind, there should be no serious confusion as to the relation of the artist to the musicologist. The artist is concerned primarily with composition or performance; the musicologist, with research. A composer or performer may devote some of his time to research, and, vice versa, a musicologist may compose or perform music. Such composers as Berlioz, Strauss, Rimsky-Korsakov, d'Indy, Busoni, and Hindemith have written scholarly works about music; and such scholars as Riemann, Tovey, Parry, and Jeppesen have been active as composers. Occasionally a man, such as Egon Wellesz, has gained almost equal distinction in both fields.

Similar reasoning may be applied, *mutatis mutandis*, to the teaching profession. The teacher may be a musical performer, composer, or research worker; or he may be something of each. He may be concerned primarily with teaching as an art, that is, with actively teaching students music; or he may be chiefly interested in research in the field of musical pedagogy; or, as frequently happens, he may divide his time among the various types of activity mentioned. The important point to realize, for present purposes, is that, although it is possible to emphasize one or another among the several activities, it is much more desirable to understand that they are fundamentally complementary.[3]

---

[3] The term *science* is commonly used in a still narrower sense to apply to such natural sciences as physics, chemistry, and biology as well as to mathematics; but it is not, primarily, in this sense that we use the word when we speak of musicology as the *science of music*. In England there has been a marked tendency to use the phrase "science of music" to refer

INTRODUCTION

THE HISTORY OF MUSICOLOGY

The science of music is coeval with the art of music.[4] There can be no art of music without some system, however naïve, for the organization of tonal relations within the work of art. In the early stages of the art, science is concerned chiefly with the organization of tones with respect to pitch. Thus, in the history of music in Western Europe, Pythagoras (sixth century B.C.) may be regarded as the first musicologist,[5] in that he worked out a mathematical-acoustical basis for the measurement and comparison of intervals.

In the centuries following, Greek philosophers and theorists worked out increasingly comprehensive systems of musical knowledge until, in about the second century of the Christian era, Aristides Quintilianus presented a system which may be outlined as on the opposite page.[6]

---

especially to physical acoustics and, to some extent, to physiology and psychology as related to music. This practice, in conjunction with the apparent aversion among some English scholars to the word *musicology* which causes them to translate the German *Musikwissenschaft* as *musical science*, has led to certain incongruities of style, if not to direct misunderstandings. For example, the new supplementary volume of *Grove's Dictionary of Music and Musicians*, although it has an extensive article on "Musicology," frequently goes out of the way, in other articles, to use the phrase "musical science" instead of "musicology" for the German *Musikwissenschaft* — with attendant inconsistency of style, if not ambiguity of meaning.

[4] *Cf.* Guido Adler, "Umfang, Methode und Ziel der Musikwissenschaft," *Vierteljahrsschrift für Musikwissenschaft*, Vol. I (1885), page 5.

[5] See Otto Kinkeldey, article on "Musicology" in *The International Cyclopedia of Music and Musicians*, page 1220.

[6] Marcus Meibom (Meibomius), *Antiquae musicae auctores septem*, Vol. II, pages 7 f. Amstelodami: apud Ludovicum Elzevirium, 1652. For further discussion of the system, see Rudolf Schäfke, *Aristeides Quintilianus, Von der Musik*, pages 66 f. and 167 f. (Berlin-Schöneberg: Max Hesses Verlag, 1937); Fr. Aug. Gevaert, *Histoire et théorie de la musique de l'antiquité*, Vol. I, pages 69–76 *et passim* (Gand: C. Annoot-Braeckman, 1875); Rudolf Westphal, *Die Musik des griechischen Alterthumes*, pages 251–254 (Leipzig: Von Veit & Comp., 1883); and Egon Wellesz, "Musicology," in *Grove's Dictionary of Music and Musicians*, Supplementary Volume, page 456.

INTRODUCTION

I. Theoretical part: θεωρητικόν (*theoretikón*)
  A. Physical or scientific section: φυσικόν (*physikón*)
    1. Arithmetic: ἀριθμητικόν (*arithmetikón*)
    2. Physics: φυσικόν (*physikón*)
  B. Technical section: τεχνικόν (*technikón*)
    1. Harmony: ἁρμονικόν (*harmonikón*)
    2. Rhythm: ῥυθμικόν (*rhythmikón*)
    3. Meter: μετρικόν (*metrikón*)
II. Practical part: πρακτικόν (*praktikón*)
  A. Section on composition: χρηστικόν (*chrestikón*)
    1. Melodic composition: μελοποιΐα (*melopoiía*)
    2. Rhythmic composition: ῥυθμοποιΐα (*rhythmo-poiía*)
    3. Composition of poetry: ποίησις (*poíesis*)
  B. Section on execution: ἐξαγγελτικόν (*exangeltikón*)
    1. Instrumental performance: ὀργανικόν (*organikón*)
    2. Vocal performance: ᾠδικόν (*odikón*)
    3. Dramatic performance: ὑποκριτικόν (*hypokritikón*)

The comprehensiveness of the system, and the detailed thoroughness of the accompanying discussion by Aristides reveal a remarkable insight into some of the problems involved in the organization of musical knowledge. Notably lacking is the historical approach.

In the subsequent centuries of the Christian era we find numerous theoretical writings on music that attempt some systematization of musical knowledge. Boethius (d. *c.* 524) divides music into *musica mundana, musica humana,* and *musica quae in quibusdam constituta est instrumentis;* and includes music in the *quadrivium,* the four branches of mathematical learning — arithmetic, geometry, astronomy, and music. Cassiodorus (d. *c.* 580) treats of music under the fol-

[5]

lowing divisions: *scientia harmonica, rhythmica, et metrica;* and is the model for such later theorists as Isidore of Seville (*c.* 570–636), Alcuin (753–804), and Aurelian of Réomé (ninth century).[7]

In general, the writers of the various periods reflect the philosophies of the ages they represent, whether scholastic, empiristic, rational, or what not. In many of the writings, discussions of problems of practical musical instruction are intermixed with theoretical speculations in an exceedingly unsystematic manner. The historical viewpoint is notably absent throughout the Middle Ages, and it was not until the seventeenth and eighteenth centuries that historical treatises began to appear in increasing numbers.[8] Finally, in 1885, Guido Adler incorporated both the systematic and historical viewpoints in a comprehensive statement of the scope, method, and aim of musicology.[9] The two views are likewise incorporated into the subsequent treatises on musicology by Hugo Riemann,[10] Ludwig Schiedermair,[11] and Fritz Volbach,[12] although, to be sure, with striking differences in emphasis and treatment of detail.

---

[7] For further details concerning Mediaeval, Renaissance, and later theorists and their relation to musicology, see especially: Egon Wellesz, *op. cit.,* pages 456 ff; Gustave Reese, *Music in the Middle Ages,* pages 117–127 (New York: W. W. Norton & Company, Inc., 1940); Wilhelm Fischer, "Musikwissenschaft," Adler's *Handbuch der Musikgeschichte,* Vol. II, pages 1234 ff. For comment on the relation of some of these writers to mediaeval learning and literature, see Loren C. MacKinney, *The Medieval World,* pages 261–273 (New York: Farrar & Rinehart, Inc., 1938).

[8] See Warren D. Allen, "History of Music Histories," *Philosophies of Music History,* Part I. New York: American Book Company, 1939.

[9] "Umfang, Methode und Ziel der Musikwissenschaft," *Vierteljahrsschrift für Musikwissenschaft,* Vol. I (1885), pages 5–20. Adler gives an outline of his system of musicology in his *Methode der Musikgeschichte,* page 7 (Leipzig: Breitkopf & Härtel, 1919). The outline is reproduced in English in the article "On Behalf of Musicology" by Waldo S. Pratt, *The Musical Quarterly,* Vol. I (1915), page 2, and by Egon Wellesz in the article "Musicology" in *Grove's Dictionary of Music and Musicians,* Suppl. Vol., page 461.

[10] *Grundriss der Musikwissenschaft.*

[11] *Einführung in das Studium der Musikgeschichte.*

[12] *Handbuch der Musikwissenschaften.*

Throughout the Middle Ages, music occupied a place in the *quadrivium,* or higher studies, of the "seven liberal arts" — at first in the monastic and cathedral schools and later in the universities. Many distinguished musical theorists held important posts at various universities during the period. After the sixteenth century, although the study of musical theory continued in the English universities, chairs of music were generally discontinued on the Continent, not to be reestablished until the late nineteenth and early twentieth centuries. At the present time, most of the better-known European universities include musicology in the curriculum, and in the United States a number of the more important universities are offering formal graduate courses in the various fields of musical research.[13]

THE SYSTEMATIZATION OF MUSICAL KNOWLEDGE

The whole history of science and philosophy exhibits the constant tendency to organize knowledge, and the more comprehensive and coherent the systematization of the facts and relations involved, the more adequate and useful the knowledge. The concepts of space and time afford the most fundamental axes for the orientation of knowledge and experience. As a particular note in a musical composition becomes significant in relation to other notes sounded at the same time, and to those that have occurred before as well as in anticipation of those to come, so, at various levels of complexity, particular experience becomes meaningful in relation to simultaneously existing facts and appropriate generic concepts, and to the course of history in which it is significantly embedded. Therefore musicology, following the lead of philosophy, adopts the epistemological concepts of space and time, and divides its subject matter under the two main headings *systematic* and *historical.*

---

[13] See footnote 3: *Preface,* page viii.

The understanding of a particular composition may be said to depend on a comprehension of what it is in itself and in relation to other similar and contrasting, contemporary style-types. This is systematic knowledge. But it can scarcely be separated from the complementary knowledge, that of understanding this particular composition in its historical perspective. Thus, we conceive of understanding as a knowledge of relations in a two-dimensional frame of reference.

The philosopher sometimes calls the *systematic* viewpoint the *philosophical*. For example, Greene speaks of the humanistic ideal as a "historico-philosophical synthesis." [14] In one passage, Greene writes: [15]

But there are two, and only two, basic modes of interpretation, the historical, in terms of temporal sequence, and the systematic, in terms of more enduring quality and structure.

On the following page, he sounds a warning against over-specialization, and adds:

Cultural, *i.e.*, historical and philosophical, synthesis, in a word, is imperative if society is to achieve spiritual unity and if men and women are to enjoy a rich and meaningful existence.

The systematic approach to musical knowledge is also sometimes very appropriately referred to as the *comparative* approach. For example, Charles Seeger, in a paper read at the annual meeting of the American Musicological Society, Philadelphia, 1935,[16] uses the terms *comparative* and *systematic* interchangeably. But the term *comparative musicology* has long been used, in a narrow sense, to denote that special branch of musicology which concerns the study of folk music and non-European musical systems, and it is in this sense that we use the term in the present work. In so doing,

---

[14] Theodore Meyer Greene (Editor), *The Meaning of the Humanities*, page xxxiii. Princeton: Princeton University Press, 1938.
[15] *Ibid.*
[16] "Systematic and Historical Orientations in Musicology," published in *Acta musicologica*, Vol. XI (1939), pages 121–128.

however, we do not mean that the use of comparison should be limited to that field, for the comparative approach may be used advantageously throughout both the systematic and historical fields.

Although for purposes of study we divide musicology into *systematic* and *historical* parts, it is important to keep constantly in mind that the two divisions of musical knowledge and research are complementary. Just as every historical study has its systematic implications, so, conversely, every systematic inquiry has its historical orientation. Historians survey the past in terms of systematic strands of events; philosophers survey the present in the light of history.

The task of musicology can never be completed; its goal cannot be attained. It must deal with a living art — with a constantly changing complex of variables — and yet, within the historico-systematic frame of reference we correlate such knowledge as may be gathered.

THE SYSTEMATIC ORIENTATION

The subdivisions of systematic musicology are based on both logic and convenience. The various auxiliary sciences which contribute to our knowledge and understanding of music are aligned as follows: (1) *acoustics*, which attempts the descriptive analysis of music in its physical nature; (2) *psychophysiology*, which treats of problems related to music as a phase of man's behavior; (3) *aesthetics*, which concerns questions of value in music; (4) *pedagogy*, which treats of problems of music education; and (5) *anthropology*, which deals with music as an element in the sociocultural make-up of the various peoples of the world. These sciences all contribute, each in its own characteristic way, to the more intrinsically musical science of *music theory*, which is the direct study of the work of art itself.

In spite of some overlapping, each of these fields affords a fairly well-defined and extensive literature of particular interest to musicology. It is therefore convenient as well as logical to subdivide systematic musicology according to the foregoing alignment of auxiliary sciences. The chapter in this book on "The Theory of Music Theory," as one branch of *applied* musical aesthetics, quite naturally and logically follows the chapter on "Musical Aesthetics." With this one exception, the subdivisions of systematic musicology are all closely related to the respective allied sciences.

Music theory is, in a sense, the principal section of systematic musicology. Dealing directly with the work of art, and leaning heavily upon all the auxiliary sciences, it attempts the descriptive analysis, if not the explanation, of the musical composition in technical terms.

Partly because the fundamental technical subject matter of this field is extensively covered in numerous formal courses in the curriculum, the subject of music theory does not receive a more extensive treatment in the present work. The same is largely true of music education. But acoustics, psycho-physiology, and aesthetics are not, ordinarily, a part of either the general musician's training or the formal school or college curriculum in music. Therefore, in the present volume, relatively more attention is paid to the content-material of these subjects.

The Historical Orientation

History offers one of the two basic ways of interpreting the experience of the individual in relation to that of the race, and in relation to the realities with which he has to deal. In musicology, this generalization means that the historical mode of interpretation, in terms of temporal sequence, supplements the systematic, in terms of quality and structure. The systematic and historical approaches constitute the two axes in the frame of reference in relation to which musical intelligence is oriented. The two approaches are, of course, complementary; the one cannot be maintained without reference to the other. Throughout our discussion of systematic musicology we constantly refer to the historical viewpoint, broadly conceived, whether by reference to the temporal nature of a melody or to the long-term processes of habituation in the formation of musical taste. The individual item of musical experience, whether scale, folk song, or symphony, can be illuminated for human intelligence only by being placed in the proper historical as well as systematic frame of reference. To determine what constitutes the proper frame of reference is naturally a fundamental concern of musicology.

That part of the present volume which concerns historical musicology attempts no account of the history of music; such content-material is the proper province of the usual courses in that subject. It deals, rather, with the theories, sources, problems, and methods basic to research and interpretation in the realm of musical history.

Musicology and the Student

The primary concern of the great majority of musicians is, undoubtedly, musical performance; the number of musicians who devote much time to composition, or writing about music, is relatively small. The preparation for performance means, primarily, the study of a musical instrument. Yet the training in the theory and history of music required in college and conservatory curricula is essential to intelligent musicianship. The extent to which this desired ideal is realized in the life of the individual student is directly proportional to the depth and spread of his insight into the nature and meaning of music, in all its complexity, from the highly specialized musical-technical aspects to the broad sociocultural implications. The development of perspective comes not only from experience, but also from reflection upon the relations involved in any situation or subject matter.

The foregoing discussion suggests one of the primary functions of an introductory course in musicology on the undergraduate level. Most students do not pursue their studies in music in the graduate field; they are not interested in, and in many instances not especially qualified to do, research work. Nevertheless, it is important that every musician should attain some synthesis of the somewhat disparate knowledge acquired through his studies in musical performance, theory, and history; and that he should develop what may be fittingly called, in a broad sense, a well-rounded philosophy of music.

The *Introduction to Musicology* is designed to assist the student of music in broadening his horizons and in gaining a synoptic view of the basic approaches to musical knowledge. It offers not so much a course in musical research as a survey of the fields in which scientific investigations have been carried on. The distinction needs to be stressed, for, although it is important that every musician have a sympathetic orientation in the meaning, scope, problems, and methods of musicology, it is not important that he be active personally in research. The essential thing is that he be able to make intelligent use of the fruits of research in his musical life.

We must constantly remind ourselves that *musicology* means, on the one hand, *the systematization of musical knowledge;* and on the other, *research in the field of music.* Although a person steeped in musical knowledge might very properly be called a musicologist, the term ordinarily refers to a research worker in the field. Herein lies the general distinction between undergraduate and graduate study: graduate work concerns not only knowledge, but especially the advancement of knowledge; and the further we go in the graduate field, the greater the emphasis on research.

INTRODUCTION

The value to the student of an introductory course in musicology lies not merely in the factual knowledge gained of subjects not ordinarily covered in other courses, not merely in the broad survey of the literature in the several fields, and certainly not in any specific formulae for the solution of this, that, or the other problem in music — but especially in the development of sound points of view that will enable him to see particular problems in true perspective and to seek answers in the light of properly oriented, well-established principles. In short, its chief value may be in the cultivation of the capacity to think — to consider impersonally, dispassionately, and without prejudice, any problem related to the art of music. One of its major goals is the acquirement of an objective, inquiring, and intelligent attitude.

MUSICOLOGY AND THE MUSIC CURRICULUM

Musicology, as systematized knowledge concerning music, is taught in every course in the music curriculum. A course in harmony attempts the systematization of knowledge within a certain area; a course in the history of music, in another; and even a course in applied music — such as instruction in piano, which we ordinarily think of in a very different sense — among other things, actually embodies a certain systematization of knowledge. The introductory, survey course in musicology differs from these courses in that it attempts a synthesis of all musical knowledge with particular emphasis on content in those divisions not ordinarily covered in formal courses. If, in any particular institution, a special, formal course in acoustics is included in the music curriculum, the subject of acoustics would naturally be treated more concisely in the survey course in musicology. The chapter on acoustics in the present work, treated in more detail, might serve as the basis of the special course in acoustics. The same applies, with necessary changes, to each of the subsequent chapters. Courses in the theory of music and in the philosophy of music history would, of course, naturally tend to be in the graduate field.

A Note of Warning

The reader is warned against assuming that the relative importance of the several subdivisions of musicology is in direct proportion to the amount of space devoted to each in the present book. Although it is impossible, if not pointless, to give the various subjects definite relative values, we are undoubtedly justified in juxtaposing *theory* with *history* in the systematic and historical framework, and in placing *acoustics, psychophysiology,* and *aesthetics* in the category of auxiliary science. This leaves musical pedagogy and comparative musicology as important practical divisions of systematic musicology, each with numerous characteristic articulations to the systematic field.[17]

Bibliography

Abert, Hermann, "Kunst, Kunstwissenschaft, und Kunstkritik," *Gesammelte Schriften und Vorträge von Hermann Abert,* pages 548–561. Edited by Friedrich Blume. Halle: Max Niemeyer, 1929.

————, "Musikwissenschaft," *Illustriertes Musik-Lexikon,* page 316.

Adler, Guido, "Musik und Musikwissenschaft," *Jahrbuch der Musikbibliothek Peters,* Vol. V (1898), pages 27–39.

————, "Umfang, Methode und Ziel der Musikwissenschaft," *Vierteljahrsschrift für Musikwissenschaft,* Vol. I (1885), pages 5–20.

---

[17] The reader may be interested in comparing this arrangement of the systematic section of musicology with that of Guido Adler (given in *Grove's Dictionary of Music and Musicians,* Supplementary Volume, page 461). *Cf.* also, Waldo Selden Pratt, "On Behalf of Musicology," *The Musical Quarterly,* Vol. I (1915), pages 1–16.

Bücken, Ernst, "Die Musikerziehung auf der Universität," *Handbuch der Musikerziehung*, pages 317–325. Edited by Ernst Bücken. Potsdam: Akademische Verlagsgesellschaft Athenaion, m.b.H., 1931.

Chrysander, Friedrich, "Vorwort und Einleitung," *Jahrbücher für musikalische Wissenschaft*, Vol. I (1863), pages 9–16.

Cohn, A. W., "Die Erkenntnis der Tonkunst," *Zeitschrift für Musikwissenschaft*, Vol. I (1918–19), pages 351–360.

Fischer, Wilhelm, "Musikwissenschaft," Guido Adler's *Handbuch der Musikgeschichte*, Vol. II, pages 1233–1240.

Haydon, Glen, "Musicology in the College and University Curricula," *Music Educators National Conference Yearbook*, Vol. XXX (1939–40), pages 414–416.

Kinkeldey, Otto, "American Higher Music Education Compared With That in Europe," *Volume of Proceedings of the Music Teachers National Association*, Twenty-Ninth Series (1934), pages 20–28.

——, "Chánging Relations Within the Field of Musicology," *Volume of Proceedings of the Music Teachers National Association*, Thirty-First Series (1936), pages 246–261.

——, "Musicology," *The International Cyclopedia of Music and Musicians*, pages 1218–1221.

——, "Musicology in American Colleges and Universities," *Yearbook of the Music Educators National Conference*, Twenty-Seventh Year (1934), pages 125–131.

——, "The Preparation of the College Music Student for Graduate Study," *Volume of Proceedings of the Music Teachers National Association*, Twenty-Ninth Series (1934), pages 165–170.

Kretzschmar, Hermann, "Kurze Betrachtungen über den Zweck, die Entwicklung und die nächsten Zukunftsaufgaben der Musikhistorie," *Jahrbuch der Musikbibliothek Peters*, Vol. XIV (1907), pages 83–96.

Láng, Paul H., "The Place of Musicology in the College Curriculum," *Volume of Proceedings of the Music Teachers National Association*, Twenty-Ninth Series (1934), pages 144–149.

Moser, H. J., "Musikwissenschaft," *Musik-Lexikon*, pages 549–552.

Ortmann, Otto, "The Contribution of Physiopsychology to Musicology," *Volume of Proceedings of the Music Teachers National Association*, Thirty-First Series (1936), pages 213–217.

INTRODUCTION

Pratt, Waldo S., "On Behalf of Musicology," *The Musical Quarterly*, Vol. I (1915), pages 1–16.

Riemann, Hugo, *Grundriss der Musikwissenschaft*. Fourth edition revised by Johannes Wolf. Leipzig: Quelle & Meyer, 1928.

——, "Musikwissenschaft," *Hugo Riemanns Musik-Lexikon*, pages 1238–1239.

Roberts, Helen H., "The Viewpoint of Comparative Musicology," *Volume of Proceedings of the Music Teachers National Association*, Thirty-First Series (1936), pages 233–238.

Schiedermair, Ludwig, *Einführung in das Studium der Musikgeschichte*. Third Enlarged Edition. Berlin: Ferd. Dümmler, 1930.

Scholes, Percy A., "Musicology," *The Oxford Companion to Music*, pages 601–602.

Seeger, Charles L., "Music and Musicology," *Encyclopaedia of the Social Sciences*, Vol. XI, pages 143–150.

——, "On the Principles of Musicology," *The Musical Quarterly*, Vol. X (1924), pages 244–250.

——, "Systematic and Historical Orientations in Musicology," *Acta musicologica*, Vol. XI (1939), pages 121–128. Abstract in *Bulletin of the American Musicological Society*, No. 1, 1936, page 16.

Smith, Carleton Sprague, "The Service of the Library to Musicology," *Volume of Proceedings of the Music Teachers National Association*, Thirty-First Series (1936), pages 239–245.

Sonneck, O. G., "The Future of Musicology in America," *The Musical Quarterly*, Vol. XV (1929), pages 317–321.

Spivacke, Harold, "The Place of Acoustics in Musicology," *Volume of Proceedings of the Music Teachers National Association*, Thirty-First Series (1936), pages 207–212.

Strunk, W. Oliver, "The Historical Aspect of Musicology," *Volume of Proceedings of the Music Teachers National Association*, Thirty-First Series (1936), pages 218–220.

——, "State and Resources of Musicology in the United States," *American Council of Learned Societies*, Bulletin 19. Washington, 1932.

Volbach, Fritz, *Handbuch der Musikwissenschaften*. 2 vols. Münster i.W.: Aschendorff, 1926, 1930.

Wagner, Peter, "Zur Musikgeschichte der Universität," *Archiv für Musikwissenschaft*, Vol. III (1921), pages 1–16.

INTRODUCTION

Wellesz, Egon, "Die Grundlagen der musikgeschichtlichen Forschung," *Archiv für Musikwissenschaft,* Vol. I (1918–19), pages 437–450.

————, "Musicology," *Grove's Dictionary of Music and Musicians,* Suppl. Vol., pages 455–462.

PART ONE

SYSTEMATIC MUSICOLOGY

Chapter II

ACOUSTICS

THE WORD "ACOUSTICS" IS DERIVED FROM THE GREEK ἀκουστικόν, *pertaining to hearing*, from ἀκούειν, *to hear.* Modern practice more commonly uses the term to refer to the physical aspects of sound.

Thus, in physics, acoustics is defined as *the study of the laws of sound*, or as *the science of sound*, including the production, transmission, and effects of sound. In architecture the term is used chiefly to describe the characteristics of an auditorium with regard to sound. In psychology the emphasis is placed upon the process of hearing itself, upon the perception of sound. Here, the study considers psychophysical and psychophysiological features.

Other distinctions, more or less well defined — such as musical acoustics or physiological acoustics — are possible. In musicology it seems advisable to consider acoustics as a branch of physics dealing primarily with the production and transmission of sound, emphasizing especially phenomena of more or less clearly defined musical import.

The Nature of Sound

The term *sound* is commonly used with two distinct meanings. On the one hand, it refers to an initial physical stimulus and its transmission; on the other hand, to the effects of this stimulus upon the hearing apparatus. The old controversy about whether a falling tree would make a sound if no creature were present to hear it is obviously due to a confusion of definitions. The study of sound, defined in the first sense as *any vibrations capable of being heard*, is the province of physics, and, more particularly, of acoustics as that word is employed in physics. Sound as a sensation is treated in physiology and psychology under such headings as audition and hearing.[1]

The various aspects of sound are so closely interrelated that most textbooks on physics have something to say of hearing, and psychology textbooks usually devote some space to the vibratory motion which produces hearing. Nevertheless, the logical division of the field is clear, and there need be no confusion between physical phenomenon and sensory perception. In musicology, some overlapping of the two fields is inevitable because of the very nature of the problems with which it is concerned. For example, the problem of consonance and dissonance has a place not only in physics and psychology, but also in aesthetics and history.

Vibratory Motion

Physically, sound is produced by vibrations. Every musical instrument is designed to produce vibrations of one type or another under controlled conditions. The vibrations must be within certain limits of frequency, intensity, transmitting medium, and so forth, in order to be characterized as sound, or as the cause of sound. Vibrations that are too slow, too fast, or too weak do not produce sound. The determination of these various limits is one of the problems of acoustics that concerns both physics and psychophysiology.

---

[1] M. Y. Colby (*A College Course in Sound Waves and Acoustics*, page 2) suggests that sound as a sensation may be defined as "an auditory sensation resulting from the action of an external disturbance upon the ear and its associated nerve ending"; and, as a physical phenomenon, as "a physical disturbance (of vibratory character) in an elastic medium which would be capable of producing an auditory sensation if received by an ear."

The Principles of Wave Motion

Sound is transmitted through a medium by means of pulsations called *waves*. To visualize these waves accurately is a task probably beyond the capacity of the human mind. Physicists usually use water waves to give some notion of the action of sound waves, or of wave motion in general.

That a medium such as air or water is necessary for the propagation and transmission of sound waves is commonly demonstrated in experiments by causing a bell to vibrate in a vacuum. The fact that no sound is heard is due, we conclude, to the absence of a medium suitable for transmitting sound waves. When we think of the movement of a wave, we must distinguish carefully between the motion of the medium and the motion of the wave itself. If we look at the waves produced by the wind blowing across a field of grain, this distinction is easily made. The waves move across the field, but the individual stalks of grain simply move to and fro. The movement of sound waves through the air is analogous to this, except that sound waves emanate in all directions from the point of origin.

A convenient way of representing a sound wave graphically is by means of the simple sine curve:

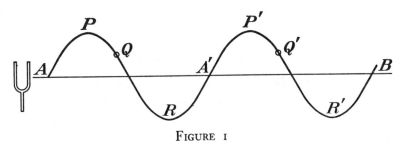

FIGURE I

This may be taken as a representation of the wave set up by the vibration of a tuning fork. The first movement of the prong in the direction from *A* to *B* compresses the air in front of it, producing the condensation *P;* and the movement in the opposite direction thins out the air, producing the rarefaction *R*. The process is repeated by each succeeding vibration of the tuning fork, and a train of similar waves is set up. The curve from *A* to *A'* represents one wave, and the points *A'*, *P'*, *Q'* are points in the same *phase* as the respective points *A, P,* and *Q*. The distance from one compression to the next, or, in general, between any two points in the corresponding phase, is called the *wave length,* and the time involved is called the *period*. This type of motion is called *pendular motion* or *simple harmonic motion*. The measure of the maximum amount of displacement of the vibrating body is called the *amplitude,* and the number of vibrations per second, the *frequency*.

The foregoing is one of the simplest ways of approaching the idea of wave motion. It is not, however, a complete statement of the actual production of sound waves. Normally, when vibrations of the type described occur, they travel outward in all directions from the source, and a moment of reflection will reveal that the process is really much more complicated than the analysis above indicates. Nevertheless, such an exposition is helpful in the study of wave motion in general, and of the transmission of sound waves in a given direction.

GENERAL CHARACTERISTICS OF SOUND

The physical disturbances or pulsations in the air which constitute sound waves have certain characteristics in common. These may be discussed under the headings *velocity, reflection, refraction, diffraction,* and *interference*. Further characteristics of musical sounds will be treated under the headings *frequency, intensity, wave form or overtone structure,* and *duration*.

Velocity

The *velocity* of sound, or the distance traveled in a given direction per unit of time, varies with the medium and with the temperature. While the velocity of sound through air is about 1090 feet per second at the freezing point, at 68° Fahrenheit it is about 1130 feet per second. This accounts, at least in part, for the fact that a wind instrument sounds flat in a cold room. The wave length of the tone depends upon the length of the tube. Since this length remains approximately constant with an increase in temperature, the number of vibrations per second emitted from the tube will be slightly augmented as the temperature of the air within the tube rises. This may be explained by the mathematical formula $n = \dfrac{V}{l}$, in which n is the number of vibrations per second, V is the velocity of sound, and l is the wave length produced by the given length of tube. If l remains constant, n will vary with V. Instruments are made to be in tune at 68° Fahrenheit, normal room temperature; marked deviations in temperature cause many difficulties in any musical performance using wind instruments.

Reflection

When a sound wave or pulsation strikes a wall surface that is large compared to the wave length of the sound, the sound is reflected. The physical basis of this phenomenon is usually explained by Huyghens' principle, which is too complex for the present discussion.[2] For practical purposes we may say that the reflected sound acts as though it emanated from a source the same distance from the wall as the actual point of origin, but on the opposite side of it. The angle of reflection is equal to the angle of incidence and is in the same

[2] For a discussion of Huyghens' principle see G. W. Stewart, *Introductory Acoustics*, pages 36 f.; or Floyd R. Watson, *Sound*, pages 40 ff.

plane. If the wall is perpendicular to the approaching sound a *simple echo* occurs, provided, of course, that the intervening. distance is great enough for the original sound impulse to be distinguished from the reflected impulse. The time necessary for this distinction is about one tenth of a second, and, consequently, the distance is some fifty or sixty feet. If the intervening distance is short, the original pulsations and their reflection are received by the ear as a single impression. This principle is used in the soundboard behind a speaker's rostrum.

Many different types of echo are caused by variations in the character of the reflecting surface. Where there are several reflectors, the result may be a multiple echo. If there is a series of surfaces, as in the open-air Greek theater in Berkeley, California, with its tiers of concrete seats, the sound is so modified that a clap of the hands on the stage comes back as a somewhat musical echo, called by some authorities a *harmonic echo.*

The reflection of sound plays an important role in a number of fields, from the construction of auditoriums to the determination of altitude in aviation. *Reverberation* is the repeated reflection of sound in a room or the persistence of sound in a room after the original sound stimulus has stopped. The *time of reverberation* is the time it takes for a sound impulse to die away to one millionth of its original intensity.[3] *Absorption* refers to the change of acoustic energy into heat energy, often spoken of as a "deadening" effect. The study and understanding of these phases of the reflection problem have made it possible to eliminate many undesirable features and to enhance certain desirable ones in the acoustics of practice rooms, studios, and auditoriums.

Reverberation has the effect of "building up" the intensity of sound. In a recital hall a certain amount of reverberation

[3] See Vern O. Knudsen, *Architectural Acoustics*, page 41.

is desirable; but the optimal reverberation times for music and for speech differ, for the amount of "build-up" that will enhance a musical performance is likely to be too much for the short-timed articulations of speech. Acoustic engineers have so worked out reverberation time formulas for auditoriums that today there is little excuse for auditoriums with insufferably bad acoustic qualities.

REFRACTION

Refraction is the change in the direction of propagation caused by a change in the medium through which the sound wave is traveling. For example, if a sound is traveling along the earth's surface during the heat of day when the strata of air nearer the ground are warmer than those more remote, the sound will be deflected upward because the pulsations travel faster in the warmer medium. This accounts for the fact that sounds cannot be heard at so great a distance during the day as they can at night, when the air is cool near the ground. Refraction also occurs when there is a wind blowing, as the air moves more slowly near the ground. In this situation a sound traveling with the wind tends to "hug" the earth's surface, whereas a sound traveling against the wind is diverted upward and hence is not audible at so great a distance.

DIFFRACTION

Diffraction is the term applied to the action of sound waves in passing around an obstacle so that sound may be distinctly heard on the other side. This "bending" of the sound impulse around an object occurring in its path is usually explained in terms of Huyghens' principle, which states, in substance, that each point in any wave front may be taken as the source of a new impulse that travels outward from this point in the form of a hemispherical wave. In accordance with this principle, we can hear a sound when we cannot see the source — for example, through a window, over a wall, or around a corner.

INTERFERENCE

One of the fundamental teachings of physics is that when two forces in the same line are acting upon a single point, the resultant effect is the algebraic sum of the two forces. If the forces are operating in the same direction, the effect is equal to the sum of the two forces, whereas, if the directions are opposed, the result is equal to the difference between the two forces. The phenomena of *interference* are related to, and depend upon, the operation of this principle. For example, if two waves of the same frequency, and in the same phase, are traveling in the same direction — that is, if the points of maximum and minimum displacement coincide — the resultant is equal to the sum of the two displacements. If, however, the waves are opposed in phase, the one displacement tends to cancel the other, and the total resultant effect is decreased. In either case, this is called *interference*. In practice, the situation becomes very complex and difficult, but interference is a significant factor in acoustics.

RESONANCE

In general, the term *resonance*, or sympathetic vibration, is applied to the stimulation of vibrations in a body by a sound wave from another source. The classic example for the demonstration of this principle is the experiment with two tuning forks of the same frequency. If the one is sounded, and then dampened with the hand, the other "catches up" the sound and continues to vibrate. If the forks are not in tune, the second fork does not respond. The operation of the principle of resonance may be further illustrated by the ringing of a large bell. Even a boy can set in motion a huge bell many times his weight if he tugs at the end of the rope at properly timed intervals. Gradually, the swing of the bell increases until, finally, it is in full motion. If he should apply his weight at the wrong time, the force of the bell might be sufficient to lift him from his feet. But if he should continue to work against the force of the bell, he would soon bring it to rest.

Resonance plays an important part in the construction and operation of most, if not all, musical instruments, as exemplified in the soundboard of the piano, the body of the violin, the tube of the clarinet, and the sound box of the mounted tuning bar, not to mention the "head cavities" in connection with the human voice.

There are two general methods of applying the resonance principle to musical instruments. One is illustrated by the increase of the rate of flow of energy from a fork in the presence of an air column, in a jar or tube of appropriate length. The other is exemplified by the increase of the vibrating surface exposed to the air, as when a vibrating fork is placed on a table top in such a way that the top of the table acts as a resonator, thus communicating more acoustic energy per unit of time to the air than could the fork alone.

Musical Sounds

Sounds are usually classified as tones or as noises. To these a third group is sometimes added — vocables. Regular, comparatively simple, periodic vibrations form the physical basis of tones. A noise is produced by irregular, and relatively complex, vibrations. Vocables are the sounds of speech; they occupy a sort of intermediate position between tones and noises.

The general distinction between tone and noise is clear, but the actual dividing line between them is not so sharp as one might at first think. A close examination will reveal that nearly every sound classified as a musical tone has a certain element of noise as a characteristic part of it; and, conversely, many noises have an easily discernable pitch or tone constituent. For example, a keen ear will detect in the tone of the wind instruments the noise of hissing; in that of the stringed instruments the scraping noise of the bow, the thud of the pianoforte hammer, or the plucking of the harp or pizzicato violin. On the other hand, a tone of well-defined pitch may be detected in the noise of the passing electric train. The point is further illustrated by the classic laboratory experiment with the falling sticks of wood. If a single stick drops to the floor, we would normally refer to the sound as a noise. But, if a series of laths, cut to the proper length, are dropped in succession, the notes of the scale may be clearly discerned. In fact, the xylophone, the orchestra bells, and the celesta are nothing but refined applications of this particular method of producing tones.

German scientists have two words at their disposal to distinguish between simple and complex tones — *Ton* and *Klang*. In English, the word *tone* is applied to both simple and complex sounds of definite frequency. A simple tone, sometimes called a pure tone, is one produced by an instrument giving forth a certain definite number of vibrations per second. A violin string making 440 vibrations per second produces the tone called A. But this A refers only to the "fundamental tone" produced by the vibrations of the string as a whole. As a matter of fact, such a simple transverse motion of the string is exceedingly difficult to produce because the string invariably tends to vibrate in smaller segments of its length at the same time, segments of one half, one third, one fourth, one fifth, and so on. Each of these partial vibrations of the string produces a tone of its own. These tones all tend to fuse with the fundamental, and the total result is what we call the tone of the violin. (There are, of course, other factors entering into the situation which we can, for the moment, ignore.) The tones produced by the partial vibrations are known as *overtones*, or *partials*. The fundamental tone and its partials are called *the harmonic series*.

The Physical Characteristics of Tones

If we analyze the physical nature of a tone, we find that it consists of a certain number of pulsations per second; that these pulsations have a certain extensity, displacement, or amplitude; and that the disturbance as a whole endures for a certain length of time. From these fundamental factors the intensity of the tone may be derived by means of a calculation involving the mass of the vibrating substance and the frequency and amplitude of the pulsations. Furthermore, the total complex disturbance in the medium has a certain structure, or formal organization, which may be represented graphically.

For practical purposes, in relation to music, frequency, intensity, form or overtone structure, and duration may be considered the most important physical characteristics of tone. It is upon these attributes that the psychological factors of pitch, loudness, quality, and duration primarily depend.

Frequency

Frequency may be defined as the number of complete vibrations per second of the vibrating medium. The term *cycle* is commonly used to signify one complete vibration. Some of the factors governing frequency will be discussed in the sections dealing with musical instruments. The relations between the physical characteristics of tone — frequency, intensity, form or overtone structure, and duration — and their psychological correlates — pitch, loudness, quality, and duration — will be discussed in the next chapter. In the sections immediately following we will turn our attention to some mathematical-physical aspects of tonal relations.

THE PHYSICAL BASIS OF PITCH RELATIONSHIPS BETWEEN TONES

Although the discussion of pitch as a sensation properly belongs in the next chapter, certain topics, such as the mathematical-physical relations between the frequencies of tones commonly used in music, naturally fall within the scope of the present chapter. The overlapping of fields is implicit in the situation; hence it is not surprising that textbooks on acoustics take up certain psychological matters, and books on psychology certain physical ones. The physical basis of pitch relationships between tones is but one of many close correlations between different fields.

The relation between the physical and psychological phenomena of intervals has an important bearing upon the selection and organization of musical tones. The frequency ratios that correspond to the musical intervals, according to the ordinary theory of pure intonation, are:

Octave	2:1
Fifth	3:2
Fourth	4:3
Major third	5:4
Minor third	6:5
Major sixth	5:3
Minor sixth	8:5

The interval of the octave, for example, means that the two notes forming this interval have frequencies that stand in the relation of 2 to 1. If a given note a has a frequency of 220, its octave a^1 will have a frequency of 440. Many of the theoretical scales of the past were derived by calculations based upon this principle.

The "scale of Pythagoras" was presumably arrived at by a calculation through the cycle of fifths. But, curiously enough, the twelfth fifth, which should have been the same as the seventh octave of the starting point, was found to be slightly more. The difference between the two tones, which is known as the *Pythagorean comma*, is expressed by the ratio 531441:524288.[4]

Another mathematical discrepancy, which causes trouble in working out a theory of tuning, is that the so-called *pure major third*, derived as the interval between the fourth and fifth partials, does not give the perfect octave when taken three times, but an interval smaller than the octave by the amount represented in the proportion of 125/128.[5] This difference is sometimes called the *enharmonic diesis*.[6]

Still another difficulty is presented by the fact that the major third derived from the fourth fifth, and the major third calculated as the interval between the fourth and fifth notes of the harmonic series, differ by the ratio 81/80. That is, the former third, known as the *Pythagorean third*, is larger than the latter, known as the *pure third*.[7] This is called the *comma of Didymus* or the *syntonic comma*.

These, and similar differences[8] in the various ways of

---

[4] In making calculations with intervals represented by proportions, it should be noted that the sum of two intervals is obtained by multiplying the fractions representing the proportions of the two intervals. Thus the sum of two fifths is obtained by multiplying: $3/2 \times 3/2 = 9/4$ or a ninth. Similarly, the difference between two intervals is obtained by division. Thus the difference between a fifth ($3/2$) and a fourth ($4/3$) is obtained by dividing: $3/2 \div 4/3 = 3/2 \times 3/4 = 9/8$ or a second. The difference between the twelfth fifth, and the seventh octave is obtained from the equation $(3/2)^{12}/(2/1)^{7} = (3/2)^{12} \times (1/2)^{7} = 3^{12}/2^{19} = 531441/524288$.

[5] $(5/4)^{3} = 125/64$, which is 125/128 of 2/1, the octave. $125/64 \div 2/1 = 125/64 \times 1/2 = 125/128$, which means that the first interval is 125/128 of the second. In other words, the third third has a smaller frequency than the octave.

[6] See "diesis" in *Grove's Dictionary of Music and Musicians*.

[7] $(3/2)^{4} \div 4/1 = 81/64$, the Pythagorean third; $5/4$ is the pure third. $81/64 \div 5/4 = 81/64 \times 4/5 = 81/80$.

[8] For a comprehensive list of tonal relations see "Tonbestimmung," *Hugo Riemanns Musik-Lexikon*.

calculating the intervals of the scale, together with certain facts of a physiopsychological nature — such as that the ear does not detect minute differences in frequency — lead eventually to the adoption of the equal-tempered scale, according to which the octave is divided into twelve equal semitones.[9] In this system of tuning the scale the difference of the Pythagorean comma is divided equally among the twelve fifths which represent the twelve degrees of the chromatic scale. Each fifth is smaller than the perfect fifth, by about one sixtieth of a semitone — one twelfth of the Pythagorean comma. *Mean-tone temperament, just intonation, artistic intonation,* and other similar expressions refer to various theories of tuning and should be distinguished from equal temperament.

COMBINATION TONES

Combination tones are heard "whenever two musical tones of different pitches are sounded together, loudly and continuously." [10]   The differential tones, whose discovery is usually attributed to Sorge, a German organist, in 1745, are tones whose frequency is equal to the difference between the two primary generating tones. For example, if two tones represented by the ratio 3:2 — the interval of the perfect fifth — are sounded together, a low tone an octave below the lower generating tone may be heard.   Thus $c^1 - g^1$ will produce the differential tone c.   Similarly, the interval $g^1 - e^2$, representing the relation 3:5 — a major sixth — produces a differential tone c^1.   Helmholtz himself claims credit for the discovery of summational tones and defines them as of a frequency "equal to the sum of the pitch numbers of the generating tones." [11]   Thus, the octave $c - c^1$, represented by the

[9] For further details see James M. Barbour, *Equal Temperament: Its History from Ramis (1482) to Rameau (1737).*
[10] Hermann L. F. Helmholtz, *On the Sensations of Tone,* pages 152 f.
[11] *Op. cit.,* page 153.

ratio 2:4, will produce a summational tone g^1. This tone is represented by the number 6, the sum of 2 plus 4.

These phenomena may be easily demonstrated in experiments, but authorities differ in their explanation of the various details.

THE PHENOMENON OF BEATS

According to the laws of interference, when two tones differ slightly in frequency, a successive waxing and waning of intensity takes place. The number of beats per second is equal to the difference in the frequencies of the two tones. Thus, if one tone has a frequency of 440 and another 443, maximum and minimum intensities will occur three times a second when the respective phases coincide and when they are opposed.

Four to six beats per second are easy to follow with the ear. As the number of beats increases, they can no longer be discerned separately but are heard as a sort of rattling sound. The relation of beats to the combination tones has not been fully determined.

The matter of consonance and dissonance is fundamentally a psychological matter, but the phenomena just discussed afford the physical basis for it. Theorists have assumed that the degree of consonance depends upon the simplicity of the relation between the frequencies of the tones forming the intervals. Thus, the octave, represented by the ratio 2:1, is the most perfect consonance; the perfect fifth, 3:2, is next; and the perfect fourth, 4:3, follows. But the fourth, although theoretically one of the most consonant intervals, is usually dissonant in effect when the lower note is in the bass. The physical explanation is probably connected, at least in part, with the fact that the perfect fourth does not occur in direct relation to the fundamental in the harmonic series; and when it is sounded against the bass, a clash occurs between it and the prominent overtones of the fundamental. The existence of such a problem throws some doubt on the unqualified statement that consonance is determined by the simplicity of the ratio between the tones of the interval, but there is some truth in it.

INTENSITY

The intensity of sound concerns the energy of the pulsations in the air which constitute the physical nature of sound. Physicists variously characterize intensity as "the amount of energy in a given volume of the space through which the sound is traveling," [12] "the energy in ergs which flows perpendicularly through one square centimeter during one second," [13] and "the time rate of flow of energy across a square centimeter at right angles to the direction of propagation." [14]

Both frequency and amplitude are factors in the intensity of sound. The relation of these factors may be stated as follows: the intensity varies as the square of the frequency and the square of the amplitude. Thus, if the frequency remains constant, the intensity is proportional to the square of the amplitude; and, conversely, if the amplitude remains constant, the intensity is then proportional to the square of the frequency.

The actual energy of sound impulses is very slight. A barely discernible sound may have an energy of about ten million-billionths of a watt. Since the expression of the intensity values of sound, in terms of energy units, involves the use of figures of fantastic size, a unit of sound intensity based upon logarithms has been generally adopted. This unit is called the *bel*. Thus if *I* represents the intensity of a sound in energy units, such as a fraction of a watt per square

[12] Harvey E. White, *Classical and Modern Physics*, page 186.
[13] Carl F. Eyring, *A Survey Course in Physics*, page 172.
[14] Henry A. Perkins, *College Physics*, page 307.

centimeter, the intensity of I in bels is the logarithm of I to the base 10 [I (in bels) $= \log_{10} I$]. But a smaller unit, one tenth the value of a bel, has been found more useful; so the term *decibel* is more commonly used. Bels may be reduced to decibels by multiplying the number of bels by 10.

The intensity of a barely audible sound is about ten million-billionths of a watt per square centimeter (10^{-16} watt/cm^2). If this is taken as the zero or reference level of the intensity scale, other values in the scale may be expressed in relation to it. Thus, if I is the intensity of a sound in watts per square centimeter, the intensity level will be given by the equation:

$$IL = 10 \log_{10} I/I_0 \text{ decibels.}$$

If a sound is increased tenfold above the zero level, its intensity level will be ten decibels ($10db$); if increased a hundredfold, $20db$; a thousandfold, $30db$; and so on. In other words, the intensity level varies as the logarithm of the ratio between the two intensities.

Form or Overtone Structure

When the frequency and intensity of a tone have been determined, the possibilities of objective descriptive analysis have not been exhausted, for it is still possible to investigate the tone with respect to its *overtone structure*. This overtone structure is ordinarily referred to as the shape, or *form*, of the sound wave or impulse. The analysis of musical tones is based upon mathematical-acoustical laws of long standing, which state, in substance, that a complex musical sound may be analyzed into a number of simple tones of definite frequency and intensity; and that, in a graphical representation of the sound as a periodic complex curve, the sine-curve components of that curve give a true representation of the constituent tones. It is through the mathematical analysis of such curves that the study of the structure of complex musical tones is carried on.[15]

Because sound waves or impulses in the air are longitudinal, they are difficult to study directly. But, through the application of the principles discussed in the preceding paragraph, means have been devised for graphically representing the linear motion of the sound wave, and for making a harmonic analysis of this representation. The *phonodeik* of Dayton C. Miller employs a diaphragm and mirror arrangement, whereby a light spot traces the "shape" of the sound wave in magnified form on a photographic film, or, for demonstration purposes, on a screen.[16]

Of the instruments which have been developed to obtain graphs of sound waves, the most satisfactory from many viewpoints are the high-quality *electrical oscillographs* [17] — especially the *cathode-ray oscillograph,* which employs a cathode-ray tube broadened at one end to hold a fluorescent screen.

Mechanical and electrical *harmonic analyzers* — instruments designed to calculate the relative amplitudes of the component frequencies of complex waves — provide the data necessary for the construction of acoustic spectra and wave pictures of the tones of the various musical instruments. Some of these instruments work from the wave forms made with the phonodeik or oscillograph; others operate directly from the sound waves themselves.[18]

The oscillograms and sound spectra of the tones of various

---

[15] For a more detailed account of Ohm's law with regard to periodic functions, and Fourier's theorem concerning harmonic analysis, see Dayton C. Miller, *Sound Waves: Their Shape and Speed,* pages 4–8.

[16] For details see Dayton C. Miller, *op. cit.,* Chapters II and III.

[17] For a discussion of various methods of recording sound waves, see Harvey Fletcher, *Speech and Hearing,* pages 14–28. New York: D. Van Nostrand Company, Inc., 1929.

[18] For details concerning the various analyzers, refer to Harvey Fletcher, *op. cit.;* Dayton C. Miller, *The Science of Musical Sounds;* and Ferdinand Trendelenburg, *Klänge und Geräusche,* pages 13–16 and 61–66.

musical instruments show their overtone structure, or composition. Although the pictures obtained by different methods vary greatly in detail, the interpretations of the data are in sufficient agreement to warrant certain general observations.

The graphs do not show the actual values of wave lengths — which vary from about 50 feet, for the lowest audible tones, to a fraction of an inch for the highest tones. Also, it should be remembered that the graphs give a greatly exaggerated picture of the displacement of air particles. An air particle does not move, at most, more than possibly a thousandth of an inch, and often perhaps as little as a hundred-thousandth of an inch.[19] The most distinctive general factors influencing the characteristic structure of musical tones are the instrument producing the tone, the frequency and intensity of the tone, and the resonance characteristics of the room.

Each instrumental tone has its own individual structure. For example, the bassoon tone shows evidence of a formant at a frequency of about 500 cycles;[20] the clarinet has a predominance of odd-numbered partials; the French horn has a formant between 200 and 600 cycles; and the violin has numerous, evenly-distributed partials.[21] Low tones generally have more partials than high tones; and tones of greater intensity have more partials than tones of lesser intensity. Furthermore, there are often pronounced changes in the relative

---

[19] John Redfield, *Music: A Science and an Art*, page 28.

[20] For examples of the tonal spectra of many instruments, see Carl E. Seashore, *Psychology of Music*, Chapters 17 and 18. New York: McGraw-Hill Book Company, Inc., 1938. Other acoustic spectra are given in Harvey Fletcher, *op. cit.*, pages 90–98; and numerous graphs are included in Dayton C. Miller, *The Science of Musical Sounds* and *Sound Waves*. In studying these illustrations the student should take into account the differences in the methods of procedure in obtaining the graphs. The present discussion is based largely on the data given by Seashore.

[21] For a discussion of the wave forms of the sounds of speech, see Harvey Fletcher, *op. cit.*, pages 28–63.

intensity of corresponding partials, with changes in frequency and intensity. In many instances partials have greater intensity than the fundamental tone. And, finally, rooms having longer reverberation times tend to increase the intensity of low partials at the expense of the higher partials.

DURATION

In addition to frequency, intensity, and form or overtone structure, the fourth physical characteristic of musical sounds is *duration*. Every tone has a finite duration as one of its fundamental characteristics. Duration is, thus, one of the four intrinsic orders of tones; it is of particular significance in relation to the rhythmic structure of music.

MUSICAL INSTRUMENTS

All musical instruments involve two fundamentals — a means of exciting a tone, and a means of reinforcing it or giving it resonance. Most instruments have some provision for the production and control of tones of different pitches — a factor exceedingly important to the acoustical construction of the individual instrument, and to its usefulness. Such instruments as the pianoforte or organ have individual strings, or tubes, for each tone. Other instruments, such as the violin or flute, produce a number of tones on a single string or tube by various mechanical devices. According to these means, musical instruments are classified in a general way as (*a*) stringed, (*b*) wind, and (*c*) percussion instruments.

STRINGED INSTRUMENTS

The stringed instruments are further divided into three classes, according to the method used to produce the vibration; that is, whether the strings are plucked, struck, or bowed. The harp, guitar, and mandolin are instruments of the first type. The pianoforte is the outstanding example of the sec-

ond type; and the violin, viola, violoncello, and double bass
are the most familiar bowed instruments.

These instruments consist of a number of strings stretched
over and attached to a more or less rigid body, which acts
as a sounding board or resonance chamber. The sounds
produced by the vibrating strings are comparatively feeble,
but when the vibrations are taken up by the rest of the instrument — which serves as a resonator — these vibrations are
intensified, and the tone is made loud enough to be musically
effective. Thus, the strings of the violin are set in motion by
the action of the bow. The vibrations are then transmitted
through the bridge and body of the instrument to the air —
greatly intensified. The air is affected not only by the surface movements of the body of the instrument, but also by
the action of the interior chamber, which serves in some measure as a resonance chamber.

Stretched strings vibrate according to acoustical laws,
which have been investigated and established theoretically
and experimentally. The general principles are based on the
tendency of a stretched string, when displaced, to return to
its position of rest, and, because of the momentum, to pass
through that position to a displacement on the other side.
Two important types of waves are distinguished: *traveling
waves*, which are those moving from the point of displacement and reflected at the ends; and *standing transverse waves*,
which are set up when the tension and speed of vibration are
sufficiently great.

With regard to the vibration of a string as a whole, the
two ends, which are fixed and stationary, are called *nodes* or
nodal points. The middle, where the transverse displacement
is the greatest, is the so-called *loop*. This simple vibration
produces a tone whose pitch or frequency depends upon
the length, tension, thickness, and material of the string.
Pythagoras and his pupils demonstrated, by means of the

monochord, that one half, one third, one fourth, and so forth, of the length of the string produced the octave: the octave plus a perfect fifth, the second octave, and so on, above the fundamental tone. As far as we know, they did not express this in terms of frequencies. In the sixteenth century, Zarlino referred to the fact that lower tones have slower rates of vibration. But Mersenne, in the first part of the seventeenth century, is usually credited with having demonstrated, for the first time, that pitch is determined by frequency. The laws governing the frequency of vibrating strings may be summarized somewhat as follows:

(*a*) The frequency varies inversely as the length of the string. That is, all other things being equal, twice the length of the string will produce a tone of one half the number of vibrations per second; or, contrariwise, one half the length produces twice the frequency; one third, three times, and so forth.

(*b*) The frequency varies directly as the square root of the tension. Thus, to produce two, three, or four times the frequency, the tension must be four, nine, or sixteen times as great, respectively.

(*c*) The frequency varies inversely as the diameter of the wire. For example, if the thickness of the wire is doubled, or tripled, the frequency is lowered by one half or one third.

(*d*) The frequency varies inversely as the square root of the density of the string. Other things being equal, the density of a string must be increased four or nine times to reduce the frequency to one half or one third.

The explanation of many phenomena, familiar to musicians in their daily experience, is to be found in the application of these principles. The length, diameter, material, and tension of the strings of the stringed instruments are determined in terms of these laws.

None of the ordinary ways of exciting the tone on a stringed instrument causes the whole length of the string to vibrate simply. Experiments show that the string vibrates in such a complex way that, when it is vibrating as a whole, it is also vibrating in halves, thirds, fourths, and so forth, of its length, each partial vibration producing an overtone. The prominence of the various overtones depends in part upon the place at which the string is struck or bowed and upon the nature of the stroke producing the motion. These factors play an important role in the construction and technique of the various stringed instruments. The tone quality of any given stringed instrument depends upon the total resultant action of the instrument as a whole. The manner and place of actuating the vibration; the length, tension, material, and other characteristics of the string itself; the way it is mounted on the main body of the instrument; and the operation of the resonator — all these enter into the determination of the tone quality of any particular instrument.

WIND INSTRUMENTS

The wind instruments may be classified, according to the means of producing the tone, into the following groups:

Means of producing tone	Instrument
Metal reeds without pipes ..	harmonium, American reed organ, harmonica or mouth organ.
Metal reeds with pipes	reed stops of the organ.
Pipes without reeds	flute stops of the organ, flute and piccolo, and a number of instruments, mostly obsolete, such as the recorder and other instruments of the fipple-flute type.
Double cane reeds with conical pipes	oboe, bassoon, and sarrusophone families.
Single cane reeds with cylindrical pipes	clarinets.

Means of producing tone	Instrument
Single cane reeds with conical pipes	saxophones.
Pipes with cupped mouthpieces, human lips as reeds	the usual brass instruments of the orchestra or band, such as the trumpets, trombones, horns, tubas, and variations.
Vocal chords as reeds	human voices.

With the exception of the first group, these instruments all have some sort of tube as an essential part of the mechanism. The most complicated of these instruments is undoubtedly the human voice. A discussion of the siren, aeolian harp, and certain other instruments using wind in the tone production, is beyond the scope of the present work.

The most prominent feature of the majority of wind instruments is the tube or pipe, which acts as a resonator to the tones and is the chief determining factor of the pitch of the tone produced. Three fundamental types of pipes are used in the various wind instruments: (1) closed cylindrical pipes, (2) open cylindrical pipes, and (3) closed conical, or noncylindrical, pipes. The expression *closed pipe* refers to the fact that one end of the tube is shut off or "stopped" so that only one end is left open. In the air column contained within the tube, "standing longitudinal waves" are set up by the vibrating agent. The operation of a stopped pipe may be demonstrated easily by blowing across the open end of a slender test tube. As Tyndall expresses it,[22]

a fluttering of the air is thereby produced, an assemblage of pulses at the open mouth of the tube being generated . . . The tube selects that pulse of the flutter which is in synchronism with itself and raises it to a musical sound.

The rigid end of the tube becomes a nodal point, because the air is kept from moving as a whole; while the open end be-

[22] John Tyndall, *Sound*, page 207.

comes an antinode or loop, where the to-and-fro motion of the air is a maximum. At the node the pressure alternates many times a second, while at the antinode the pressure remains constant. The distance from a node to an antinode is one fourth the wave length of the tone produced. Thus, a stopped pipe will produce a fundamental tone whose wave length is approximately four times the length of the pipe.

Important in the operation of all band and orchestral wind instruments is the principle of *overblowing*. This refers to the phenomena, familiar to every wind instrument player, which occur when the performer forces the tone slightly in an appropriate manner. The instrument then produces, not the fundamental, but one of the overtones or upper partials. In other words, a pipe of a given length will afford resonance to certain frequencies corresponding to the integral multiples of the given fundamental. However, a stopped cylindrical pipe — because the closed end is always a node and the open end an antinode — will produce only the odd-numbered overtones. This is best explained by means of a diagram, in which x and y represent the nodes and antinodes, respectively.

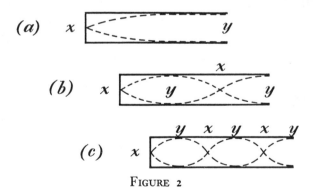

FIGURE 2

The distance from x to y represents one fourth of a wave length. The length of xy in Figure 2b is obviously one third of that in Figure 2a and, therefore, the total wave length is also one third (which means that frequency in 2*b* is three times what it is in 2*a*). The tone produced, then, is a twelfth higher. Similarly, in Figure 2*c*, the wave length is one fifth of the fundamental, the frequency five times as great, and the resultant tone is two octaves and a major third higher — the fifth harmonic.

An open pipe has an antinode at each end. The lowest tone or fundamental would have one nodal point, that is, in the middle of the tube. The wave length of the fundamental is approximately twice the length of the open pipe, which means that the fundamental tone of an open pipe is an octave higher than that of a stopped pipe of the same length. Furthermore, since the open pipe can be overblown so as to contain two, three, four, or more nodal points, it can produce both the even- and odd-numbered overtones.

Both theory and experiment have established the fact that the third type of pipe — that is, a closed pipe with an appropriately designed conical bore — acts like an open pipe, overblowing in the octave and producing both even- and odd-numbered overtones.

With the exception of the flute and clarinet families, all the ordinary wind instruments belong to this general class. The flute is an open cylindrical tube type of instrument, and the clarinet — notwithstanding the opening in the mouthpiece — is, in principle, a closed cylindrical pipe.

In instruments of the *flute* type, the tone is excited by means of a comparatively narrow column of air, directed across an opening near one end of the tube. The principle of tone production is the same as in the familiar experience of producing a tone by blowing across the mouth of a bottle. The effective length of the tube is regulated by means of a series of lateral openings, the ordinary finger holes of the tube. A simple example of this is the penny whistle, with six finger holes which are sufficient to produce the seven tones of the diatonic scale. Then, according to the principle of overblowing, the same fingerings produce the tones of the second octave, and the tones above that are still higher partials. The orchestral flute operates in a similar manner, except that additional holes, controlled by an elaborate key mechanism, are introduced in order to produce the complete chromatic scale.

The flute, although it is now generally made of metal instead of wood, is classed with the wood-wind instruments — the material of which the instrument is made being of secondary importance in determining the quality of tone. General similarity of tone quality, and the fact that the tones of the scale are produced by a similar system of lateral openings in the tube, seem to be the chief criteria for the classification of the wood-wind instruments. In this connection, it is of interest that the French horn is a regular member of the classic wood-wind quintet — probably because of the remarkable similarity of tone quality between the French horn and the bassoon, which makes it so well suited to the wood-wind ensemble.

The tone of the *clarinet* is generated by means of a single reed of bamboo cane which vibrates on the facing of a suitably designed rigid mouthpiece. The reed is comparatively weak as a vibrating agent, so that its frequency is determined chiefly by the length of the tube, which is controlled in a manner similar to that of the flute. The clarinet, however, acts as a stopped pipe — which means that the tones of the fundamental scale are an octave lower than the tones produced by a similar length of tube on a flute or oboe. This fact, together with its corollary — that is, that the clarinet overblows in the twelfth — accounts for the remarkable range of the instrument. Another attendant peculiarity of the clarinet is that its lowest tones may be easily produced pianissimo; whereas, the lowest tones of the oboe, and bassoon especially, tend to be louder than the tones of the medium register.

The *oboe* tone is actuated by a double-reed mouthpiece, made of two strips of bamboo cane attached to a small metal tube by means of an appropriately wrapped thread. An ordinary wheat straw, with the end pressed together between the thumb and forefinger so that a narrow slit is formed, through which one may blow, will serve as a simple, practical illustration of the double-reed principle. The tube of the oboe, with its finger hole and key arrangement similar to the flute and clarinet, is conical throughout, and overblows in the octave, so that both the even- and odd-numbered harmonics may be produced.

The *bassoon* is also a double-reed instrument, operating according to the same principle as the oboe. It has, however, a peculiarly characteristic tone quality partly due to the difference in the size and proportions of the reed and resonance tube, and especially to the way in which the long, narrow finger holes are bored in the body of the instrument to bring the principal lateral openings within reach of the fingers of the player.

The *saxophone* is a hybrid instrument in a sense — combining a single-reed mouthpiece, like that of the clarinet, with a conical tube, like that of the oboe. That the main body of the instrument is made of metal is apparently unimportant in determining the tone quality. Of prime importance are the size and proportions of the resonance chamber, the type of mouthpiece or reed, and, of course, the skill of the performer in manipulating the instrument as a whole. The adjustment of the lips to the mouthpiece in producing the tone is called the *embouchure*.

The *brass* instruments have tubes that are of the noncylindrical type, that is, none of these instruments is cylindrical throughout the entire length of the tube. They are all more or less conical in bore, so that they overblow in the octave, and may produce both the even- and odd-numbered partials, as do closed pipes of conical bore in general. The tone of these instruments is generated by the action of the human lips vibrating, within the cupped mouthpieces, like stretched membranes actuated by the breath of the performer.

In general, the narrower the tube in proportion to the length, the easier it is to produce the higher tones of the harmonic series. The ordinary bugle is so constructed as to favor the production of the third, fourth, fifth, and sixth partials. In such an instrument there is no practical way of producing the intermediate tones. The horn and trumpet of the classical orchestra were of this type, except that the tubes were longer and narrower, so that the eighth to the sixteenth harmonics were also usable. Thus, it was possible to approximate the diatonic scale, in this register, on the natural horn or trumpet. Slight modifications of the pitches of the natural tones were obtained by inserting the hand into the bell of the instrument.

The problem of finding a means to modify the length of tube effectively has played a most important part in the development of the brass-wind instruments. Attempts to use lateral openings, like those of the wood-wind instruments, did not prove permanently successful. The principle of the long, movable slide, as still used in the modern slide trombone, was more practical; but the perfecting of a valve mechanism, as a means of varying the length of the tube, was a most important step in expanding the usefulness of the brass-wind instruments. Thus, a three-valved instrument became chromatic — capable of producing every semitone of the scale, from the second harmonic of the lowest fundamental tone, upwards throughout its entire range.

In principle, the brass-wind instruments may be divided into four categories: horns, saxhorns, tubas, and trumpets or trombones.[23]   In actual practice, manufacturers have deviated considerably from type, so that the distinctions made here must be regarded as only approximate.   This applies to members of the saxhorn and tuba families particularly.

The *French horn* has three valves, a deep, conic-cup mouthpiece, and a long, narrow tube that is conical throughout and culminates in a side bell.

The *saxhorn* has a bell-cup mouthpiece, a short, conical tube, and a bell that usually faces the front.   There is a whole family of saxhorns, extending from the small sopranino to the large contrabass instrument.   The most common representative of this family in America is the fluegel horn. Some of the other brass instruments use this type of mouthpiece, but have a modified bore.

The members of the *tuba* family are characterized by a deep bowl-cup type of mouthpiece, and tubing that is short and approximately one third cylindrical and two thirds conical. Most of the brass instruments of the American wind band, from the cornet to the large contrabass tuba, seem to be of this general type, although many of them use mouthpieces more nearly of the saxhorn type.

Trumpets and *trombones* have shallow, bowl-cup mouthpieces, and tubes that are two thirds cylindrical and one third conical, with "front" bells.[24]

The *human voice* is one of the most important of the wind instruments.   The tone is excited by means of the passage of air from the lungs through the vocal cords, which vibrate like stretched membranes.   The mouth and associated cavities provide the resonance chamber.   The detailed study of the many complexities involved in the operation of the

---

[23] See Stanislao Gallo, *The Modern Band*, Book I, pages 56–74.
[24] For illustrations of the four types of mouthpieces used by the brass-wind instruments, see Stanislao Gallo, *op. cit.*, page 60.

voice as an instrument extends through the fields of acoustics, anatomy, physiology, and psychology.

Percussion Instruments

Books on instrumentation usually classify the *percussion instruments* into two main groups with definiteness or indefiniteness of pitch as the criterion.[25]   Physicists commonly divide these instruments into such groups as membranes, rods (bars and tubes), and plates.   An entirely logical and complete classification is difficult, because of overlapping among the bases of classification.   The pianoforte, for example, is classed as a stringed instrument, but, since the strings are set into motion by percussive means, it might logically be classed as a percussion instrument.   Other keyboard instruments, such as the celesta, are ordinarily classed with the percussion instruments.   For present purposes, it will be sufficient to consider briefly the chief acoustical types and the more common musical instruments associated with each.

The vibration of *membranes* is very complex.   Roughly speaking, a membrane is the two-dimensional counterpart of a stretched string.   The membrane is usually attached to a circular frame, so that the circumference may be regarded as a nodal point, and the center as the point of maximum displacement.   Researches carried on in this field show that the partials of vibrating membranes are generally nonharmonic in character.   This fact is important in accounting for the tone quality of the drum.   The kettle drum, or tympany, is constructed so as to provide for the tuning of the fundamental tone to a definite pitch, whereas the bass drum, the snare drum, and the tambourine have pitches that are less clearly defined.

---

[25] See Cecil Forsyth, *Orchestration*, pages 22 ff. London: Macmillan & Co., Ltd., 1914. Forsyth makes the rather remarkable classification of "unmusical" and "musical" percussion instruments.

Plates differ from membranes in that the stiffness of the former is due to the rigidity of the material, whereas, in the latter, the stiffness is caused by its being stretched. With due allowance for this fundamental difference, there are marked similarities between the vibrations of plates and membranes. The details are too complex to warrant discussion here. The cymbal is the most prominent musical instrument that uses this type of construction. The circumference, being free, is an antinode; and the center, where the handle is attached, is a nodal point. The pitch is so indefinite, and the quality of the sound produced so complicated, that the result is usually classified as a noise. The gong, or tam-tam, and the bell are modified forms of instruments using plates.

Among the percussion instruments that belong to the *rod*, *bar*, or *tube* type are the tuning fork, triangle, xylophone, and celesta. A thin, horizontal bar supported at appropriate distances from the two ends will produce transverse waves, analogous to those of a stretched string, but with antinodes at the ends, and with nodes at the points of suspension.

A tuning fork is a bar of this type, bent into a U shape with an additional mass of metal at the bend, which serves as a handle. One of the chief characteristics of a tuning fork is that it produces a clear, fundamental tone, free from prominent overtones. The first overtone is said to be about six times the frequency of the fundamental.[26] The triangle, on the other hand, has many relatively strong overtones that are nonharmonic. This fact tends to give the effect of indefinite pitch, and explains why the triangle is usually classed with the instruments of indeterminate pitch. The ordinary orchestral bells, which are not to be confused with church bells, are made of bars, of the type mentioned in the preceding paragraph, arranged so as to produce the various tones of the scale. The xylophone is similar, but made of wood. The

---

[26] George W. Stewart, *Introductory Acoustics*, page 191.

celesta is, roughly speaking, a set of orchestral bells, with a keyboard attachment in which the tone is strengthened and improved by means of resonators. In some types the bars are replaced by thin-walled tubes.

ELECTRIC INSTRUMENTS

In recent years, many musical instruments which use electricity in the production of tones have been developed. Two principal types of electric instruments may be distinguished: (1) *electromechanical* instruments which produce the tone in more or less the conventional manner, but increase the intensity by electrical amplification; and (2) *real electric*, or *electronic*, instruments which use electrical means both for producing the tone and for amplifying it. Photoelectricity, beat frequencies of radio frequency vacuum tubes, and rotating alternating current generators are the chief means used for tone production in the second type of instrument.[27]

The best-known of the electric instruments is undoubtedly the Hammond organ. This is a real electronic instrument, producing its tones by means of small electromagnetic generators. Each of these generators, consisting of a metallic disk, rotated continuously before a permanent magnet surrounded by a coil, gives rise to a frequency which depends upon the speed of the rotating disk and the number of projections on its edge. Drawbars, analogous to organ stops, permit the introduction of harmonics — in various combinations, and with adjustable intensity. The harmonics used are restricted to those already available in the equal-tempered scale. Hence, although the octaves are pure, the thirds are

---

[27] J. Murray Barbour, "Music and Electricity," *Volume of Proceedings of the Music Teachers National Association,* Thirty-Second Series (1937), page 255. See also Percy A. Scholes, "Electric Musical Instruments," *The Oxford Companion to Music,* pages 286–289; and F. W. Galpin, "Electrophonic Instruments of Music," *Grove's Dictionary of Music and Musicians,* Supplementary Volume, pages 189–191.

sharp, and the fifths flat. The depression of a key on the keyboard simply closes the proper electric circuit.

Innumerable other kinds of electronic instruments have been and are being made, including types such as the violin, guitar, piano, and others, such as the theremin and nova-chord.[28]

PROBLEMS AND METHODS

The field of acoustics as a branch of musicology is somewhat narrower than the general field of acoustics. The theories of sound production and transmission are basic to all work in acoustics. The application of these theories brings about a division of the field according to the interests served. For example, the study of the acoustical properties of rooms and auditoriums belongs logically to the physicist working in conjunction with the architect. The results of these studies are of real importance to the musician, and the musicologist should properly cooperate with the physicist and architect in the solution of many problems.

The design and manufacture of musical instruments affords occupation to a large number of specialists, most of whom probably learn their trade by the apprentice method. Progress in this field affects directly the course of musical development. Compare, for example, a Beethoven score with one of Wagner's, with respect to the use of the brass-wind instruments, particularly the horns and trumpets. Beethoven was greatly handicapped in the use of these instruments, because the valve mechanism which completely revolutionized the technique of these instruments had not been perfected in his time. The improvement of old instruments, and the

---

[28] For a discussion of such instruments, see J. Murray Barbour, *loc. cit.*, pages 250–258; also, Benjamin M. Miessner, "The Electronic Piano," *Volume of Proceedings of the Music Teachers National Association*, Thirty-Second Series (1937), pages 259–272; and John Mills, *A Fugue in Cycles and Bels*, pages 186–198.

invention of new instruments, such as the electric organ, will undoubtedly continue to expand the resources of composers.

In music theory, systems of chord classification, problems of tuning and temperament, principles of orchestration, and many related problems have acoustical implications. Other acoustical problems are connected with the field of performance.

Studies of the acoustical principles involved in playing instruments in tune are important. How to vent notes on the wood-wind instruments, the effects of "lipping" on the brass-wind instruments, the vibrato on wind and stringed instruments, the effect of different ways of striking the keys of keyboard instruments on the tone quality, phonetics — these and many other similar problems are largely acoustical in nature.

The study of sound transmission, and many related problems in connection with the radio and the sound films, fall chiefly in the province of electrical engineers. Obviously, they are not without significance to the musician and the musicologist.

The methods used in research in these various fields are as many and varied as the problems themselves. In many of the great universities of the world, physics departments maintain laboratories for study and research in the countless general problems of acoustics; engineering departments have laboratories for the investigation of problems of sound transmission by electrical means; language departments occasionally have laboratories for phonetic studies; and psychology departments often maintain acoustical laboratories. Large instrument factories maintain divisions of research, and other commercial concerns, such as the Bell Telephone Company, have laboratories for investigations that are largely acoustical. An acoustical laboratory should be available to every well-rounded musicological department. The equipment of such a laboratory should include the apparatus and material essential for the demonstration of the various acoustical phenomena and for advanced research on special research projects.

BIBLIOGRAPHY

Akustische Zeitschrift. Edited by Martin Grützmacher and Erwin Meyer. Leipzig: S. Hirzel, 1936 to date.

Barbour, James M., *Equal Temperament: Its History from Ramis (1482) to Rameau (1737).* Dissertation, Cornell University, 1932.

————, "Music and Electricity," *Volume of Proceedings of the Music Teachers National Association.* Thirty-Second Series (1937), pages 250–258.

Barton, Edwin H., *A Textbook on Sound.* London: Macmillan & Co., Ltd., 1922.

The Bell System Technical Journal. A journal devoted to the scientific and engineering aspects of electrical communication. New York: American Telephone & Telegraph Co., 1922 to date.

Blackwood, Oswald, *Introductory College Physics.* New York: John Wiley & Sons, Inc., 1939.

Bragg, Sir William, *The World of Sound.* (First published in 1920.) London: G. Bell & Sons, Ltd., 1936.

Braunmühl, H. J. von, and Walter Weber, *Einführung in die angewandte Akustik.* Leipzig: S. Hirzel, 1936.

Buck, Percy C., *Acoustics for Musicians.* London: Oxford University Press, 1928.

Chavez, Carlos, *Toward a New Music: Music and Electricity.* (Tr. by Herbert Weinstock.) New York: W. W. Norton & Company, Inc., 1937.

Colby, M. Y., *A College Course in Sound Waves and Acoustics.* New York: Henry Holt & Company, Inc., 1938.

Combarieu, Jules, *Music, Its Laws and Evolution.* New York: D. Appleton-Century Company, Inc., 1910.

Crandall, I. B., *The Vibrating Systems of Sound.* New York: D. Van Nostrand Company, Inc., 1926.

Davis, A. H., *Modern Acoustics.* New York: The Macmillan Company, 1934.

Dupont, Wilhelm, *Geschichte der musikalischen Temperatur.* Kassel: Bärenreiter, 1935.

Emmanuel, Maurice, "Notions d'acoustique grecque," *Encyclopédie de la musique et dictionnaire du conservatoire*, Part I, Vol. I, pages 453–470.

Encyclopaedia Britannica. Eleventh Edition. "Ear," "Music," "Organ," "Sound," "Violin."

Eyring, Carl F., *A Survey Course in Physics*. New York: Prentice-Hall, Inc., 1936.

Gallo, Stanislao, *The Modern Band*, Book I. Boston: C. C. Birchard & Company, 1935.

Hamilton, Clarence G., *Sound and Its Relation to Music*. Philadelphia: Oliver Ditson Company, Inc., 1912.

Helmholtz, Hermann L. F., *On the Sensations of Tone as a Physiological Basis for the Theory of Music*. (Tr. from the fourth German edition of 1877 by Alexander J. Ellis. First German Edition, 1862.) New York: Longmans, Green & Company, 1912.

Jeans, Sir James, *Science and Music*. New York: The Macmillan Company, 1938.

Jones, Arthur Taber, *Sound: A Textbook*. New York: D. Van Nostrand Company, Inc., 1937.

The Journal of the Acoustical Society of America. Published for the Acoustical Society of America by the American Institute of Physics, Inc., Lancaster, Pa., and New York, N. Y. 1929 to date.

Knudsen, Vern O., *Architectural Acoustics*. New York: John Wiley & Sons, Inc., 1932.

————, *Modern Acoustics and Culture*. Berkeley: University of California Press, 1937.

Lamb, Sir Horace, *The Dynamical Theory of Sound*. Second Edition. London: Edward Arnold & Co., 1931. (First Edition, 1910.)

Lanz, Henry, *The Physical Basis of Rime*. Palo Alto, California: Stanford University Press, 1931.

Lloyd, Ll. S., *Music and Sound*. London: Oxford University Press, 1937.

McLachlan, N. W., *The New Acoustics: A Survey of Modern Development in Acoustical Engineering*. London: Oxford University Press, 1936.

Meyer, Max F., *The Musician's Arithmetic*. Philadelphia: Oliver Ditson Company, Inc., 1929.

Miessner, Benjamin Franklin, "The Electronic Piano," *Volume of Proceedings of the Music Teachers National Association*, Thirty-Second Series (1937), pages 259–272.

Miller, Dayton Clarence, *Anecdotal History of the Science of Sound*. New York: The Macmillan Company, 1935.

————, *Sound Waves: Their Shape and Speed*. New York: The Macmillan Company, 1937.

————, *The Science of Musical Sounds*. New York: The Macmillan Company, 1916.

Millikan, Robert A., Henry G. Gale, and Charles W. Edwards, *A First Course in Physics for Colleges*. Revised Edition. Boston: Ginn and Company, 1938.

Mills, John, *A Fugue in Cycles and Bels*. New York: D. Van Nostrand Company, Inc., 1935.

Morse, Philip M., *Vibration and Sound*. New York: McGraw-Hill Book Company, Inc., 1936.

Olson, Harry F., and Frank Massa, *Applied Acoustics*. Second Edition. Philadelphia: The Blakiston Company, 1939.

Ortmann, Otto, *The Physical Basis of Piano Touch and Tone*. New York: E. P. Dutton & Co., Inc., 1925.

Perkins, Henry A., *College Physics*. New York: Prentice-Hall, Inc., 1938.

Pole, William, *The Philosophy of Music*. Sixth Edition. New York: Harcourt, Brace & Company, Inc., 1924.

Rayleigh, J. W. S., *The Theory of Sound*. 2 vols. Second Edition. London: Macmillan & Co., Ltd., 1929. First Edition, 1877.

Redfield, John, *Music: A Science and an Art*. New Edition. New York: Tudor Publishing Company, 1935.

Richardson, E. G., *The Acoustics of Orchestral Instruments and of the Organ*. London: Edward Arnold & Co., 1929.

————, *Sound: A Physical Text-book*. Second Edition. London: Edward Arnold & Co., 1935.

Riemann, Hugo, "Akustik," "Tonbestimmung," etc., *Hugo Riemanns Musik-Lexikon*.

Sabine, P. E., *Acoustics and Architecture*. New York: McGraw-Hill Book Company, Inc., 1932.

Sabine, W. C., *Collected Papers on Acoustics*. Cambridge: Harvard University Press, 1922.

Scholes, Percy A., "Acoustics," *The Oxford Companion to Music*, pages 6–15.

Scripture, E. W., *Researches in Experimental Phonetics: The Study of Speech Curves*. Washington: The Carnegie Institution of Washington, 1906. Publication No. 44.

Stanley, Douglas, *The Science of Voice*. Third Edition Revised and Enlarged. New York: Carl Fischer, Inc., 1939.

Stewart, George Walter, *Introductory Acoustics.* New York: D. Van Nostrand Company, Inc., 1933.

————, and R. B. Lindsay, *Acoustics: A Text on Theory and Applications.* New York: D. Van Nostrand Company, Inc., 1930.

Stringham, Edwin J., "Acoustics," *The International Cyclopedia of Music and Musicians,* pages 9–13.

Trendelenburg, Ferdinand, *Klänge und Geräusche.* Berlin: Julius Springer, 1935.

Tyndall, John. *Sound.* Third Edition. New York: D. Appleton-Century Company, Inc., 1898.

Watson, Floyd Rowe, *Acoustics of Buildings.* New York: John Wiley & Sons, Inc., 1923.

————, *Sound: An Elementary Textbook on the Science of Sound and the Phenomena of Hearing.* New York: John Wiley & Sons, Inc., 1935.

White, Harvey E., *Classical and Modern Physics.* New York: D. Van Nostrand Company, Inc., 1940.

Wood, A. B., *A Textbook of Sound.* New York: The Macmillan Company, 1930.

Wood, Alexander, *The Physical Basis of Music.* Cambridge: Cambridge University Press, 1913.

Zahm, John A., *Sound and Music.* Chicago: A. C. McClurg & Company, 1892.

CHAPTER III

PHYSIOLOGY AND PSYCHOLOGY IN RELATION TO MUSIC

DEFINITION OF THE FIELD

W HEN THE "PULSATIONS" IN THE AIR STRIKE THE EAR-drum, we pass from physics into the realms of physiology and psychology. The line of demarcation between the physical and physiological is clear-cut at this point, but, from here on, the fields overlap more and more.

Each new subject in the sequence depends directly on all the fields previously mentioned, but includes certain material peculiar to the new field: physics rests upon mathematics; zoology (including morphology or anatomy, physiology, and taxonomy) upon physics and chemistry; psychology upon physiology; and aesthetics upon psychology.

Whereas anatomy concerns the structure of living organisms, physiology concerns their function. The study of the sensory processes — seeing, hearing, feeling, and the like — is, therefore, a physiological study. But, since these processes are linked closely with others which are classed as mental or psychological, it is convenient to treat these fields together. The term *psychophysiology*, describing the study of the mutual interrelation of physiological and psychological processes, suggests the close interrelationships of these subjects.

[60]

Anatomy and Music

Anatomy, physiology, and psychology reveal many principles of significant interest to the musicologist. The structure of the human body has played an important determinative role in the development of music. This fact is particularly obvious in the structure of musical instruments, which, designed for manipulation by human hands, are accordingly limited to structures that can be manipulated. Certain anatomical considerations are basic in the study of many, if not all, musical instruments. In acquiring a technique on the piano, for example, many heartaches could be avoided if the teacher but knew enough elementary anatomy not to urge students beyond their anatomical capacities.

The Central Nervous System, Sensory and Motor Nerves, Reflex Action

Physiology, the science dealing with the functions of an organism as distinct from its structure, concerns such topics as nutrition, circulation and respiration, the nervous system, and the effectors (or muscles) and glands.

The central nervous system, consisting of the spinal cord and brain, is connected by nerves with the sensory organs and the motor apparatus. The sensory nerves are the paths into the central nervous system; the motor nerves, the paths out. The sensory-motor arc, being the basis for the single action-unit, stimulation-and-response, is the anatomical unit around which both the physiologist and psychologist build their accounts of various physiopsychological phenomena.[1]

When a violinist performs, the relations among his various sensory and motor (receptor and effector) apparatus are very complex. The attempt to describe such an opera-

---

[1] See Vernon H. Mottram, *Physiology*, pages 44 ff.; John F. Dashiell, *Fundamentals of General Psychology*, pages 40 f.

tion, even though inadequate, may, nevertheless, explain the musicologist's interest in physiopsychological matters.

Let us take the printed page of musical notation as the external origin of the stimulus. The light energies, which fall upon the organ of vision, are ordinarily described as electromagnetic vibrations of very short wave lengths. The eye, as receptor, transmits the energy to the brain by the visual nerve. From the brain, the impulses are transmitted through the central nervous system to the various motor apparatus that participate in the manipulation of the violin and bow.

Among the operations involved are: the control of the fingers on the finger board with respect to position, pressure, vibrato, and the like; the control of the right arm, wrist, and fingers, with respect to pressure of the bow on the strings, its motion across the strings, and its position in relation to the strings, finger board, and so forth; the control of the left shoulder and chin in supporting the body of the instrument; and the control of other parts of the body having less direct connection with the operation.

At the same time, other sensory apparatus are sending their messages to the brain. Receptors for pressure stimuli, located in the skin, transmit cutaneous excitations. Kinesthetic receptors in muscles and tendons report changes in the position and movement of parts of the organism. Still others in the canals and vestibule of the inner ear report changes in the position and movement of the whole body. These concern static sensitivity. The ear is another receptor making an important contribution to the performance. All these receptors send in their various messages to the brain, and contribute, each in its own peculiar modality, to the performance of the violinist.

The pulsations of the air, set up by the action of the instrument, are transmitted to the brain as auditory neural impulses, which, in turn, produce appropriate responses in the effector system — correcting an intonation, modifying a tone quality, and so forth. With the experienced artist, this reaction is, ordinarily, almost pure reflex activity. Through long training and experience it has become habit, or mechanized activity. The study of the processes at this level is primarily in the province of physiology, or at least in that of psychophysiology.

For a detailed account of the nervous system, the sensory and motor apparatus, and the related topics pertaining to the way the human body works, the student may consult the standard textbooks on the subject. A general knowledge of physiology is, as has been suggested, basic to the investigation of many problems of musical significance. The studies which Ortmann and others have carried on, concerning piano technique, should be carried on for all important musical instruments.

The Structure and Function of the Ear

There are three distinct divisions of the ear, known as the outer, middle, and inner ear. The outer ear consists of the *pinna*, and a tube a little over an inch long — called the *ear canal* or *auditory meatus* — leading to the *tympanum* or *eardrum* which separates the outer from the middle ear.

The middle ear is a sort of air chamber, containing a passage to the throat known as the *Eustachian tube*, and three small bones popularly called the *hammer, anvil*, and *stirrup*, all linked together in the order named. The first of these bones is attached to the tympanum or eardrum; the last connects with the *oval window* — the upper of two membrane-covered holes — which leads into the inner ear.

The inner ear is by far the most intricate portion of the entire organ of hearing. It is situated in the *bony labyrinth* — a cavity in the petrous bone — and consists of a structure known as the *membranous labyrinth*. Its three principal parts are (1) the *vestibule*, or part just beyond the oval window, (2) the *semicircular canals*, which contain the sense organs of equilibrium and have nothing to do with the hearing process, and (3) the *cochlea*, a spiral, snail-shaped passage containing the auditory receptors. Beyond the cochlea is a second opening, connecting with the middle ear, which is known as the *round window*. Adjoining this is the Eustachian tube, which joins the middle ear with outside air through openings in the upper part of the throat behind the nasal cavity.

The cochlea is divided along its length into three canals, by thin membranes which readily transmit any vibratory energy from one canal to the other. One of these membranes, known as the *basilar membrane*, supports the *organ of Corti*, which consists of the hair cells and the termini of the afferent nerve fibers.[2]

Numerous theories have been advanced to explain how the various parts of the inner ear function during the process of hearing. That of Helmholtz is undoubtedly the best-known. According to this theory, the fibers along the basilar membrane are laid alongside one another like the blocks of a xylophone. Each of these fibers is presumably tuned to a note of a certain frequency, and vibrates in that frequency when the vibrations of the note reach the inner ear.[3]

How the nervous impulses travel along the nerves constitutes another interesting physiological problem. The auditory nerve contains about 3,000 fibers, not unlike the insulated wires of a telephone cable. Nervous impulses, however, do not travel at all as do electric currents. Apparently, an

---

[2] A diagrammatic sectional view of the human ear is given in *Webster's Dictionary* and in almost every textbook on psychology.

[3] For more detailed discussion of the theories of hearing, see Harvey Fletcher, *Speech and Hearing*, pages 118–131; Hermann L. F. Helmholtz, *Sensations of Tone*, pages 137–151; and Henry J. Watt, *The Psychology of Sound*, pages 139–175.

elemental nerve fiber does not respond unless it responds with full force. According to this theory, the loudness of a tone would depend upon the number of nerve ends stimulated, and upon the rate at which the excitations occur.[4] Presumably, the pitch is determined by the position of the maximum stimulation on the membrane (that is, on the particular nerve fibers excited), and the quality by the pattern of the stimulation on the basilar membrane. These various theories of the nature of the hearing process have not been fully verified, but are illuminating in the study of the various phenomena of audition.

Finally, the ear is an asymmetrical or nonlinear vibrator. A symmetrical vibrator would be, for example, a simple membrane which would vibrate in exact sympathy with the sound impulses which come in contact with it. The eardrum, however, because of the connections with the bony mechanism of the middle ear, does not respond in this fashion. Furthermore, the operation of the linked series of bones itself is nonlinear, thus adding to the asymmetry of the response of the ear. This means that even a simple tone, represented by a sine curve, causes complex vibration forms and certain subjective phenomena which will be discussed under the heading of subjective tones.

TACTILE ASPECTS OF SOUND AND BONE CONDUCTION

The close relation between hearing and some aspects of tactile sensation seems obvious. Some lower aquatic animals have sensory organs which respond to pulsations in water that are subaudible. In the lower vertebrates, the external ear is not always present. Thus, the evidence seems to indicate that the ear may have developed from a sense organ which was tactile rather than auditory.

The upper threshold for the intensity of sounds has been

---

[4] Fletcher, *op. cit.*, pages 126 f.

defined as the point at which the sensation becomes one of feeling, rather than of hearing. Cutaneous vibratory sensation may be easily demonstrated by humming through the partially closed nostrils. Performers on instruments report tactile sensations. Listeners, also, report the perception of vibrations through the various cutaneous receptors. Although the close relation between the tactual and auditory perception of sound has been quite generally recognized, the subject has not yet been thoroughly investigated.

Somewhat similar observations may be made with respect to bone conduction of the vibrations of sound. That the bony structure of the head is a good medium for the transmission of sound vibrations is easily demonstrated by placing the base of a vibrating tuning fork against the teeth. But it seems doubtful whether vibrations transmitted through the air cause any pronounced transmission effect of this type.

Sensory Thresholds and Reaction Times

We have defined physiology as the study of the functions of various organs of the body. With the study of reactions which arise through and depend upon the functioning of these organs, we enter the field of psychology. Originally, psychology was regarded as the scientific study of the nature and activities of the mind. But, with the great advances in the science of physiology, especially since the middle of the nineteenth century, psychology has come to mean, rather, the study of human behavior. With these differences in definition may be associated differences in method. The attempt to describe mental processes observable by reflection and analysis is subjective or introspective, while the attempt to describe mental processes by the methods of the natural sciences is an objective or behavioristic approach.[5]

---

[5] Gardner Murphy (*General Psychology*, pages 619–647) gives a brief discussion of some of the more important psychological "schools."

One of the first concerns of psychology is to correlate physical stimuli and phenomena of the stream of consciousness. The study of the sensory thresholds and reaction times affords a natural point of departure. One problem is to determine what minimal intensity a stimulus must have to excite the organ of hearing.

The investigation of the lower threshold of audibility has revealed that the intensity threshold varies with the frequency of the tone. Thus, the intensity of a tone at a frequency of 64 is greater at the auditory threshold than that of a tone at a frequency of 2,048. The minimal intensity threshold is, accordingly, indicated graphically on a curve.[6]

In the field of audition, the upper intensity threshold may be defined as *the point at which the sensation changes from one of audition to one of feeling.* In other words, if a tone is increased in intensity, a point is finally reached at which the sensation of sound is supplanted by a feeling of pain. Since this intensity limit also varies with the frequency of the tone, it, too, may be represented graphically on a curve.

The determination of the lowest frequency that will produce the sensation of tone is somewhat difficult, because it is necessary to differentiate the sensation of tone from that of feeling. There is a certain sensation of feeling in frequencies of the middle range. As the frequency decreases, this sensation of feeling changes from a tickling to a flutter, and becomes gradually more prominent, until it is difficult to distinguish which sense modality is more affected.

Seashore [7] says that the lowest audible tone is usually about 16, but that under the most favorable circumstances tonal fusion may be obtained at a frequency as low as 12. He gives the upper frequency limit at from 16,000 to 25,000, according

---

[6] For a discussion of the methods used in determining these thresholds, see Harvey Fletcher, *op. cit.*, pages 132 ff.

[7] Carl E. Seashore, *Psychology of Music*, page 54.

to the variable factors. Fletcher[8] indicates that the two points on the graph, where the upper and lower threshold lines meet, represent the upper and lower frequency limits for audibility. The *difference limen*, or the minimum perceptible differences in pitch and intensity, will be discussed under the headings *pitch* and *loudness*.

Reaction times of various types are basic in the field of musical performance. Investigations have not been carried very far, but the information available on simple reactions is not without interest to musicians. Dashiell summarized the published findings as follows: ". . . simple responses to auditory stimuli vary from 120 ms. to 180 ms.; to visual stimuli from 150 ms. to 225 ms.; to tactual pressure, from 130 ms. to 185 ms."[9] The simple response referred to is some such muscular motion as closing or opening a key in an electric circuit. Woodworth gives a more extensive discussion of the topic.[10]

Although the data as to the minimum time that a pure tone must excite the ear for definite pitch to be perceived are rather limited, Fletcher suggests that it is about one twentieth of a second, and that it is nearly independent of frequency.[11] Seashore states that, to be heard as a definite pitch, a tone at a frequency of 128 must have a duration of .09 of a second; at 256, about .07; at 384, about .04; and at 512, about the same.[12]

FATIGUE

The physiopsychological study of fatigue is important, in many ways, in relation to diverse musical activities. The phenomena of fatigue are, roughly, of three kinds: *muscular*, *sensory*, and *attentive*. In their physiological basis, the three

---

[8] *Op. cit.,* page 141.
[9] John F. Dashiell, *Fundamentals of General Psychology,* page 45. The abbreviation *ms.* means millisecond, the thousandth part of a second.
[10] Robert S. Woodworth, *Experimental Psychology,* pages 298–339.
[11] *Op. cit.,* pages 152 f.
[12] *Op. cit.,* page 62.

kinds of fatigue are undoubtedly related; but, apparently, a great deal of further research is necessary before we can expect a comprehensive exposition of the relationship.

In general, however, it is well known that there is a reduction of the capacity to do voluntary muscular work if the movements are long continued; that auditory fatigue is practically negligible for sounds within the ordinary range of musical experience; and that attentive fatigue limits the span of attention, but is, apparently, very different from the first two kinds of fatigue mentioned. For further details the student must be referred to the standard textbooks on physiology and psychology.[13] We shall have further occasion to refer to attentive fatigue in treating some of the basic laws of aesthetic design.

PITCH [14]

Pitch, a psychological term, is that fundamental characteristic of a tone which affords us the data for classification of tones in a series running from *low* to *high*. For musical purposes, pitch values are judged in relation to the tones of musical scales. For scientific purposes, pitch values are judged in terms of their relation to a given reference tone.[15] The physical characteristic of tones to which our experience of pitch is most closely related is that of *frequency*. Therefore, in a sense, we may say that pitch depends upon frequency.

Pitch, as a sensory process, depends upon the response of the organ of hearing to the physical stimulus; and, further, it seems to depend upon something like what Mursell has

---

[13] With reference to the psychology of attention, see, especially, Dashiell, *op. cit.*, pages 314-341; and Woodworth, *op. cit.*, pages 684-712.

[14] For a concise account of the subject of pitch, see Don Lewis, "Pitch: Its Definition and Physical Determinants," *Objective Analysis of Musical Performance*, University of Iowa Studies in the Psychology of Music, Vol. IV, pages 346-373.

[15] See Fletcher, *op. cit.*, page 155.

called "central or mental integration." [16]   But, pitch also depends to some extent upon the other physical characteristics of tone.   Large changes in intensity produce only slight changes in pitch, but certain changes in overtone structure may produce large changes in pitch.[17]

The pitch of complex tones in music is ordinarily taken to be that of the fundamental tone, which is described approximately in terms of frequency.   It would be more accurate to speak of the frequency of the complex wave, since the fundamental, and even several of the partials, may be eliminated without changing the pitch of the tone.   Fletcher explains this as a result of the phenomena of "subjective difference tones," while Lewis points out that the complex wave pattern would still have the same frequency as the fundamental, even if the latter were missing.[18]   Fletcher concludes that, if a complex tone sounds any four consecutive tones in the harmonic series (up to the tenth harmonic), the pitch of the fundamental remains constant.   Other changes in the harmonic structure of a complex tone cause corresponding changes in the pitch of the tone.

But, the term *pitch* may logically be used in a sense other than the one discussed so far.   For example, noises, vocables, chordal complexes, and the like may be assigned approximate relative positions in a pitch scale, according to the total resultant effect of the stimulus.   Thus, we distinguish between the high-pitched rustle of leaves, and the low-pitched rumble of a train; between the high-pitch character of the vowel "a," and the low-pitch of the vowel "oo"; between the total pitch effect of a complex chordal structure in the high woodwinds, and a similar structure in the low brass instruments.   In this

---

[16] James L. Mursell, *The Psychology of Music*, page 71.
[17] See Harvey Fletcher, "Newer Concepts of the Pitch, the Loudness and the Timbre of Musical Tones," *Journal of the Franklin Institute*, Vol. CCXX (1935), pages 427 f.
[18] Fletcher, *Speech and Hearing*, pages 175 f.; Lewis, *op. cit.*, pages 364 f.

sense, it seems reasonable to conclude that pitch is affected by relative intensity of the components in a complex tonal structure. This aspect of the problem of pitch has been mentioned by psychologists, but it needs further investigation. It suggests, among other things, how closely pitch and quality are related.

The fractional change in frequency necessary to produce a perceptible difference in pitch, as reported by Knudsen, is approximately 0.3 of one per cent for frequencies above 512 and below 4096, for tones of moderate loudness.[19] This implies that the ear could detect a difference in pitch between the frequencies 500 and 501.5. This must be taken as an approximation, however, since many factors are involved. There is a great deal of individual variation. Much depends upon the way the tones are presented to the ear: whether or not they are pure; whether they are sounded in succession with slight separation, with no separation, or simultaneously; and so on.

The intensity of the tones is also a factor. The most important practical consideration is that tones have a certain *breadth*. That is, the frequency of a given tone may vary within certain limits without a perceptible change in pitch. Beyond the frequency limits mentioned, the percentage of change in frequency increases to a marked degree.

The physiological limits for pitch discrimination are determined by the hearing organ itself. The cognitive limits do not coincide with the physiological limits. Apparently, the physiological limits do not change perceptibly during the life of the individual, unless the organ of hearing is affected by disease, extreme old age, or injury. Cognition, however, improves with maturation, experience, and training.

In dealing with the problems of pitch discernment, one

---

[19] Vern O. Knudsen, *Architectural Acoustics*, page 78. New York: John Wiley & Sons, Inc., 1932.

should remember that there is a great difference between the simple matching of tones, and the comprehension of pitch relationships in the complex tonal structure of musical performance. For example, it is one thing to distinguish differences of one or two vibrations, in comparing tones which are almost in unison; but quite another to make such fine discriminations in tonal relationships at the interval of the major sixth, or in the more complex melodic, harmonic, and rhythmic situations of actual music. The available evidence would seem to indicate considerable opportunity for improvement with training in these more complex relationships. There is room for much further investigation in this as well as in related fields.

An interesting corollary of the psychophysiological limits for pitch discrimination is the fact that an individual can perceive only a limited number of tones as being of different pitch. It is estimated that the average person can distinguish approximately 1,400 different pitches of a pure tone of average loudness.[20] Of course, with differences in intensity, the number of perceivable pure tones is greatly increased. Fletcher calculates the number as being several hundred thousands and points out that the number of complex tones would, logically, be very much larger.[21]

Many interesting and baffling problems arise in the study of the musical phenomenon known as absolute pitch. It is a well-known fact that many people possess a remarkable ability to identify pitches, even apart from musical contexts. A satisfactory physiopsychological explanation of this phenomenon has not been found, although a growing body of literature concerns it. The evidence seems to indicate that, though tonal memory may be somewhat developed with training and experience, so that many musicians have something

---

[20] Seashore, *op. cit.*, pages 60 f., and Lewis, *op. cit.*, pages 353 f.
[21] Fletcher, *op. cit.*, pages 159 ff.

like a sense of absolute pitch, the same ability shown by some people, otherwise unmusical, is a gift.[22]

INTERTONES, SUBJECTIVE TONES

Of the many other interesting aspects of the problem of pitch, we can mention only a few in passing. The so-called *intertone* is the tone heard when two beating primary tones differ in frequency by only a few vibrations. Its pitch is between that of the two primaries. As the difference in frequency increases, Woodworth says, the intertone grows more faint, and the primary tones become audible separately.[23] Other investigators suggest that two intertones may be heard — one below the upper primary, and the other above the lower primary.[24]

Fletcher describes *subjective tones* of three types, which he calls *harmonics, summation tones,* and *difference tones.* He tells of the presence of tones of frequencies of 1200, 2400, and 3600 when the harmonic analyzer showed the presence of a single frequency — namely, 1200. He attributes this to the nonlinear response of the hearing mechanism.[25]

A number of interesting studies have been made of the relation between pitch and the frequency vibrato. The available data show that the principal pitch of a tone with a frequency vibrato varies from the geometric mean tone. For vibratos whose extents are small (less than a quarter of a tone) the principal pitch is slightly above the geometric mean, while for vibratos greater than .6 of a tone, it is lower.[26]

---

[22] For further discussion and bibliography, see Mursell, *op. cit.,* pages 132–137, and Seashore, *op. cit.,* pages 162 f.

[23] Woodworth, *Experimental Psychology,* page 515.

[24] See H. Banister, "Audition," *Handbook in General Experimental Psychology,* page 899.

[25] For further details see Fletcher, *Speech and Hearing,* pages 175 ff., and Seashore, *Psychology of Music,* pages 64 ff.

[26] For a summary of the findings in this field, see Lewis, *op. cit.,* pages 355 ff.

LOUDNESS

Loudness is a psychological term used to distinguish that fundamental characteristic of sound which most nearly corresponds to the physical characteristic of intensity. Experiments show that loudness of tones depends upon three physical qualities, *intensity, frequency*, and *overtone structure*. But, since the sensation of loudness changes more rapidly with changes of intensity than with changes in frequency or overtone structure, the common idea is that loudness depends upon intensity.

For scientific purposes, measurements of loudness are most conveniently made by comparison with a standard tone of reference. The standard reference tone commonly used is a pure tone of moderate loudness, with a frequency of 1000. This tone has been selected as a reference tone because it falls within the limits in which the relation between the physical measurement of the intensity and the subjective judgment of the loudness approximately conforms to the formula, *the sensation of loudness varies as the logarithm of the intensity* — a formula which can be conveniently stated in mathematical terms, and applied in objective physical measurements.

The important fact to remember, in this connection, is that the subjective perception of loudness does not vary directly with the change in the physical energy of the stimulus. It varies approximately in terms of the so-called Weber-Fechner law, which dates from 1834. According to this law, the amount of increase in the stimulus necessary to produce a just-noticeable change in the loudness is proportional to the intensity of the original stimulus.

A method commonly employed in determining the minimum perceptible difference in intensity is to take two tones of the same pitch and intensity and sound them alternately. Then, one of the tones is increased in intensity until a difference is detected; or the investigator begins with the difference plainly perceptible, and gradually reduces the difference until it is no longer distinguishable.

The Weber-Fechner law applies with reasonable accuracy to the perception of pure tones of moderate intensity in a frequency range from 700 to 4000. Beyond these limits the divergence from the law increases. For example, the fractional increase in intensity necessary to produce a just-noticeable difference in loudness for low and soft tones is disproportionately larger than it is in the frequency and intensity range indicated above.[27]

The application of the logarithmic formula to the intensity-loudness relationship means, for example, that if an intensity were increased from 10 to 100, the loudness would only increase from 1 to 2, since the logarithm of 10 to the base 10 is 1, and that of 100 is 2. On the other hand, if the intensity is increased from 10 to 20, the loudness increases only to 1.30103.

Because the sensation of loudness does not conform to the Weber-Fechner law outside the limits indicated, the term *decibel* is not satisfactory as a unit for the expression of the degree of loudness. The term *equivalent decibels* has been used, but a new word *phon* would seem to offer the best way out of the difficulty.[28]

By selecting a reference tone within the limits where the logarithmic law holds, loudness of tones outside these limits can be compared; and, when they are judged equal, the outside tone may be said to have the same number of phons of loudness, or to be at the same loudness level. Within the limits phons and decibels would be equal in number, but outside the limits they would differ. For example, a pure tone with a frequency of 150 and an intensity level of 65

[27] For a more detailed discussion of this topic, see Fletcher, *op. cit.*, pages 145 ff.
[28] See Ll. S. Lloyd, *Decibels and Phons*. *Phon* is pronounced to rhyme with *gone*.

decibels will have a loudness, in phons, of 50. In other words, it will have a loudness equal to that of a tone with a frequency of 1000 at a sound level of 50 decibels. Ordinary conversation ranges from 60 to 70 phons, while other sounds vary from 10 to 130 phons from the lower to the higher thresholds of audition.

Though accurate results have not been attained, in attempts to determine the minimum perceptible difference in intensity, several significant observations can be made. In the first place, we can say roughly that if a sound of moderate frequency and intensity is increased by one decibel, the difference will be just noticeable to the average person.[29] In the second place, the total number of intensity differences which can be perceived for a pure tone of constant pitch is relatively small. If the Weber-Fechner law were accurate, the number of perceptible intensity differences would be equal to the number of decibels across the auditory area, which is, at most, about 130.[30]

Something of the musical implications of the intensity-loudness relation may be illustrated by an example or two. Suppose one flute is playing at a loudness of 40 phons. Assuming that the addition of another flute would double the intensity of the sound, the resultant increase in terms of phons would be only 3, or a total loudness of 43 phons. Ten flutes would increase the loudness to only 50 phons. If an 80-piece band has a loudness value of 70 phons, a 160-piece band would sound louder by only 3 phons, or a total of 73.

---

[29] Seashore, *op. cit.*, page 84, gives one *db* as the magnitude of just-noticeable difference, but states (page 87) that "a fine pianist may be able to hear and reproduce differences as small as 0.1 *db* in the middle register." Cf. George W. Stewart, *Introductory Acoustics*, pages 129 ff. (New York: D. Van Nostrand Company, Inc., 1933); John Mills, *A Fugue in Cycles and Bels*, pages 35 f. (New York: D. Van Nostrand Company, Inc., 1935); Fletcher, *op. cit.*, pages 69 and 159; and especially Lloyd, *op. cit.*, pages 7, 12, *et passim.*

[30] Cf. Seashore, *op. cit.*, pages 85 f.

Twenty players would have to be added to an 80-piece band to produce a just-noticeable difference in loudness. Doubling the intensity of a sound does not mean doubling the loudness. On the other hand, the phon is not a unit for measuring the increase in loudness in the sense that twice the number of phons means twice the loudness. There is very little information available on this particular matter, but Lloyd, for one, writes: [31]

> For sounds with a loudness-level of, say, 80 phons it is found, however, that broadly speaking a tenfold increase of intensity, that is, an increase of 10 decibels in the intensity-level, is judged to correspond to a doubling of the loudness.

In terms of these observations, an 800-piece band would be necessary to increase the given intensity from 70 to 80 decibels, and thereby produce the impression that the loudness had been doubled.

Whether these samples are scientifically accurate or not, there is overwhelming evidence to indicate the futility of trying to increase the size of musical organizations — bands, orchestras, choruses — beyond certain limits. The facts presented also suggest reasons for there being so relatively few degrees in the loudness scale as compared to the pitch scale. The ambiguity of the conventional dynamic markings may some day be clarified by indications, in phons, of the desired loudness, just as tempos are defined by metronomic indications.[32]

QUALITY

Tone quality or *timbre*, as a psychophysiological attribute of tonal sensation or perception, is ordinarily defined as *that aspect of tonal perception which enables us to distinguish between tones of the same pitch and loudness, sounded by*

---

[31] Lloyd, *op. cit.*, page 15.
[32] In Seashore, *Psychology of Music*, page 89, see reference to a suggestion by Scott Reger.

different instruments. It may also be truthfully said that it is that aspect of tone which enables us to identify a certain tone as that of a given instrument, regardless of pitch and loudness. Thus, an experienced musician can identify the tone of a clarinet at various pitch and loudness levels.

Except for differences in wave form due to differences in phase, the physical correlate of *quality* would seem, in a most comprehensive way, to be the wave form. This means that quality depends chiefly upon the response of the organism to the overtone structure of the tone, and, to a lesser degree, upon its response to the absolute intensity and frequency. Thus, the intensity pattern of the partials of an oboe differs from that of a clarinet. Ordinarily, we point to this difference in overtone structure as the physical basis of the difference in quality, which is a psychological matter. But, we also distinguish between the tone quality of the different registers of most, if not all, instruments, as when we speak of the *chalumeau* register of the clarinet as compared to the *middle* and *high* registers. The general pattern of the overtone structure may remain sufficiently similar, in the different registers, for us to recognize the tone as that of the clarinet, but differences in frequency and intensity undoubtedly contribute to the resultant differences in quality.

The sameness of quality in different registers of the same instrument is also partly accounted for by the so-called *formant* theory. According to this view, the partial tones within a certain register are prominent, regardless of the pitch of the fundamental. This phenomenon may be due to the noise element caused, in part, by the characteristic vibration of the reed in certain wind instruments, or by the scraping of the bow in the stringed instruments. The pitch of these high, often inharmonic, overtones might remain fairly constant for tones produced in different registers of the instrument. The formant theory is generally accepted as the best explanation of the various vowel qualities, and there seems little doubt that it partly accounts for the characteristic tone quality of many musical instruments. This particular problem needs further investigation.

An oscillograph will reveal absolute differences in the form of the waves produced by tones of different frequencies and intensities. Similarly, tones of different durations will have different absolute wave forms and, consequently, different qualities within certain psychological limits. It is probably more meaningful to explain the difference in quality in such cases as due to the difference in wave form, than it is to attribute it in a causal sense to duration.[33]

Another aspect of tone quality which requires special attention is that which Seashore and his associates have designated as *sonance*. This term has arisen particularly in the study of the vibrato, and refers especially to that aspect of tone quality which results from the fusion in perception of certain fluctuations in pitch and intensity. The average frequency for a good vibrato is 6.5 pulsations per second, with an average pitch variation of .5 of a tone.[34]

THE SENSE OF TIME

Insofar as the *sense of time* is taken to mean *the ability to compare the length of tones sounded in succession*, or to judge the comparative lengths of intervals of time measured off between clicks, as in the Seashore tests, this sense depends upon the objective factor of duration. The psychological response to the temporal aspects of tonal relations is undoubtedly of fundamental importance in musical experiences or activities; but the situation is so complex, that we are hardly in a position to evaluate the ability to make nice discriminations in duration, as this ability has been tested in the Seashore experiments.

---

[33] *Cf.* Otto Ortmann, "What Is Tone-Quality?" *The Musical Quarterly*, Vol. XXI (1935), pages 442–450.
[34] Carl E. Seashore, *Psychology of the Vibrato in Voice and Instrument*, University of Iowa Studies in the Psychology of Music, Vol. III, page 151.

More generally, the sense of time would logically include other, perhaps related, capacities: the ability to set a tempo, to maintain a uniform tempo, or to modify it in accordance with the demands of intelligent performance; as well as the ability to deal successfully with the complexities of the rhythmic patterns which occur in music.

The values given by Seashore for the minimum perceptible difference in the lengths of tones vary from .01 of a second, for a fine musical ear, to .2 for an inferior ear. Apparently, sensitivity to differences in duration is not dependent upon the structure of the ear in the same manner as is sensitivity to differences of frequency, intensity, and form or overtone structure.

VOLUME AND BRIGHTNESS AS CHARACTERISTICS OF TONE

A psychological attribute of tone different from any of those already discussed is *volume*. It may be roughly defined as *that subjective characteristic of sound which most nearly corresponds to the physical factor of extensity*. Low tones seem to be greater in volume than high tones; but pitch is not the sole determinant of volume, because, with pitch constant, volume will vary with loudness. Again, if the pitch and loudness are kept the same, volume will vary with quality. For example, a soprano voice seems to have less volume than a mezzo-soprano, even in the same range. In an analogous manner, tones of short duration seem, within certain limits, to be smaller in volume than longer tones. Thus Seashore seems to have considerable justification for saying: [35]

Volume as a musical characteristic of tone is a complex experience resting upon the frequency, the intensity, the duration, and the harmonic constitution of the physical stimulus, and largely influenced by associational, affective, and motor factors in perception.

[35] Seashore, *Psychology of Music*, page 134. See also Mursell, *op. cit.*, pages 62 ff.; and Henry J. Watt, *The Foundations of Music*, pages 6 ff.

The case for *brightness, density,* and *vocality* or *vowel quality* as separate dimensions of tonal sensations is not so well established.[36]

MASKING EFFECT

If, in the presence of a given sound, another sound is introduced and gradually increased in intensity until the original given sound can be no longer heard, it is said to be *masked* by the second sound. In general, low tones of considerable intensity show a marked tendency to mask higher tones, while high tones do not mask low tones so much. The masking effect is most pronounced when the masked tone is almost identical with the masking tone.

A low tone, however, does not produce a marked masking effect upon a tone that is very much higher in pitch. Thus, while a trumpet might easily mask the tone of a clarinet at approximately the same pitch, a tuba would scarcely mask the tone of a piccolo, in a high register, to any great extent. Fletcher, for example, shows a chart indicating that a 200-cycle tone would have to be increased to 55 decibels before it would have any interfering effect upon a tone of 3000 cycles.[37] The masking results given by Fletcher are based upon the use of pure tones. The problem would be very much modified if complex tones were used.

BINAURAL PHENOMENA

It is a well-known fact that we possess, to a considerable extent, the ability to tell the direction from which a sound comes to us. The normal use of two ears in hearing seems to make this possible. Two different theories are offered to explain this effect of *binaural* hearing. One is the *intensity* theory, and the other is the *phase* theory.

---

[36] For a review of some of the more important investigations in this field, see Woodworth, *op. cit.*, pages 507 ff.

[37] Fletcher, *Speech and Hearing*, page 171.

According to the intensity theory: the direction is determined by the difference in intensity with which the sound reaches the two ears, since the ear on the side of the head opposite from the source of the sound receives a stimulus of lesser intensity. The angle from which the sound is perceived as coming is said to be proportional to the difference in intensity. But, according to the phase theory, when a sound comes from an angle, the waves at the two ears are different in phase, and this difference enables the individual to distinguish the direction from which the sound comes.[38]

With regard to binaural beats, Fletcher points out that under certain conditions objective beats, undoubtedly due to physical interference in one ear from vibrations coming from the other ear by means of bone conduction, may be observed.[39] It is suggested that the phenomenon of subjective beats is produced in the brain, and, further, that the term *beat* is scarcely accurate — since, in the place of waxing and waning of tone as in ordinary beats, there is an apparent swinging from side to side of the source of sound.

THE MUSICAL INTERVAL

Thus far, in this chapter, we have been considering some physiopsychological matters fundamental to the musical ex-

---

[38] A summary of the experiments in this field will be found in Fletcher, *op. cit.*, pages 188 ff., and Woodworth, *op. cit.*, pages 518 ff. Stewart (*op. cit.*, page 144) concludes that "the binaural intensity effect cannot account for the ability to locate sounds," and that ". . . the binaural phase effect can do so in the limited region here discussed." Cermak ("Akustik," Müller-Pouillet, *Lehrbuch der Physik*, Braunschweig, Friedr. Vieweg und Sohn, 1929, Vol. 1, pt. 3, pages 163 ff.) suggests the difference in time between the arrival at the two ears of the sound stimulus coming from the side as a supplement to the phase theory, but points out that this would apply chiefly to noises and intermittent sounds. Mills (*op. cit.*, pages 178 ff.) explains and describes an important application of the binaural principle of audition in the electrical transmission of an orchestral concert, whereby the music may be presented in auditory perspective.

[39] Fletcher, *op. cit.*, pages 193 ff.

perience. It has been repeatedly emphasized that tones in isolation do not constitute music; and the topics studied so far, although fundamental, are, in a sense, introductory or preliminary to the psychology of music proper. In other words, when we begin to study the psychological aspects of tonal relations as expressed by such terms as *interval, scale, rhythm, melody,* and *harmony,* we are getting closer to actual music. We must try to keep in mind that the psychology of the interval, the scale, rhythm, melody, harmony, and so on, is not synonymous with the musical significance of these terms. Nor is it the same as the physical or aesthetic implications of these terms. Many of these topics will recur under the headings of musical aesthetics and music theory and practice, but there they will be studied from different viewpoints. Thus, when we study the interval in psychology, we ask how and why we perceive these tonal relations as we do; in aesthetics, we consider the interval as an element of musical design with certain potential expressive values; and in music theory we stress still other, although no doubt related, meanings.

An interval, psychologically, is the perception of the relation between two tones with reference to pitch. The notion of the interval, or the interval effect, depends, in a rather complex way, upon the reaction of the organism to the frequency relationship between the tones; and the reaction itself is further conditioned by the musical context in which the tones occur. For example: whether an interval is perceived as an augmented fourth or a diminished fifth, or whether it is heard as a major third or a diminished fourth, and so on, depends upon the context.

From these considerations it should be clear that *interval* is not synonymous with *difference in pitch,* although, of course, difference in pitch will ordinarily affect the situation. Thus.

the fundamental musical intervals may be mistuned, but still maintain their identity as fifths, sixths, seconds, and so forth.[40] In other words, the amount of change in frequency necessary to produce a noticeable difference in pitch is very much less than that necessary to produce a change in interval classification.

When two tones are sounded simultaneously, the interval effect is produced. This is called the *harmonic interval.* Without attempting to enter upon a discussion of the nature of perception, we may simply say that the interval so produced is a *Gestalt* (a unit of perception). We may suggest something of the reason for the relative stability of these intervallic units of perception, by pointing out the comparatively simple proportions between the frequencies of the tones; by referring to the degree of fusion obtained between the two tones; and in various other ways. But, whatever the final explanation may be, we must be content for the present with the statement that the interval is a fundamental unit of perception.

The interval effect is also produced when two tones are sounded in succession. This is called the *melodic interval.* Many of the observations concerning the simultaneous, or harmonic, interval apply, with necessary changes, to the melodic interval. In addition, the melodic interval is perceived as movement, or at least as involving a kind of movement. From this fact, it is easy to see how Kurth and others have arrived at the concept of the melodic interval as possessing a kind of kinetic energy — a concept psychologically fundamental in certain aspects of the theory of musical aesthetics.[41]

---

[40] Carroll C. Pratt, *The Meaning of Music*, pages 119 ff.

[41] *Cf.* Ernst Kurth, *Musikpsychologie*, page 76 *et passim;* and Pratt, *op. cit.*, pages 185–190, 228–232. For a discussion of further details in connection with the interval, see Mursell, *op. cit.*, pages 81–98, and Watt, *op. cit.*, pages 36–44 *et passim.*

SCALES

The *scale*, in a psychological and in a general sense, is a schematic organization of the tones used in music in a pitch series. Although the term is closely related to the concepts of tonality, modality, and key, it is not synonymous with any of them. The idea of scale is contingent on the perception of pitch relationships, and, in this relationship, it should be thought of as a succession of intervals.

The psychological considerations basic in the development of the conventional scale formations used in music may be summarized briefly as follows. One fundamental factor is the organizing activity of the human mind or central nervous system — the tendency of the individual to organize sensory perceptions. Another important psychological factor is the fact that tones, as perceived, have breadth of pitch. That is: within limits, the frequency of tones may be varied without noticeable difference in pitch. A third factor is interval quality — more specifically, the fact that intervals may be slightly mistuned and still retain their characteristic quality as intervals. Further, the limits of our powers to discriminate pitch and interval set natural limits on the size of interval practicable in scale structure. Other psychologically determinative factors probably, to some extent at least, exist in the laws of habituation and association.

The effect of these and similar considerations, in conjunction with the underlying physical and psychological factors already discussed, has been the selection of a limited number of the psychologically discriminable intervals in the audible range, and the organization of them into the familiar patterns used in music for aesthetic purposes.

RHYTHM

In psychology, musical *rhythm* depends upon the fact that tones presented in temporal sequence are perceived as having not only pitch, loudness, quality, and duration, but also *movement*. Movement is so exactly *progression from one note to another in a melody* that the term is a literal use of the word. And yet, the objective stimulus which produces the sense of movement is a movement, not through space, but rather through time, as one frequency is superseded by another, or, more comprehensively, one tonal complex is followed by another. A succession of tones of the same pitch is perceived as a kind of hopping motion, up and down in the same place; and tones in stepwise succession, and other tonal progressions, are perceived variously as smooth swaying movements, skips, dizzy plunges, cascades of movements, and so on. This multiplicity of effects, a result of the organizing activity of the human mind, shapes into patterns called *rhythm*.

As the literature dealing with psychological theories of rhythm is immense, we can attempt only the barest outline of a few basic facts. In view of the complexity of the problem, the many controversial issues, and the lack of unanimity of opinion among psychologists, it is difficult to make a satisfactory brief statement about it. Nevertheless, we may say that the ultimate psychological foundation of rhythm lies in mental activity and kinesthetic (muscular) sensations, or factors, organized as bodily movements.[42] Or, following Seashore, we may say that the perception of rhythm involves the whole organism, the sense of time, the sense of intensity, auditory and motor imagery, motor impulses, emotional type and temperament, logical span, and creative imagination.[43] Other implications of rhythm would logically be discussed under such headings as musical aesthetics, musical theory, and musical pedagogy. The psychology of rhythm has an important bearing on all these fields.

---

[42] See, for example, Pratt, *op. cit.*, pages 228–239.
[43] Seashore, *Psychology of Music*, pages 138–148.

MELODY

In general, the psychology of *melody* has to do with the study of how the temporal sequences of tones in music are perceived. It is concerned with the application of the various psychological laws of perception, attention, association, habituation, memory, and the like, in our experience of the melodic structure of music. From studies in this field we learn much that is of significance for aesthetic theory and for the practice of music. Gestalt theory points out that a melody is more than the sum of its parts, insofar as a sequence of tones is "apprehended in terms of a unified and single response." [44]

The further psychological study of melody is not to be separated from the study of the constitutive elements, or factors, of interval, scale, rhythm, harmony, tonality, and so forth, so that in the end it is difficult, if not impossible, to draw hard and fast lines of demarcation among the various related special fields of investigation. On the other hand, the study of the psychological factors significant to our conception of melody should not be confused with more purely aesthetic or music-theoretical factors.

HARMONY

The term *harmony* is ordinarily taken to mean, or to refer to, tones sounding simultaneously. From this central idea, two other well-defined conceptions of the word have developed, one more primitive or fundamental, and the other more advanced and complicated. On the one hand, it means the study of tonal relations in general, especially with the determination and definition of the pitch relationships in intervals, scales, melodies, and chords. On the other hand, it concerns the relations between the successive combinations

---

[44] See Mursell, *The Psychology of Music*, page 104.

of tones that occur in music. Thus, when Helmholtz tries to explain the relationship of tone C to tone D, in terms of the relation of each to another tone G, which is a fifth above the one and a fifth below the other, he is discussing melodic relations in terms of harmonic relations. And, when Rameau and other theorists discuss the chord of the added sixth as distinguished from the first inversion of the supertonic seventh chord, they are concerned with the functional relation between chords, which is, of course, one of the fundamental concerns of harmony.

The fundamental problems of psychology in relation to harmony include the effort to explain how, and why: first, tones are perceived as related; second, certain simultaneous combinations of tones are perceived as well-defined chordal entities though others are not; third, a given chordal structure may sound utterly different in a different tonal environment; and fourth, certain chordal progressions produce a feeling of finality, though others create a feeling of suspense. And, of course, psychology can contribute to our understanding of many other detailed problems of harmony. Much fumbling in this field would seem due to the fact that so few professional psychologists have had a thorough technical training in music, and, vice versa, that so few technically trained musicians have been thoroughly trained psychologists.

The laws of harmony of a musical system — such as that of music from Bach to Brahms — may be said, in the main, to represent the practical application of musical aesthetic principles which are themselves conditioned by psychological, physiological, and physical factors. Psychology can, by the investigation of special problems such as those already mentioned, and others yet to be mentioned, contribute much to the musician's understanding of the fundamental problems of harmony.

TONALITY AND CADENCE

The psychological study of *tonality* refers to certain so-called laws which psychologists have set up, known as the *law of the tonic*, the *law of the cadence*, the *law of return*, and the *law of equal intervals*. The following account of these laws is based chiefly upon Ogden.[45]

The law of the tonic may be formulated somewhat as follows:

> Other things being equal, the trend of a two-tone sequence is always toward the one whose ratio-number is 2, 4, 8, 16, 32, and so on, whenever such a tone is present.

If we strike C and G in succession, the greater satisfaction comes from ending on C; similarly, with C and F, the better ending note is F. Why? Because C–G, 2–3, and C–F, 3–4, give C and F respectively as the ratio numbers 2 and 4. It is suggested that the reason for this is that these numbers represent the fundamental tone in the *Klang*.

The law of the cadence is stated thus:

> Other things being equal, finality attaches to the lower tone, an effect which is also enhanced by the decreased intensity that usually attaches to low tones.

The operation of this law is seen in the falling inflection at the end of a sentence, and in such familiar expressions as *tick-tock, knick-knack, flip-flop,* and so on. Here, the tonic is not necessarily present in the sequence of sounds.

The law of return is expressed in the following words:

> Other things being equal, it is better to return to any starting-point whatsoever than not to return.[46]

---

[45] Ogden, *Hearing*, pages 152 ff.

[46] See W. Van Dyke Bingham, "Studies in Melody," *Psychological Review*, Monograph Supplements, Vol. XII, No. 3, Whole No. 50 (1910), pages 33 f.

This is a rather complex matter, involving many such factors as accentuation of tones, rhythmical setting, duration, and the pitch distance traversed.

The so-called law of equal intervals, operating in sequences of tones that do not comply with the conditions of a harmonic series, provides for the organization of tones upon a unit whose ratio serves as a recognizable interval. The octave is divided into equal parts, and this proportion differs from the proportions of the harmonic ratios — precluding the use of a tonic, and only approximating harmony — but arousing attitudes of expectancy through sequences of tones. Oriental music, in some cases, follows this principle, using cadence and return, but with the equal interval as a measure for the melodic sequence. Ogden concludes that tonality is not an attribute of sound, but a perceptual characteristic of tones in their sequential setting, depending upon all the attributes of sound.[47] The detailed application of these principles in musical composition is what the rules of music theory, harmony, counterpoint, and so forth, attempt to accomplish.

CONSONANCE AND DISSONANCE

In order to gain some insight into the psychological problem of *consonance and dissonance* it is necessary to review briefly some of the acoustical, aesthetic, music-theoretical, historical, and other factors involved. One of the central problems is the definition of the terms, and another is that of finding a basis for a clear-cut distinction between consonance and dissonance.

From the physical-acoustical viewpoint, consonance and dissonance are defined in terms of the simplicity of the relationship between the frequencies of tones. Thus, two tones having the same frequencies constitute a perfect consonance

---

[47] *Op. cit.,* pages 165 f.

because of the one-to-one agreement, or complete synchroni-
zation, of the frequencies. The octave, represented by the
proportion of 2 to 1, is the next most perfect consonance;
while, at the other end of the series, the major seventh or
minor second, and other intervals represented by much more
complex proportions, are extreme dissonances.

In between these extremes are tonal combinations which
are variously classed as *imperfect consonances* or *mild dissonances*. Where to draw the line of distinction between
consonance and dissonance is a question which the science of
acoustics cannot answer adequately in its own terms.

Psychophysiological attempts to define and explain the
terms have varied, from the naïve statement that consonance
is a pleasing and dissonance a displeasing sensation, to the
more sophisticated observations of Watt with his volumetric
theory. Helmholtz has related the problem to beats, while
Stumpf has developed his theory of fusion. Although the
findings of these scientists cannot be regarded as conclusive,
they are nevertheless valuable and are suggestive in many
ways.

The statement that the dissonance of one period in musical
history becomes the consonance of another seems to assume
a definition in terms of what is pleasing or displeasing, or
in terms of the feeling-of-a-need-for-resolution. Although
there is some evidence supporting such a statement, in neither
case is it strictly accurate. It seems to refer to changes of
taste, rather than to changes in the intrinsic character of dissonance and consonance. People may grow increasingly
fond of dissonance, and composers may treat it more and more
freely, but that scarcely justifies calling such intervals as
sevenths and seconds consonances.

This feeling-of-a-need-for-resolution is one of the most
stable psychological criteria for the distinction between consonance and dissonance, at least in the history of music up

to the twentieth century.[48]   In accordance with this idea,
the dissonance would be defined as a combination of, or a
relationship between, tones in which one or more tones seem
to require resolution.   The tone which seems to demand
resolution is normally the dissonant tone.   In the light of
such a definition, it is easy to see how an interval, ordinarily
classed as a consonance, may be so used as to give rise to the
feeling of a need for resolution and, consequently, be classed
as a dissonance.   For example, the interval of the sixth and
the six-three chord are ordinarily classed as consonances; yet
the six-three combination, especially when it is found on the
dominant, is naturally felt as a dissonance resolving in the
conventional manner to a consonance.   This familiar effect
has been called the *conceptual dissonance* — the *Auffassungs-
dissonanz* of Louis and Thuille.[49]   Music theory sets up its
definitions of these terms, and classifies its tonal combinations
with due regard for both the physical and the psychological
factors in the situation.

THINKING, IMAGINATION, AND INSPIRATION

Thinking is a concept that is not very well or sharply defined psychologically.   Types of thinking responses vary
from routine thought sequences, such as going through a
familiar melody silently, to reasoning, which psychologists
regard as "thinking in its most explicit, its most articulated
form." [50]   The psychology of thinking, as related to musical
activities, affords a broad field for study and scientific investigation.

Combarieu has defined music as "the art of thinking in

---

[48] In spite of the fact that modernistic composers may say they do not
have such a feeling with regard to sevenths, seconds, and the like, the author
thinks this thesis can be defended.

[49] R. Louis, and L. Thuille, *Harmonielehre* (8th ed.), pages 46 f.   Stuttgart: Klett, 1913.

[50] John F. Dashiell, *Fundamentals of General Psychology*, page 551.   *Cf.*
Woodworth, *Experimental Psychology*, pages 783 ff.

sounds." [51] He supports this definition, in part, by giving an example of a melody, and pointing out that the tones are perceived, not in isolation, but in terms of their relations to each other and to the tonic. Thus, in a sense, a melody is a system of relations. One type of relationship involved — the interval — is, as we have previously defined it psychologically, an abstraction; but the individual intelligence has been used to compare and appreciate. This, Combarieu believes, is the kind of activity that constitutes musical thinking, since philosophers define thinking as *abstracting and uniting*.

The development of concepts in the field of music seems to be similar to that in other fields. When Combarieu speaks of thinking in sounds as thinking without concepts, he is apparently identifying concepts with linguistic ideas. Without going into a detailed discussion of the problems involved, it is safe to assume that musical concepts are as real and substantial as any other concepts, and, with necessary changes, follow similar psychological principles.

Ideational activity in general and imagery, inspiration, creative thinking, and the like in particular, as applied to music, are ordinarily considered in this field. The word *idea* is used loosely to mean a great many different things: a plan or project, a notion, a fancy, or something contrasted to fact or actuality. However it is defined, we think of ideas as the fundamental objects of thought.

Objectively considered, thinking is an indirect process: when we think about a thing, we are at least one step removed from direct manipulation of it. The psychological description of what goes on in the organism must be, as Dashiell suggests, "in terms of responses that are set up and that serve in turn as stimuli." [52] Adapting or paraphrasing

---

[51] Jules Combarieu, *Music, Its Laws and Evolution*, page 7.
[52] *Op. cit.*, page 561.

the words of Dashiell to illustrate musical thinking, we might say: a tone or combination of tones arouses as an implicit reaction a sensation of tone or a perception of a configuration of tones, and that reaction in turn arouses a new implicit reaction as some kind of a musical experience, until, sooner or later, the implicit reaction arouses overt behavior — whether in some act related to musical composition or performance, or even in listening.

Subjectively or introspectively considered, the ideational processes seem to involve some kind of imagery. Thus, a musician can think through a composition when no physical stimulus is present. While the value of imagery to thinking has been challenged,[53] there can be little doubt that it is very considerably used in music. The composer has in mind a vivid image of many, if not all, details of his composition before ever a note is sounded, or before his pen is put to the paper. Before he produces a sound, the performer has in mind a clear-cut image of the tone quality he wishes to attain, how a given phrase will sound, and so on. In his chapter on "Imagining in Music," [54] Seashore gives many other examples, and stresses its importance as one of the most important marks of the musical mind.

For a discussion of other details of the nature of thinking, the student must be referred to the technical psychological literature. Much of what psychologists tell us concerning problem solving, inspiration, creative thought, and similar problems applies to thinking in music.

One or two comments may be made, in passing, on *inspiration* and creative thought. Most of the large amount of literature on the subject seems to be devoted to descriptive accounts of the circumstances under which ideas come suddenly and unexpectedly to the thinker. Nevertheless, what

---

[53] See Dashiell, *op. cit.*, pages 563 f.
[54] *Op. cit.*, pages 161–172.

theorizing has been done tends to indicate that the process of creating is not simply haphazard waiting for the inspiration to come, but, rather, taking some fairly well-defined steps to stimulate the desired end. For example, Woodworth suggests that, in the creative work of poets and artists, three overt stages — preparation, illumination, and revision — have been identified.[55] Stages not unlike these are to be found in the creative processes of many composers.

EMOTION, FEELING, AND MOOD

Because the musical experience is fundamentally emotional, what psychology has to tell us of *emotion* is of especial interest to musicians. The complexity of the subject as well as the limitations of space make impossible more than a brief discussion of this important topic. Modern psychology tries to explain and describe the emotions in terms of changes of diffuse internal conditions within the organism. The literature of psychology shows on every hand the difficulty of distinguishing between such terms as *emotion, feeling,* and *mood.*

Traditionally, feeling is considered an elementary process, and emotion a complex of feeling and sensation. At one time, the attempt was made to classify elementary feelings as pleasant and unpleasant. Wundt broke with tradition in postulating three classifications: pleasantness-unpleasantness, excitement-calm, and tension-relaxation or expectancy-relief. Titchener and others questioned these distinctions, and suggested numerous revisions and modifications in the general theory of the emotions, without achieving definitive results. Woodworth sums up the situation as follows: [56]

A general conclusion, not exactly forced by the evidence from introspective studies of feeling, but at least rendered attractive, is that the feelings are reactive attitudes of the organism. Pleasant-

---

[55] *Op. cit.,* page 821.
[56] *Op. cit.,* page 241.

ness and unpleasantness correspond to the attitudes of acceptance and rejection, excitement and depression to the momentary level of muscular activity or readiness for activity, tension and relaxation to the degree of muscular tension. The various emotions may correspond to more specific attitudes.

While emotions are ordinarily thought of as related to certain feelings of bodily changes, certain other feelings or bodily states, such as hunger and thirst, are not called emotions. It has been suggested that the basis for the distinction is that, while the typical emotion is aroused by an external stimulus and is directed outside the organism, a bodily state, such as hunger or thirst, is basically an intraorganic process and has no relation to the environment.[57] Another difficult distinction is that between emotion and desire.

Of greater importance, perhaps, is the attempted distinction between feeling and valuation. In connection with a spontaneous aesthetic judgment expressed in the words, "That is beautiful," we ordinarily have a feeling of pleasure. For this reason, Woodworth says, aesthetics is sometimes included in the psychology of feelings. However, he thinks it belongs, rather, under the heading of judgment, where experimental aesthetics is the study of response to the beautiful.

Pepper, identifying emotion with the quality of an event, suggests that emotion, mood, and feeling differ not so much in kind as in intensity. Speaking in terms of fusion of quality, he says: [58]

An extensive fusion spread out over the fringe and lacking in intensity and concentration, we are likely to call a mood. If there is concentration of quality, but no great massiveness or intensity, we call it sensuous feeling. Absorption in the violet of a night sky would be sensuous feeling. The spell of a soft evening saturating thought, movement, and utterance would be a mood. A surge of passion such as inspired Shelley's "Swiftly

---

[57] See Woodworth, *op. cit.*, page 234.
[58] S. C. Pepper, *Aesthetic Quality*, page 82. New York: Charles Scribner's Sons, 1937.

walk o'er the western wave, Spirit of Night" would be an emotion. If sensuous feeling acquires intensity, it rapidly gathers up extensity and turns into emotion. The same with mood. There is only a difference of degree among them.

Lanz, in a very interesting chapter entitled "The Logic of the Emotions," reviews some of the more important psychological theories of the emotions, and concludes that the field of emotional experience is broader psychologically than is commonly believed. He points to the fact, long established in psychology, that all our sensations, and possibly our perceptions as well, are accompanied by slight emotional reactions — called by the Germans *Gefühlstöne*.[59] In stating that "melody is not an auditory sensation, but a form of emotional response" he shows how far the meaning of emotion can be extended. Further discussion of the relation to music of the psychology of the emotions will be found in Mursell and Pratt.

LEARNING AND MEMORY

The topics of learning and memory have been dealt with extensively in the literature of psychology. In view of their importance in music, surprisingly little scientific investigation has been carried on in specifically musical aspects of these problems. *Learning* means the acquisition and retention of knowledge on the one hand, and of skills on the other. Memory plays the more important role in the first type of learning, but habit the more important in the latter. The word *memory* is commonly used in two different senses; one refers to the recall of a fact, and the other to the retention of a skill. We *recall a date* and we *remember how to swim*. Obviously the second type of memory is closely related to habit. Learning, then, may mean roughly either the acquisition of knowledge or the formation of habits. The same

---

[59] Henry Lanz, *The Physical Basis of Rime*, pages 268 ff. Palo Alto: Stanford Univ. Press, 1931.

facts and findings, the same general psychological laws, seem to apply equally to both activities. The experimental psychologist regards memory not so much as a faculty, but rather as an activity — the process of remembering.

The problems of memory are ordinarily divided into three or four stages: *acquiring* or *learning, retaining,* and *remembering* (which last may be subdivided into *recalling* or *reproducing,* and *recognizing.*) What general and educational psychology tell us about the learning process needs to be interpreted and applied to musical situations. Some work has already been done in this field, but much more is needed. Attention has been devoted to effecting economy in the learning process. Many principles, of which only a few can be mentioned here, have been at least tentatively set up. A favorable attitude, usually expressed as a desire to learn, is important. Spacing the practice intervals or study periods so as to get the maximum results requires special attention. Studies of the relative rates at which rote and meaningful material can be learned or memorized emphasize the value of musical analysis in connection with musical performance.

Psychology teaches us that forgetting, the negative expression of retention, is not merely some kind of passive "fading out," but, rather, a phase of an active process in which the impairment of the process is due to disuse of the structure involved — not unlike the atrophy of an unused muscle — or, perhaps, to a kind of competition with other activities. Experiments show that retention is better if a rest period follows the original practice period than if another kind of activity follows it. An acquired habit is probably never lost. Relearning takes less time and makes for a more permanent fixation. There is normally a rapid drop in the retention curve unless the lesson is followed by review or is "overlearned" in the first place.

Less progress has probably been made in the study of recall than in that of learning, but the findings in this field are none the less full of implications for the musician. Reproducing is a kind of reacting, and the stimuli to recalled reactions are of many types — words, symbols (musical notation), bodily postures, environmental situations of many kinds, and many other less well-known varieties. Laboratory experiments have verified applicability of the so-called secondary laws of association as objective determinants of recall. These are the well-known laws of *frequency, recency,* and *intensity,* and the auxiliary law of *primacy.*[60]

Briefly, the law of frequency means that the connection which has been made most frequently, other things being equal, will be most readily recalled or re-established. The law of recency means: other things being equal, the more recent the response, the more readily it will be invoked. The law of intensity implies that the more vivid the experience emotionally, the more easily it will be retained in memory. And finally, the law of primacy signifies that first impressions are most lasting. These laws seem to operate in musical recall in an intermixture of the modalities of vision, audition, and motor response. For the average musician, remembering in performance probably involves all three types of imagery — visual, auditory, and kinesthetic; although with a given individual, one or the other type will tend to be predominant. One suggestion here is that the improvement of one's powers of memory, or abilities in remembering, is not so much a matter of exercise, like that of a muscle, as it is training in the ways of learning.[61]

The second kind of remembering — recognizing — differs from recalling functionally in that recognition starts from the object, whereas recall must find its object. The processes

---

[60] For a more detailed discussion of the laws of association see Dashiell, *op. cit.,* pages 423 ff., or almost any standard textbook on psychology.

[61] Dashiell, *op. cit.,* pages 437 f.

of recognition are closely related to those of perception. The problems in this field are fundamental to many, if not most, kinds of musical activity, such as reading musical notation or listening to the development section of a symphony. Psychologists have done some work in the general field, but very little in more specifically musical problems.

MUSICAL INTELLIGENCE

In taking up the consideration of the nature of musical intelligence from the psychological point of view, we must keep in mind that intelligence is not a thing, but rather a quality of behavior. Dashiell formulates a rough definition which emphasizes this viewpoint when he says: ". . . intelligence is the ability to acquire and perfect through individual experience new and more efficient modes of adaptation." [62] The phrase, "capacity to learn," is very suggestive as a definition of intelligence, especially for the field of education.

Thorndike describes intelligence in terms of *level*, which has to do with the degree of difficulty of problems solved; *range*, the variety of fields or types of problems; *area*, the total number of situations successfully met, including both level and range; and *speed*, how quickly a person responds to a situation. [63]

Pratt, following Spearman, favors a definition of intelligence in terms of a *general factor*, which is common to all cognitive acts and remains constant for any individual, and a *specific factor*, which not only varies from individual to individual but with the same individual with respect to his various abilities in different fields. [64]

Seashore cites Stoddard and Wellman's analysis of intel-

---

[62] *Op. cit.*, page 342.

[63] A. M. Jordan, *Educational Psychology*, pages 392 f. New York: Henry Holt & Company, Inc., 1933.

[64] Pratt, *op. cit.*, pages 100 ff.

ligent behavior, which uses the slogans *difficulty, complexity, abstractness, economy, adaptiveness to goal, social value,* and *the emergence of originals,* as the criteria of intelligence.[65] According to this view, intelligence would imply the successful solution of problems considered in the light of these criteria.

Keeping in mind the general characterization of intelligence as a quality of behavior, we might define musical intelligence as *the ability of the individual to deal successfully with the problems in the various kinds of musical activity,* whether composition, performance, or listening to music. An evaluation of one's musical intelligence would have to take into consideration all types of responses — whether sensory, emotional, or more purely intellectual — to all kinds of musical situations. Such a psychological conception of musical intelligence would allow for great individual differences in capacities in the manifold varieties of activities which can properly be called musical. It would give a basis for showing many correlations between general and musical intelligence, and yet allow for the consideration of more specifically musical capacities. Obviously musical intelligence, like general intelligence, is a very complex matter and any extremely simple statement of the matter must be looked upon skeptically.

Tests and Measurements

If we think of intelligence in general and, *a fortiori,* of musical intelligence not as a thing but as a quality of behavior, then we should think of tests and measurements of musical intelligence as dealing with the activity of the organism in relation to the specifically musical aspects of its environment. They are attempts to test and measure certain qualities of behavior, or, more specifically, one's "ability

---

[65] Seashore, *Psychology of Music,* pages 175 ff.

to acquire and perfect through individual experience new and more efficient modes of adaptation" to musical situations. In short, if intelligence means, roughly, *the capacity to learn,* musical intelligence should logically mean *capacity to acquire musical skill and knowledge.* Tests and measurements of musical intelligence should be evaluated in terms of their effectiveness in affording objective data on this capacity.

Seashore's Measures of Musical Talent attempt to measure certain basic discriminatory capacities with respect to pitch, intensity, time, consonance, tonal memory, and the like.[66] Insofar as these tests measure capacities not susceptible to improvement with training, experience, or maturity, they cannot be tests of musical intelligence. They may yield valid information concerning capacities or limitations of the organism in responding to certain specific situations,[67] but one should be very cautious about assuming that ratings in sensory capacities alone afford the final index to musical intelligence. The crux of the matter is not merely these relatively persistent and unchanging capacities, but, more particularly, the individual's capacity for improvement in dealing with musical situations, whether in composition, performance, or in listening to music.

Tests of melodic apprehension and response,[68] interval recognition and reproduction,[69] chordal and harmonic perception,[70] — these and similar tests, especially if worked out to show capacity for improvement, would seem of fundamental importance in determining musical intelligence in a

---

[66] See Carl E. Seashore, *The Psychology of Musical Talent.*

[67] See, for example, Pratt, *op. cit.,* pages 133 ff., and Mursell, *op. cit.,* page 293. Pratt questions chiefly the consonance test, and Mursell both the consonance and rhythm tests.

[68] See Mursell, *op. cit.,* pages 300 ff., for a discussion of the work of Révész, Brehmer, Serejewski and Maltzew, Vidor, and others in this field.

[69] See Mursell, *op. cit.,* pages 303 f., for a brief account of the work of Van Briessen, Révész, and others in this field.

[70] Mursell, *op. cit.,* pages 304 ff., discusses the investigations of Kwalwasser, Drake, Lowery, and others in this field.

scientific manner. Other tests which have received attention are those for musical achievement and knowledge.[71] Violent controversies have arisen over the value and significance of the various tests and measurements, but these have had a salutary effect upon research as they have called attention to flaws in various theories and procedures, and have led to serious critical thought on the fundamental problems. They have yielded a substantial body of psychological data of enduring value.

COMPOSITION

The psychology of musical *composition* is peculiarly difficult, as it cannot readily be approached by the experimental method. Mursell conceives musical composition as the act of transmuting emotion into tone.[72] There is no doubt truth in this theory, especially if emotion is taken in a very broad sense to include vague "feeling" attitudes which the composer may have toward the tonal materials of music. Such feelings are very attenuated forms of emotion as compared with those relatively vivid emotions called love, hate, joy, sorrow, and the like.

To name the specific emotional attitude which the composer has in writing a string quartet, for example, is a difficult, if not impossible, task for the psychologist. One must obviously be careful not to confuse an *emotional state* with the *emotion* being translated. Further pursuit of this line of thought would soon lead one out of the field of psychology proper into aesthetics, speculative philosophy, and metaphysics. The psychologist is likely to become obnoxious when he presumes to disparage the technical training of the composer.[73] Psychology can undoubtedly assist in improv-

---

[71] See bibliography under Kwalwasser, Kelsey, Knuth, and others.
[72] *Op. cit.*, pages 268 ff.
[73] See Mursell, *op. cit.*, page 259.

ing methods of teaching music by its contributions to our understanding of the nature of composition; but it is scarcely within its proper field when it aspires to replace the mastery of the techniques of composition by studies of the psychological processes involved in composition.

The composer is concerned with the specifically musical imagery presented in the stream of consciousness, and it is doubtful whether any present consciousness of the underlying psychological processes would be of material assistance. Nevertheless, the psychology of musical composition properly contributes to the musicologist's knowledge of musical composition, and gives him a deeper insight into the nature of music. Psychology may show much of practical value to the composer, the performer, the listener, and, probably most of all, the teacher. The question of whether or not musical composition can properly be regarded as a "transposition of human feeling into a pattern of tone and rhythm," as Mursell expresses it,[74] is a problem for aesthetic theory rather than for psychology, although, naturally, aesthetic theory will lean heavily upon psychological investigations in formulating its answer.

The psychology of the three overt stages in creative work in general — *preparation, illumination,* and *revision* — has been investigated to some extent, and certain general principles have been set up; but, obviously, much more detailed work remains to be done. Only a few of the most general findings can be mentioned.

Preparation includes not only the technical equipment the composer brings to his work, but also whatever special work he may do by way of reading, study of other works, formulation of general and specific plans, sketching, and the like. *Illumination,* or *inspiration,* seems to be a very elusive psychological matter, but available evidence indicates that it

---

[74] *Op. cit.,* page 260.

is not so elusive as it seems. Saturation with the subject matter, and even fruitless effort to get an idea, may not be in vain; for, after a rest, some diversion, or other type of work, the idea may be suddenly there either as a whole or in part. *Revision*, or *working out the details*, is a phase of creative activity closely related psychologically to problem solving.

In general, the psychological methods used in studying the problem of creative work fall into three main types: (1) studying the procedures of men of genius through biographical data, (2) using questionnaires and interviews for the purpose of obtaining the views of composers concerning the subject, and (3) setting up laboratory experiments involving the solution of creative problems under observation.

PERFORMANCE

The study of the psychological aspects of musical *performance* has been receiving more and more attention in recent years. If we observe a violinist playing in a symphony orchestra, we see that many complex interactions are taking place between the organism and its environment. The performer is watching his music, which is one stimulus guiding his behavior. At the same time, he is watching the conductor and is sensitive to his gestures, which are cues governing his behavior. He is listening to the sounds produced by the other players, and adjusting his own playing in relation to what he hears. The scientific study of the various aspects of his behavior in such a complex situation is, naturally, approached in different ways involving many different methods.

Two stages or phases of the methodology may be roughly distinguished: (1) the collection of objective data, and (2) the interpretation of the data leading to the formulation of pertinent psychological principles. Photographic records of the sounds produced in performance provide one type of data which gives objective material for psychological interpretation. Seashore gives a number of illustrations of the problems and methods of the work in this field dealing with violin, piano, and voice.[75] More details and further bibliography will be found in the Iowa series of publications in the psychology of music.[76] An excellent example of the studies of overt movements in piano performance is afforded in Otto Ortmann's *The Physiological Mechanics of Piano Technique.* Slow-motion pictures and many other devices are used to obtain further material. Other methods and techniques must be worked out for the investigation of the psychological processes involved in the reading of musical notation, in the response of the performer to the gestures of the conductor, in the adjustment of the individual performer's actions to what he hears in the performance of other members of the orchestra, and in the relation of the concert artist to his audience.

The interpretation of the data obtained through all the specialized studies will lead to the formulation of the fundamental psychological principles underlying musical performance in all its complexity. These principles might pertain to such matters as economy of motion in performance; various types of co-ordination; control of frequency, intensity, quality, duration and their derivatives; memory; and similar items. These psychological principles themselves will, in turn, become important factors in determining the materials and methods used in musical pedagogy and in developing the technique of the performing musician.

Listening to Music and the Effects of Music

What psychology has to say about *listening to music* and *the effects of music* is of fundamental importance for the

---

[75] Seashore, *Psychology of Music*, pages 199–285.
[76] See especially *Objective Analysis of Musical Performance*, University of Iowa Studies in the Psychology of Music, Vol. IV. Iowa City: University Press, 1936.

theory of musical aesthetics. Psychologically speaking, music may be regarded as a certain type of experience involving both the organism and its environment. The most critical problem is probably that of explaining how it is that the tonal-rhythmic patterns of sound constituting the stimulus or tonal environment, or what we objectively call *music*, can produce the effects they do within the organism. Experimental psychology attacks the problem, with all the means at its disposal, in the attempt to obtain scientific data as to the effects of music. In collecting its data, it tries to take into account the specific nature of the stimulus, the condition of the organism, and whatever other pertinent factors there may be. In the interpretation of the material, psychology tends to become speculative, and a further pursuit of the inquiry leads naturally into the field of aesthetic theory. There, one of the basic questions is: In what sense, if any, can it be said that music is the language of the emotions? The contribution of psychology to answering that question seems to be, at least in part, the study and analysis of the problems of auditory sensation and perception, in relation to the other sense modalities and the affective or emotional experience of the individual, or, perhaps, what Greene calls "emotive-conative" states.[77]

We may summarize the findings in this particular problem in several points. Auditory sensation has certain tactual aspects. In fact it has been suggested that the organ of the internal ear, as well as the lateral line sense organs and cutaneous organs, may all have "developed phylogenetically from some more general type of tactile structure."[78] Further, there is something in common between a sound which increases in loudness and a pressure which increases in intensity over a similar period of time. In this and other related facts,

---

[77] Theodore M. Greene, *The Arts and the Art of Criticism*, page 46. Princeton: Princeton University Press, 1940.
[78] Pratt, *op. cit.*, page 223.

we probably have the key to the problem of how it is that tones sounded in succession are perceived as movement. But psychology tends to explain the emotions, or affective states in general, in terms of movement, or bodily changes. This statement of the case is greatly oversimplified, but it will serve to suggest the psychological basis of the explanation of how tones and tonal patterns in all their complexity are translated into emotive-conative states.

Tones, intervals, chords, melodic figures, rhythmic patterns — all the elemental and structural characteristics of music — have affective qualities, felt qualities; and this lays the psychological foundation for the study of the effects of music. On the other hand, listeners to music bring to the listening situation certain attitudes, certain organic sets, which condition the experience. These attitudes have been classified as: (1) *physiological* or *subjective*, when the individual has a tendency to think of the music in terms of its effects upon him, that is, as stimulating or soothing him, or making him feel gay or sad; (2) *objective*, when the person is, rather, conscious of the quality of tone, of the forms of rhythmic and harmonic structures and the like as attributes, properties, or intrinsic qualities in the music "out there"; (3) *associative*, when the tendency is to like the music because of the pleasant scenes or fond recollections it calls to mind; and (4) *character* or *expressive*, when the music gives rise to felt qualities, but the listener tends to attribute them to the music. In this last case the music may be characterized as restless, calm, agitated, passionate, or triumphant, but these qualities are ascribed to the music itself.[79]

From the foregoing analysis, it becomes obvious that listening to music involves a very complex response. As the ex-

---

[79] For a more detailed discussion of this topic, see, for example, Pratt, *op. cit.*, pages 150 ff.; Mursell, *op. cit.*, pages 218 ff.; Aram Torossian, *A Guide to Aesthetics*, pages 29 ff. (Stanford University Press, 1937).

perience is analyzed from different viewpoints, it is seen to have at least three fairly well-defined aspects: *intellectual, emotional* or *affective-conative,* and *motor.*

From an intellectual standpoint it seems that the response is selective, since in accordance with the laws of attention it is possible to attend to only a limited number of the multiplicity of possibilities in or suggested by the tonal-rhythmic complex. In listening attentively to a symphony concert, for example, one follows now the first violins, now the violas, now the oboe, and so on. The next time the individual hears the same symphony, he may attend to different factors, such as melodic or harmonic structure. He may listen to the tonal quality or to the formal design, or, neglecting these, he may be more or less lost in a kaleidoscopic orgy of mental imagery, based on associations of various kinds far removed from the intrinsically musical details of the performance. It is, perhaps, in this sense that Ortmann has classed listeners as *sensorial, perceptual,* and *imaginal.*[80] The total resultant experience must contain something of each type of response, regardless of which is dominant.

In closing this section, we must sound one note of warning. Although the study of the effects of music may throw light on the nature of the psychological processes involved in listening to music, one must be cautious in drawing conclusions as to the sense in which music may be said to be *the language of the emotions.* The musical experience may have its emotional or affective tone, but that does not justify the assumption that it is merely a play of the emotions.

---

[80] Otto Ortmann, "Types of Listeners. Genetic Considerations," Max Schoen (ed.), *The Effects of Music,* Chapter III, pages 38–77.

Bibliography

Banister, H., "Audition," *Handbook of General Experimental Psychology*, pages 880–923. Worcester, Mass.: Clark University Press, 1934.
Bourguès, Lucien, and Alexandre Denéréaz, *La Musique et la vie intérieure*. Paris: Alcan, 1921.
Bücher, Karl, *Arbeit und Rhythmus*. Fifth Edition. Leipzig: E. Reinicke, 1919.
Combarieu, Jules, *Music, Its Laws and Evolution*. New York: D. Appleton-Century Company, Inc., 1910.
Dashiell, John F., *Fundamentals of General Psychology*. Boston: Houghton Mifflin Company, 1937.
Diserens, Charles M., *The Influence of Music on Behavior*. Princeton: Princeton Univ. Press, 1926.
————, and Harry Fine, *A Psychology of Music: The Influence of Music on Behavior*. Cincinnati: by the authors for the College of Music, 1939. (Bibliography, pages 349–400.)
Flemming, Cecile White, and Marion Flagg, *A Descriptive Bibliography of Prognostic and Achievement Tests in Music*. New York: Bureau of Publications, Teachers College, Columbia University, 1936.
Fletcher, Harvey, "Loudness, Pitch, and the Timbre of Musical Tones and Their Relation to the Intensity, the Frequency, and the Overtone Structure," *Journal of the Acoustical Society of America*, Vol. VI (1934), pages 59–69.
————, "Newer Concepts of the Pitch, the Loudness and the Timbre of Musical Tones," *Journal of the Franklin Institute*, Vol. CCXX (1935), pages 405–429.
————, *Speech and Hearing*. New York: D. Van Nostrand Company, Inc., 1929.
Graf, Max, *Die innere Werkstatt des Musikers*. Stuttgart: Ferdinand Enke, 1910.
Gurney, Edmund, *The Power of Sound*. London: Smith, Elder, & Co., 1880.
Helmholtz, Hermann L. F., *On the Sensations of Tone as a Physiological Basis for the Theory of Music*. (Tr. of Fourth German Edition of 1877 by Alexander J. Ellis. First German Edition, 1862.) New York: Longmans, Green & Company, 1912.
Howell, William H., *A Text-book of Physiology for Medical Students and Physicians*. Thirteenth Edition Thoroughly Re-

vised. Philadelphia and London: W. B. Saunders Company, 1937.

Knuth, William E., *Knuth Achievement Tests in Music*. Minneapolis and Chicago: Educational Test Bureau, 1936.

Kurth, Ernst, *Musikpsychologie*. Berlin: Max Hesse, 1931.

Kwalwasser, Jacob, *Tests and Measurements in Music*. Boston: C. C. Birchard & Company, 1927.

————, and Peter W. Dykema, *Kwalwasser-Dykema Music Tests*. New York: Carl Fischer, Inc., 1930.

Lewis, Don, "Pitch: Its Definition and Physical Determinants," *Objective Analysis of Musical Performance*, University of Iowa Studies in the Psychology of Music, Vol. IV, pages 346–373. Iowa City: The University Press, 1936.

Lloyd, Ll. S., *Decibels and Phons*. London: Oxford University Press, 1938.

Meyer, Max, *Contributions to a Psychological Theory of Music*. Columbia: University of Missouri, 1901.

Mottram, Vernon H., *Physiology*. New York: W. W. Norton & Company, Inc., 1928.

Murphy, Gardner, *General Psychology*. New York: Harper & Brothers, 1933.

Mursell, James L., *The Psychology of Music*. New York: W. W. Norton & Company, Inc., 1937. (Bibliography, pages 353–384.)

Ogden, Robert Morris, *Hearing*. New York: Harcourt, Brace & Company, Inc., 1924.

Ortmann, Otto, *The Physiological Mechanics of Piano Technique*. New York: E. P. Dutton & Co., 1929.

————, "What Is Tone-Quality?" *The Musical Quarterly*, Vol. XXI (1935), pages 442–450.

Pratt, Carroll C., *The Meaning of Music*. New York: McGraw-Hill Book Company, Inc., 1931.

Reuter, F., *Das musikalische Hören auf psychologische Grundlage*. Leipzig: Kahnert, 1925.

Révész, Geza, *The Psychology of a Musical Prodigy*. New York: Harcourt, Brace & Company, Inc., 1925.

————, *Zur Grundlegung der Tonpsychologie*. Leipzig: Veit, 1913.

Ruckmick, C. A., "A Bibliography of Rhythm," *American Journal of Psychology*, Vol. XXIV (1913), pages 508–519; Vol. XXVI (1915), pages 457–459; Vol. XXIX (1918), pages 214–218; Vol. XXXV (1924), pages 407–413.

Schoen, Max, "Bibliography of Experimental Studies on the Psychology of Music," *Volume of Proceedings of the Music Teachers National Association*, Thirty-Fifth Series (1940), pages 498–527.

————— (Editor), *The Effects of Music*. New York: Harcourt, Brace & Company, Inc., 1927.

—————, *The Psychology of Music*. New York: The Ronald Press Company, 1940.

Schole, Heinrich, *Tonpsychologie und Musikästhetik*. Göttingen: Vandenhoeck & Ruprecht, 1930.

Seashore, Carl E. (Editor), *Objective Analysis of Musical Performance*, University of Iowa Studies in the Psychology of Music, Vol. IV. Iowa City: The University Press, 1936.

—————, *Psychology of Music*. New York: McGraw-Hill Book Company, Inc., 1938. (Bibliography, pages 387–397.)

—————, *The Psychology of Musical Talent*. New York: Silver, Burdett & Company, 1919.

—————, *Psychology of the Vibrato in Voice and Instrument*, University of Iowa Studies in the Psychology of Music, Vol. III. Iowa City: The University Press, 1936.

————— (Editor), *The Vibrato*, University of Iowa Studies in the Psychology of Music, Vol. I. Iowa City: The University Press, 1932.

Stanton, Hazel M., *Measurement of Musical Talent: The Eastman Experiment*, University of Iowa Studies in the Psychology of Music, Vol. II. Iowa City: The University Press, 1935.

—————, *The Prognosis of Musical Achievement*. Rochester: Eastman School of Music, University of Rochester, 1929.

—————, *Psychological Tests of Musical Talent*. Rochester: Eastman School of Music, University of Rochester, 1925.

Stumpf, Carl, *Tonpsychologie*. 2 vols. Leipzig: S. Hirzel, 1883, 1890.

Tronnier, Richard, *Vom Schaffen grosser Komponisten*. Stuttgart: Carl Grüninger, 1927.

Vidor, Martha, *Was ist Musikalität?* Munich: Beck, 1931.

Watt, Henry J., *The Foundations of Music*. Cambridge: Cambridge University Press, 1919.

—————, *The Psychology of Sound*. Cambridge: Cambridge University Press, 1917.

Woodworth, Robert S., *Experimental Psychology*. New York: Henry Holt & Company, Inc., 1938.

CHAPTER IV

MUSICAL AESTHETICS

IN SYSTEMATIC MUSICOLOGY, ACOUSTICS TREATS OF MUSIC from the physical viewpoint as "pulsations in the air"; physiology and psychology deal with the behavior of the human organism in relation to physical phenomena; and aesthetics concerns, fundamentally, problems of value in music. As a science responsible for the organization of knowledge within this area, aesthetics depends upon many related areas of inquiry, and draws upon them freely as the occasion demands. Various branches of the natural and social sciences, the arts, and philosophy all contribute to the science of aesthetics.[1] And, in turn, the science of aesthetics makes its proper contribution to each of the other branches of knowledge.

Because many of the topics that would logically be included in a work devoted entirely to musical aesthetics are discussed in other chapters in the present work, they are omitted here. The present chapter is limited to a survey of some important problems of aesthetic theory, with special emphasis on their musical implications. Although we ordinarily suppose musical criticism to be the field most directly related to aesthetics, *musical aesthetics* is applied in composition, performance, and listening to music.

---

[1] For a more extended discussion of this point in relation to musical aesthetics, see, for example, Charles Lalo, *Esquisse d'une esthétique musicale scientifique*, pages 5–38.

Approaches to Aesthetics

The literature on aesthetics is extensive, and, for purposes of orientation, it may be well to distinguish, at least roughly, among various typical approaches to the subject. Philosophers writing on aesthetics often treat it as one division in a large systematic scheme. That is, they attempt to deduce the principles of aesthetics from the premises established or assumed in their general systems of philosophy. Not being versed in the arts, their writings have often tended to be highly theoretical, dealing chiefly with metaphysical problems. Notable pieces of aesthetic literature of this type are the works of Kant, Hegel, and Schopenhauer.

On the other hand, there is a considerable body of aesthetic literature written by men experienced in the arts, but not especially trained as philosophers. Such men are not concerned so much with metaphysical theories as with practical criteria of value. In the field of music, writers of this type include composers, performers, and critics — such men as Wagner, Liszt, and Hanslick. The literature on aesthetics has further been greatly enriched by the contributions of psychologists. The writings of Fechner, Lipps, and Bullough are examples of general works on psychological aesthetics; those of Schoen, Ortmann, and C. C. Pratt, of special studies related to musical aesthetics. In addition there are, of course, innumerable books and monographs on aesthetics that fall somewhere in between the main types mentioned.[2]

Artistic and Scientific Methods

In the several approaches just discussed, we may distinguish further among certain characteristic methods of ap-

---

[2] For a summary of the main tendencies in recent aesthetics, see Melvin M. Rader, *A Modern Book of Esthetics*, pages xi–xxxv *et passim;* and Katharine E. Gilbert and Helmut Kuhn, *A History of Esthetics*, pages 550–558. For a survey of German writings on musical aesthetics, see Felix M. Gatz, *Musik-Ästhetik in ihren Hauptrichtungen*, pages 5–50 *et passim.*

proach to the problems of aesthetics. These methods are variously described in the literature on aesthetics as *artistic, critical, scientific, philosophical, historical, psychological, experimental, empirical, eclectic,* and *systematic.* A great deal has been written about differences among the methods, and about the dangers and advantages of each; but it can easily be shown that, in spite of obvious differences, the various methods have much in common. Consider, for example, the *artistic method*, that of the creative artist, and the *scientific method*, that of the investigative scientist.

The scientist ordinarily works by analysis; by the isolation of the elements; by the reduction of the whole to its least common denominator. The artist, on the other hand, works by synthesis; by placing the elements together into a whole in such a way that the details become expressive by reason of their relation to the context. The work of art tends to be original and unique. Just as the scientist works for simplification by breaking the whole up into its parts, and the artist for complication in which each detail is individually expressive and the whole work of art has more meaning than the sum of the parts, so the scientific and artistic methods are opposite and complementary. The scientist, through analysis, seeks to generalize — to formulate universal laws; the artist, through synthesis, seeks to individualize — to give an idea or feeling unique expression. If what the scientist discovers were lost, it might be rediscovered by another scientist; if the individual work of art were lost, it could not be re-created by another artist. For example, if Newton's law of gravity were lost, it might be worked out again; but if, on the other hand, Beethoven's *Third Symphony* were destroyed, it could not be so reconstructed.

However, the two methods really go hand in hand, for the artist undoubtedly arrives at the general principles of his art through the analysis of many particular works of art.

Thus, Bach built upon the work of the seventeenth-century contrapuntal writers, and Beethoven absorbed something from the works of Mozart and Haydn before he found an individual expression. And yet, even in science, the great man has something of the artist in him. There is much that is individual and characteristic in his work. Creative imagination and insight illuminate analysis and logical method.

THE FUNCTION OF ANALYSIS

Much has been written on the dangers of analyzing a work of art. Pepper, for example, suggests that, when the psychologist adopts or attempts the method of the physical scientist with the "ideal of control by isolation and disintegrative analysis," he is in danger of destroying the very thing he is trying to study.[3] Thus, when the psychologist studies the effects of intervals apart from context, he is certainly reducing the significance of the intervals studied, for the same interval may have different meanings in different contexts. The validity of this criticism is undoubtedly responsible in part for the growth of the *Gestalt* theory in psychology.

Analysis need not destroy the work of art; on the contrary, only through analysis can we fully apprehend it. As Greene says,[4] "rigorous analysis is the *only* method at our disposal for apprehending the generic structure of art and the factors which condition artistic quality." Faced with the objection that analysis always omits something, and is, therefore, not the whole truth, we realize that nothing is the whole truth. We cannot know everything at once from all points of view, for, as Prall says,[5] "we always have, or are *at* some *one* point of view, physically, emotionally, intellectually, and in every

[3] Stephen C. Pepper, *Aesthetic Quality*, pages 11 f.
[4] Theodore M. Greene, *The Arts and the Art of Criticism*, page 16.
[5] David W. Prall, *Aesthetic Analysis*, page 23.

other way." If we listen to a musical composition, we cannot *know* it all; that is, we cannot grasp all its significance at once. We can get some impression of it as a whole, but this impression is vague and probably inexpressible.

Even if we listen closely, our attention is psychologically limited to a half dozen items at one time; awareness flits from one aspect of the composition to another. And whether it is the tone of the oboe, the swing of the rhythm, or the contour of the melody, the particular aspect is always something less than the whole. In listening to a string quartet, for example, we can follow the various motives or themes as they pass from instrument to instrument, and leave the harmonic and other details more or less in the background of consciousness. We can pay attention to the cello especially, and, although we may be vaguely aware of what the other instruments are doing, the cello part will stand out in our experience; or we may derive great pleasure from concentrating upon almost any aspect of the composition. But, certainly, we do not hear all the details of the composition at once; we cannot make one all-inclusive synthesis of the experience.

Because great works of art have some complexity either of detail or of implication, we do not grow tired of them after a few hearings. We hear a great symphony again and again, and constantly find new interest. Why? Partly, at least, because of this analytic nature of intelligent listening. Aesthetic analysis is not aesthetic appreciation, but, as Prall [6] and others suggest, "if we are to have any knowledge at all," we must "use the methods of abstraction and analysis."

[6] *Op. cit.*, page 24. For further discussion of methodological problems, see: Greene, *op. cit.*, pages 3-4, 12-25, and 242-255; Louis A. Reid, *A Study in Aesthetics*, pages 13-31; Pepper, *op. cit.*, pages 3-18; George Santayana, *The Sense of Beauty*, pages 1-13; Albert R. Chandler, *Beauty and Human Nature*, pages 5-9; Max Schoen, *Art and Beauty*, pages 13-20; DeWitt H. Parker, *The Principles of Aesthetics*, pages 1-15; Aram Torossian, *A Guide to Aesthetics*, pages 3-10; and Harold N. Lee, *Perception and Aesthetic Value*, pages 215-228.

Definition of the Term "Aesthetics"

The term *aesthetics* is used in a variety of senses. Like many generic concepts, aesthetics is an ultimate scarcely to be defined except in terms of itself; hence, most definitions are suggestive rather than definitive. Definitions necessarily vary with the angle of approach; that is, the philosopher may define aesthetics in terms of value in relation to the beautiful; the psychologist, in terms of behavior; and the art historian, critic, or artist, in terms of normative standards in art. For present purposes, we may indicate some of the important implications of the term.

The word *aesthetics* is derived from the Greek word αἰσθητικός, *perceptive, especially by feeling*, from αἰσθάνεσθαι, *to perceive, feel*. Thus, originally, it concerned sensuous rather than conceptual data. The word was used in this general sense until about 1750, when Alexander Baumgarten, a philosopher, defined it in a more special way as *the theory or science of the beautiful*. As a follower of Leibnitz, he is said [7] to have reached this definition from a consideration of the epistemological statement: "If the perfect in the world is conceptually grasped through logical thinking, we call it truth; if we recognize it by means of the senses, we call it beauty." Thus, after Baumgarten, aesthetics, or sensuous knowledge, was used to signify the theory of the beautiful. Later, aesthetics came generally to mean the science of the fine arts.

The dictionary definition of aesthetics is: "The theory or philosophy of taste; science of the beautiful in nature and art, esp. that treating of the expression and appreciation of beauty." Recently, there seems a general tendency to return toward the original meaning of the word, although aesthetic investigations are still chiefly concerned with the arts. The

---

[7] See Olga Stieglitz, *Einführung in die Musikästhetik*, page 2. *Cf.* Robert Ogden, *The Psychology of Art*, pages 3 f.

great activity in psychological aesthetics is indicative of this tendency. The emotional and intellectual aspects of the problems are being studied more or less together, possibly in recognition of Croce's doctrine that knowledge has two forms: intuitive and logical.[8]

Aesthetics is generally supposed to be primarily concerned with our perceptual knowledge of the beautiful, as distinguished from our conceptual knowledge of the true and the good. But, since our perceptual experiences are organically intertwined with conceptual ideas, it is doubtful whether limiting the field of aesthetics to perceptual experience is proper.[9] No doubt an aesthetic experience begins in perception, actual or imaginal,[10] but conceptual knowledge immediately affects the experience, and cannot be separated from it. And there is a question whether certain types of aesthetic experience may not be closer to intellectual or conceptual activities than to emotional or sensuous; for example, the enjoyment of a mathematical solution, or, perhaps, a Bach invention.[11] Such complications as these obviously increase the difficulties of defining aesthetics.

Another serious difficulty arises in such a definition as *the science of the beautiful* or *the theory of beauty* because the words *beautiful* and *beauty* have been assigned numerous meanings. Ogden and Richards in a chapter on "The Meaning of Beauty" [12] offer sixteen different definitions. A fundamental problem, for instance, is whether to regard beauty sub-

---

[8] Cf. Benedetto Croce, *Aesthetic: As Science of Expression and General Linguistic*, page 1.

[9] Cf., for example, Torossian (*A Guide to Aesthetics*, pages 2 f.), who, speaking of the study of aesthetics from a scientific viewpoint, says, "It deals with that department of human experience which involves self-expression through sensuous objects in terms of our affective instead of our intellectual selves."

[10] Cf. Reid, *A Study in Aesthetics*, pages 31 ff.

[11] For a further discussion of this point, see Reid, *op. cit.*, pages 34–37.

[12] C. K. Ogden and I. A. Richards, *The Meaning of Meaning*, pages 139–159.

jectively as a quality of an experience, objectively as a quality of an object, or, with Santayana,[13] as a quality of experience attributed to an object.

Although the foregoing discussion has not brought us to a final definition of aesthetics, it indicates some of the essential factors in the attempt to formulate a definition. Some of the problems touched upon are treated further in the sections following.

THE FIELD OF AESTHETICS

Defining the *aesthetic field* presents a difficulty analogous to that of defining sound; that is, it may be defined objectively in terms of *things*, — objects of awareness capable of stimulating experience; or, subjectively, in terms of experience. As the situation involves "an organism and its environment," it represents a typical *stimulus-response* relation. We may speak of variables in objective factors, and assume a stable organism with consistent response; or, conversely, we may consider that variations in response are due to inconstancy in the organism, and assume the constancy of the stimulus. In more complex situations both factors may vary. Whether we suppose the problem objective or subjective may be immaterial, if we recognize that the aesthetic experience concerns both art and the reaction to it.

Broadly conceived, the aesthetic field may include the whole surface of the world as experienced, if its qualities are concretely had and emotionally felt, with no thought of some ultimate practical purpose. Whether or not an object or an experience is aesthetic depends, in part, upon the attitude of the individual. Max Eastman illustrates this point significantly with the example of people on a ferry boat.[14] Those who sit inside and read are simply getting across the

---

[13] *Op. cit.*, page 49.
[14] *Enjoyment of Poetry*, pages 3 ff.

river, whereas those who sit out on deck to enjoy the scenery only regret completing the trip. To the former, crossing the river is a "practical" matter; to the latter, an aesthetic experience.

Aesthetics is concerned, therefore, with the perception of a certain kind of value.[15] This value is found especially in the six major arts — music, the dance, literature, architecture, sculpture, and painting. These arts constitute the main fields of aesthetic inquiry.

Within each area mentioned in the preceding paragraph, the field of aesthetics includes the investigation of many diverse problems: for example, the nature of the aesthetic experience; the criteria of value; the distinctions among the arts; the role of the emotions in the aesthetic experience; the problems of material, form, and content, meaning, or expression; the nature of the creative activity in the work of art; and the relation of art to the individual and to society. In musical aesthetics, these problems have their own implications; of special importance is the question whether music is *sui generis*, a thing unique in itself, or whether it is, instead, the vehicle for expressing something not music. A large portion of the literature on musical aesthetics is devoted to this question.

One of the popular theories has long been that music is, in some way, the language of the emotions. But this view has been steadily opposed by those who feel that music does not, primarily, refer to something outside itself. Indeed, most theories of musical aesthetics can be classed as *heteronomous* or *autonomous*, according to whether or not they hold that music has a non-musical content. Much of the literature in modern psychological aesthetics is devoted to some aspect of this question.[16]

---

[15] *Cf.*, for example, Santayana, *op. cit.*, page 16; and Harold N. Lee, *Perception and Aesthetic Value*, page 5.

[16] See, especially, C. C. Pratt, *The Meaning of Music: A Study in Psychological Aesthetics*. *Cf.* also Gatz, *op. cit.*

Closely related is the psychological question as to the effects of music.[17] Lipps' psychological theory of empathy, or *Einfühlung*, is of particular importance in connection with the problems just mentioned. According to this theory, the aesthetic state in which we perceive a given work of art as beautiful is produced by our identifying ourselves emotionally with the work of art; in other words, the observing subject tends to project himself into the pattern of the work of art.[18]

Among the other psychological matters important in the theory of aesthetics are: the laws of association, especially in connection with the formation of types;[19] the mechanization of behavior through the formation of habit, which, although an aid to performance, tends to dull aesthetic enjoyment; the spans of apprehension and attention, which are conditioning factors in formal design; and habituation, the long-time development of taste.

THE AESTHETIC EXPERIENCE

Although *aesthetic experience* is not easy to define simply and concisely, it has several characteristic features whose discussion may lead to a tentative definition. Thus, (1) the aesthetic experience involves a subject-object relationship — "the organism in its environment"; (2) it primarily concerns perceptual intuition — our emotional, rather than our intellectual, nature — our power to feel, rather than our power to reason; (3) it normally exhibits an organic structure with a beginning, a growth, and an end; (4) it is the experience of a

---

[17] *Cf.*, for example, Max Schoen (Editor), *The Effects of Music* (New York: Harcourt, Brace & Company, Inc., 1927); also Max Schoen, *The Psychology of Music*, pages 70–147 (New York: The Ronald Press Company, 1940).

[18] See the excerpts from Theodor Lipps and Vernon Lee in Melvin M. Rader, *A Modern Book of Esthetics*, pages 285–310.

[19] See, especially, Santayana, *op. cit.*, pages 112–126; and Pepper, *op. cit.*, pages 136–159.

certain kind of value — distinct from moral, religious, political, economic, or other values, and attributed to an object; and (5) it depends upon a "contemplative," not a "practical," attitude.

The first statement implies that the aesthetic experience is conditioned by both objective and subjective factors. In music, for example, the objective factor is the whole tonal-rhythmic structure of a composition in all its complexity; the subjective factor, the total personality of the individual with all his likes and dislikes, experience, training, and natural aptitude.[20]

The second statement means that the aesthetic experience depends upon a kind of immediate intuitive awareness incompatible with discursive language. This awareness has been referred to, somewhat vaguely, as "the emotional faculty," or "feeling"; but Lee has suggested the term *perceptual intuition*, which he identifies as "the direct awareness of that organization of data immediately apprehended through the senses or in sense imagery." [21] This faculty of perceptual intuition differs fundamentally from the intellectual faculty, which is essentially discursive, logical, and analytic in its methods.

The third statement is based upon Dewey,[22] who emphasizes the difference between experience in general, which occurs continuously, and particular experiences, which have a kind of organic unity. Thus, according to Dewey, any experience — even the intellectual experience of thinking — may have its own aesthetic quality, may be an aesthetic experience.

The fourth statement raises the question of *value*. The nature of value is a problem of philosophy which we can treat

---

[20] *Cf.*, for example, Torossian, *op. cit.*, page 11.
[21] Lee, *op. cit.*, page 30. For a further discussion of this topic, the student should read Lee's whole chapter on "Perception" (*op. cit.*, pages 22–47); *cf.* also Greene, *op. cit.*, pages 242–248.
[22] John Dewey, *Art as Experience*, pages 35–57.

only very briefly. In general, aesthetic value is identified more or less vaguely by the term *beauty*. We have already suggested, under (2), that it concerns feeling, rather than reason. It is intrinsic, rather than instrumental — an end in itself, rather than a means to something else. It is based on an interest in continuing the present experience, rather than in passing on to something not experienced in the present.[23]

The fifth statement is a corollary of the fourth; the kind of value derived from a particular experience depends upon the attitude. The contemplative attitude leads to no action, whereas the practical attitude tends to induce action of some kind. If we define the aesthetic field in terms of things liked for themselves, the criterion of the definition is *attitude*. The aesthetic attitude is commonly characterized in terms of "psychical distance"; that is, the object is regarded for its own sake, apart from practical or other values, and our subjective affections are attributed to it.[24]

We may summarize the significance of the foregoing discussion in a tentative definition, as follows: *The aesthetic experience consists of an awareness of the intrinsic values in a subject-object situation in which the felt qualities of the experience are attributed to the object.*

The Aesthetic Object

Defining the *aesthetic object* is not unlike defining sound, or any other concept that may be regarded from both objective and subjective points of view. From one viewpoint, it is "the thing out there"; from another, it is something in

---

[23] See *infra*, pages 146–149.
[24] *Cf.* Edward Bullough, " 'Psychical Distance' as a Factor in Art and an Aesthetic Principle," *The British Journal of Psychology*, Vol. V (1912), pages 87–118. See also Lee, *op. cit.*, pages 17 f.; Reid, *op. cit.*, pages 55–60; Pratt, *op. cit.*, page 97; Greene, *op. cit.*, pages 238–241; and especially Schoen, *op. cit.*, pages 134–144.

the stream of consciousness. Speaking generally, the aesthetic object is anything capable of giving rise to an aesthetic
experience — the stimulus of the experience. From this broad
point of view, the aesthetic object may be anything we can
perceive or conceive of, whether concrete or abstract.[25]
Thus, an aesthetic object may be a sense pattern, a conceptual
pattern, or a combination of the two.

Sense patterns offer the richest aesthetic possibilities; visual
and auditory sense material is most suited to aesthetic treatment. It is more suitable than "taste" or "smell" material,
particularly because it lends itself to more refined and varied
qualitative differentiation.[26]

From the other viewpoint, however, the aesthetic object
is more than "the thing out there"; it is the thing-as-perceived.
The response of the organism must be taken into account.
Suppose two individuals, A and B, are exposed to the same
stimulus; let us say they listen to a symphony. A, because
of his peculiar endowment and training in music, gets a profound response; whereas B, who has neither natural capacity
nor training in music, hears only an inarticulate confusion of
sounds. What A responds to is a well-organized, significant
work of art; what B responds to is a meaningless cacophony.
From this viewpoint, the work of art is something in the
consciousness which may, or may not, exhibit a high degree
of correspondence with the stimulus. Any judgments expressed by A or B are not based upon the stimulus, but upon
their perception of it. The sounds as organized in the symphony are the potential symbols for meanings which are subjective — within the individual and not outside. The aesthetic
object thus becomes *the stimulus plus all relevant elaboration
by the organism.* Nevertheless, it is ordinarily more convenient in practice to assume a certain normal response, and

---

[25] *Cf.* Torossian, *op. cit.*, page 31; and Reid, *op. cit.*, pages 43 and 52 f.
[26] *Cf.* Prall, *Aesthetic Judgment*, pages 59 ff.

to regard the aesthetic object as anything capable of evoking an aesthetic experience.

The Relation of the Arts

The arts are commonly divided in terms of time-space criteria into the temporal (music, dance, and literature) and spatial arts (architecture, sculpture, and painting). The temporal arts are further distinguished according to their respective materials. But the spatial arts have a temporal character, as their objects endure in time, and as time is required for the perception of individual works.[27] Conversely, in the so-called temporal arts, the dance occurs in space; literature is spatial insofar as the mind creates images. In music, the spatial dimension is suggested by the fact that tones have a certain extensity, and, further, there is evidence that tones are perceived as phenomenologically higher and lower in space.[28] That music is perceived as motion also suggests a spatial quality, for movement implies space. Although music is most significantly a temporal art, one should not lose sight of its spatial quality.

The arts may also be classified on an auditory-visual basis, or on the principle of whether they are representative or non-representative, that is, directly expressive. The arts may further be distinguished according to their characteristic techniques, or according to their several functions. Each of these criteria is valuable for bringing out certain similarities and differences among the arts; but none is entirely adequate in itself. Particularly troublesome is the classification of the mixed arts, such as opera, drama, or ballet.[29]

---

[27] Cf. Dewey, *op. cit.*, pages 23, 163, *et passim;* and Greene, *op. cit.*, pages 222–226.

[28] Cf., for example, Pratt, *op. cit.*, pages 46–54; and Georg Anschütz, *Abriss der Musikästhetik*, pages 182–190.

[29] For a further discussion of the problems of classification see, for example, Prall, *Aesthetic Judgment*, pages 190 ff., and Torossian, *op. cit.*, pages 150–166.

Material

Material means, first of all, merely the physical stuff from which the artist creates the work of art. In sculpture, the artist works directly with such material as stone or marble; in architecture, indirectly through drawings and specifications, which are later realized in the use of the materials specified. Music is, ordinarily, similar to architecture, in that the composer indicates his composition by means of notation which is later realized in performance. There is no question that buildings are built of physical materials — stone, brick, steel, or wood. Likewise, it should be clear that the material of music is physical sound; just as a brick is potential material for the architect, so a tone of an oboe is potential material for the composer.

The materials of music, then, are sounds — tones, vocables, and noises — with all their qualitative richness. Perhaps, for the sake of completeness, we should include silences — rests. The problem as to whether the materials of music are physical (pulsations in the air) or psychological (sensations) is no problem if we assume that the one is the complement of the other — that the one implies the other.

Separate works on aesthetics, especially those on musical aesthetics, usually include a discussion of the characteristics of sound as the material of music — matters which have been covered in the two preceding chapters. For systematic purposes, in our descriptive analysis of musical aesthetics, we may try to confine our account of materials to a consideration of the generic characteristics of sounds in isolation — apart from their implications for form and content. But this is difficult, if not impossible, because any comprehensive account of the fundamental characteristics of sound naturally includes a discussion of the intrinsic orders, bordering the field of the organization of tones into formal designs.

For example, the intrinsic order of pitch is expressed primarily in scales; of loudness, in dynamics; of quality, in the specific tone qualities of the various instruments — hence, especially, in instrumentation; of duration, in agogics and rhythm. These intrinsic orders are basic to further organization in formal design. Moreover, these qualitative characteristics have expressive significance in many ways, as indicated by such adjectives as *small*, *thin*, and *piercing*, for describing high tones; *strong*, *virile*, and *majestic*, for loud tones; *rough*, *harsh*, and *strident*, for tones of a certain quality; or *lively*, *spirited*, and *agitated*, for rapid tones. It was probably this relationship between materials, on the one hand, and form and content, on the other, that led Riemann to organize his discussion of musical aesthetics under such topics as "Pitch," "Quality," and "Dynamics and Agogics," rather than under "Material," "Form," and "Content." [30]

The variety and nicety of the discriminative and manipulative possibilities within the several dimensions of the intrinsic orders of sounds provide an incomparable basis for the formal and expressive richness of music. It would be futile to argue about the superiority of auditory over visual or other sensory perceptions, but it may be illuminating to consider, briefly, a single example. The mixture of a number of different-colored pigments on a canvas presents a total resultant visual effect upon the eye in which the individuality of the constituent elements is almost completely lost. An analogous mixture of musical sounds produces a total effect upon the ear that is susceptible to a remarkable degree of almost automatic discrimination of the constituent elements.

Imagine listening to a concert by a symphony orchestra and a full chorus. The complexity of sounds presented to the ear at a given moment may be tremendous; and yet, a great variety of tones of different pitch, loudness, quality, and dura-

[30] See Hugo Riemann, *Die Elemente der musikalischen Aesthetik.*

tion may be easily distinguished. In addition, many relationships of a higher order of complexity may be perceived with little or no effort — intervals, chords, and melodic, harmonic, and contrapuntal patterns in almost limitless variety — not to mention extraneous sounds from shuffling feet, coughing, and passing streetcars.[31]

The physical and psychological characteristics of sounds, taken separately and in the various modes of combination, constitute the underlying, generic differentia of the materials of music. But, in another, more properly aesthetic, sense the materials with which compositions are made are the specific musical ideas, the elementary tonal-rhythmic patterns called *motives*, or *themes*.

The approach to the materials of music, at this level, constitutes the most significant basis for the study of musical materials, whether in composition, performance, or listening. But the physical, psychological, and aesthetic approaches are interdependent, and, taken together, they constitute the essential frame of reference in terms of which the musical experience may unfold, at higher levels of synthesis, in its formal and meaningful or expressive aspects.

FORM

The term *form* in aesthetic theory has at least three fairly distinct meanings — each subject to further distinctions in meaning, according to whether it is regarded from the objective or subjective point of view. Thus, *form* may mean (1) the "body" of the work of art, regarded as the intermediary between material and content, the vehicle for the expression of meaning; (2) the structural organization of the work of art, regarded as the relations between the parts, or the ways the materials are molded or patterned in a particular

[31] *Cf.* William Pole, *The Philosophy of Music*, pages 26 f. Sixth Edition. New York: Harcourt, Brace & Co., Inc., 1924.

work; or (3) a generic pattern or scheme of organization common to a number of different works of art, such as the *sonnet, suite, sonata,* or *fugue*.

We get very different accounts of form, according to whether we regard it as a function of objects or of experience, as the structure of "things" or of perception. It should be repeated that form is conditioned by both physical and psychological factors — that the one implies the other. Sometimes it is more illuminating and convenient to think in terms of the objective factor; at other times, in terms of the subjective factor.

INTRINSIC ORDERS

The general theory of form is ordinarily concerned with the formulation of the principles of design. However these principles are expressed, they are conditioned by the orders *intrinsic* to the materials of the particular art and by the psychological nature of the organism.

The basic orders constitute the dimensions in terms of which designs or patterns of greater and greater length and complexity are created. Since they are characteristic of every tone, they can scarcely exist in isolation, except for purposes of abstraction.

The schematization of the *frequency-pitch* dimension of tones results, primarily, in scales. Further elaboration in this dimension leads to the development of such concepts as *mode, tonality, cadence, melody, harmony,* and *counterpoint*. In many of these concepts rhythmic factors play an important role.

The *intensity-loudness* dimension, apart from the application as stress accent in rhythm, has not resulted in typical formal patterns — but the dynamic design of a particular composition constitutes an important formal element.

A similar observation applies, *mutatis mutandis*, to the dimension of *tonal quality*. *Duration* factors are basic in the realization of both small and large rhythmic patterns; and in this connection it is well to note the importance of the agogic factor. According to Riemann,[32] *agogics* refers especially to the lengthening or shortening of time values, or to the increase or diminution of dynamic values.

PSYCHOLOGICAL FACTORS

Innumerable psychophysiological factors are important in relation to the problems of form. Of these we shall consider only a few that are especially significant: *span of attention*, *memory*, and *types*.

Although the psychological status of the concept of attention may be somewhat doubtful, certain implications of the topic are worth mention at this point.[33] The *span of attention* refers to (1) the span of apprehension or perceptual grasp and (2) the fluctuation of attention or interest. Concerning (1) it should be noted, first, that the number of objects that can be "attended to" — clearly apprehended at one time — is limited; and second, that where the objective material permits, the mind tends to group numerous details into larger units, thus extending the number of items that can be perceptually grasped. Concerning (2) we may remark that, in fluctuations of attention — probably a kind of fatigue phenomenon — the tendency to shift the attention after a few seconds of attending an unchanging object may be avoided by appropriate changes in the stimulus. This matter of fluctuation is sometimes discussed in terms of interest, rather than attention.[34]

---

[32] Hugo Riemann, *Grundriss der Musikwissenschaft*, pages 67 f. Fourth edition, revised by Johannes Wolf. Leipzig: Quelle & Meyer, 1928. *Cf.* Mathis Lussy, *Traité de l'expression musicale*. Paris: Heugel et Cie., 1877.

[33] For a more extended discussion of the topic, see Woodworth, *Experimental Psychology*, pages 684–712.

[34] See, for example, Pepper, *op. cit.*, pages 186–211.

The limit of the span of apprehension is a determinative factor in the formal organization of the materials of music; for example, in determining how many contrapuntal lines can be successfully followed at one time, and in determining the effective metrical and formal schemes such as the number of beats in a measure, the number of measures in a phrase, the number of sections that can be included in a movement, and the number of movements in a larger form such as a symphony or suite.[35] The limit for the fluctuation of attention or span of interest is, similarly, the basis of certain principles of design, such as those discussed by Pepper[36] under the headings of *contrast, gradation,* and *theme and variation.* As disregard for the psychological limits leads to monotony, these principles suggest ways of avoiding monotony.

The intuiting of a temporal work of art as a whole depends upon *memory.* In the appreciation of a work of spatial art, such as painting, we have the whole before us and, in a sense, work from the whole into the parts; in temporal art such as music, we have the parts presented *seriatim* and, in a sense, work from the parts to the whole.[37] Apprehension of the whole, therefore, depends upon memory. The psychological determinants of recall or memory, the so-called laws of *primacy, frequency, recency,* and *intensity* or *vividness,* operate in the organization of the materials of music into forms of a higher order or greater complexity.

In terms of musical composition, these principles might be interpreted somewhat as follows. The first theme presented enjoys the advantages of primacy. Other things being equal, the themes to be given emphasis must recur most frequently. The material presented in the coda, or closing measures, of a composition has a preferential position in recall. Thematic

---

[35] For further discussion, see Pepper, *op. cit.,* pages 160–185; also, Lee, *op. cit.,* pages 50–60.

[36] *Op. cit.,* pages 194–211.

[37] *Cf.* Greene, *op. cit.,* pages 222 f.

material not emphasized in accordance with one of the other principles may be aided by vividness of presentation — for example, by a solo instrument with an appealing tone quality. Countless examples of the application of each of these principles, singly or in combination, will probably occur to all musicians.

Although the matter of *types* is important in relation to aesthetic value and expression, type is, in its fundamental nature, a matter of *form*. Types, roughly speaking, are groups of associated elements constituting recognizable wholes. The constant association of different qualities leads to the formation of the concept. A dogwood tree consists of certain colors, shapes, masses, and so forth, that are associated in our experience to form our conception of the type. The psychology of the formation of types is that of the development of concepts.[38]

Several kinds of types may be distinguished: *natural* types such as plants and animals; *formal* types such as the sonnet, novel, sonata, and fugue; *technical* types such as the technique of performance on the violin, and the technique of musical composition; and *utility* types such as chairs, libraries, dinner music, martial music, or religious music. All these types exhibit, in one sense or another, distinctive forms; each is in its own way a determinative factor in the relevant forms of art.

With reference to *form* in music, the concept of the formal types, such as the sonata and fugue, is an abstraction of qualities common to numerous individual compositions, in terms of which a particular composition can be intelligently perceived or apprehended.[39]

---

[38] For further details, see, for example, Dashiell, *The Fundamentals of General Psychology*, pages 554–560; Woodworth, *Experimental Psychology*, pages 800–807; Santayana, *op. cit.*, pages 119–120; and Pepper, *op. cit.*, pages 140–141.
[39] For a further discussion of the significance of types in relation to form, see, especially, Pepper, *op. cit.*, pages 136–159.

Principles of Design

The general principles of formal design in the various artistic fields can be stated only in terms so abstract that they tend to be vague and almost meaningless; and yet it is important that they be at least tentatively formulated as suggestive guides in theoretical and practical work. Abstract principles may take on profound significance as they are applied in a particular medium.

The most general principle is undoubtedly *unity in variety*. Coherence and interest are determinative factors, in terms of which the principle of unity in variety may be realized. Coherence is conditioned by perceptual grasp; interest, by pleasure. The problem of form thus resolves itself into the question of how to get and hold attentive interest. The form must be organized to make the experience pleasurable; and pleasure depends, in part, on its being intelligible — within the perceptual grasp — and upon its conforming to the other psychological conditions for attentive interest.

The phrase, "unity in variety," implies a certain balance between unity and variety; for rigid unity leads to monotony, whereas great variety results in chaos. If unity were all that were needed, we might select a particularly pleasing chord and sound it indefinitely; or, if variety were the only factor, we might simply wander from chord to chord with no thought of their patterned relationship.

The organizing principles for the achievement of unity in variety have been variously expressed by different writers. The exact terminology is not so important as the main ideas. One writer [40] calls the main principles leading to unity those of *dominance, harmony*, and *balance;* those leading to variety, the corresponding antithetical principles of *thematic variation, contrast*, and *rhythm.*

---

[40] Torossian, *op. cit.*, pages 85–103.

The principle of *dominance* demands the use of one or two principal ideas — in music, one or two primary themes — to which other ideas, or thematic materials, are subordinated in a hierarchical manner.

The principle of *harmony* demands the exploitation of certain similarities among the elements. In music, harmony might be effected by the frequent recurrence of tones of the same pitch, loudness, quality, or duration; by the repetition of motives, or even of accompaniment figures in different keys or at different pitch levels; or by the use of various freer types of imitation.

The principle of *balance* supplies the feeling of rest that arises from the juxtaposition of elements of corresponding dimensions or qualities. In music, examples may be found in the antecedent and consequent phrases of a simple period; in the two sections of an ordinary binary form; in the disposition of a chord in instrumentation; in the use of tonic and dominant harmonies in a simple harmonic design; or in the fairly even mixture of notes of long and short duration. Whatever the elements involved, the principle of balance implies a feeling of equilibrium between them.

The principle of *thematic variation* affords one of the most effective means of obtaining unity in variety. In music especially, themes may be varied in units of all sizes from a simple motive to whole sections. The principle may be applied in innumerable different ways: by slight changes in the pitch, loudness, quality, or duration patterns in the successive appearance of the thematic materials, or in simultaneous variations in two or more dimensions.

The principle of *contrast* demands the introduction of new and different thematic material as a foil to previously stated elements. It may be applied to small or large units. Although significant in all the arts, it is of particular importance in music: in the middle section of the simple ternary forms;

in the second theme of the sonata; in the successive sections of the rondo; and in the various movements of the sonata or suite.

Rhythm, as a constructive principle in music, is the antithesis of balance — an essentially static idea. It refers chiefly to the feeling of movement engendered in the progression from short to long, or from unaccented to accented, notes or beats; and to the swing from one complementary element to the other: for example, from tonic to dominant harmonies (or the reverse), from antecedent to consequent phrase, from high tones to low tones, from soft tones to loud tones, or from a thin tone quality to a rich tone quality.

Obviously, these principles of organization are articulated rather than discrete; almost always, if not always, they operate in conjunction with each other. One of the highest ideals of formal organization in music is a structure in which all the elements or units are so articulated, closely knit, and interwoven into an organic whole that the dropping of a single note would be felt as a distinct loss. This ideal may be unattainable, but it suggests the importance in artistic form of organic unity in variety.[41]

Manners of Treatment

The application of principles of formal design to the materials of the several arts leads to the development of charac-

---

[41] For other formulations of basic structural principles, see, for example, Greene, *op. cit.,* pages 213–226; Pepper, *op. cit.,* pages 101–211; and Parker, *The Analysis of Art,* pages 31–62. Greene formulates certain general factors of formal unity under the categories of "artistic simplicity and complexity," "artistic integration," and "artistic rhythm." Pepper discusses methods of organization through (1) *emotion,* called the principle of dominant emotion, and that of emotional sequence; (2) *types;* (3) *pattern* — referring especially to modes of organization growing out of the limits of human attention (span of apprehension); and (4) *design* — modes of organization resulting from the limitations of human interest. Parker attempts "a logic of aesthetic form" in terms of six principles: namely, organic unity, or unity in variety, theme, thematic variation, balance, hierarchy, and evolution.

teristic modes of treatment, or technical types; and to the crystallization of the numerous formal or compositional types of each art. The detailed study of these basic techniques and forms in music is the special province of musical theory in the narrow sense; it is in this sense that music theory has been called "applied music aesthetics." For present purposes it will be sufficient to discuss briefly the significance of these topics in relation to the general problems of form in musical aesthetics.

The chief manners of treatment of the materials of music may be called *melodic, contrapuntal,* and *harmonic.* When tones, sounded one at a time in succession, are organized in temporal patterns according to certain artistic principles, the treatment is called *melodic.* When successions of two or more simultaneously sounding tones are organized into temporal patterns according to certain artistic principles, the treatment may be called either *contrapuntal* or *harmonic,* according to whether it is primarily the simultaneous combination of melodic lines, or the temporal succession of chords.

Hard and fast lines of demarcation between the different modes of treatment cannot be drawn because they tend to overlap. For example, arpeggiated chords may be treated either melodically, or harmonically, or both; and, in a single composition, contrapuntal and harmonic features may be equally balanced. But such details are problems for musical theory; as far as aesthetic theory is concerned, these manners of treatment constitute one phase or aspect of the means of realizing the principles of formal organization in musical composition.[42] They are not, in themselves, principles of formal organization, but they are conditioning factors in all compositional patterns.

---

[42] *Cf.* Greene, *op. cit.,* pages 143–149.

COMPOSITIONAL PATTERNS

The principal musical forms are generic structural patterns that have been found by experience to afford satisfactory solutions of the problems of formal design. A full measure of the aesthetic significance of these forms can be grasped only through wide experience and extended systematic and historical studies of music. A large portion of musicological research has been devoted to this and related problems. Here we can give only a very brief, synoptic discussion of some of the systematic aspects.[43]

The most elementary musical idea is the compositional unit consisting of a small number of notes or chords called a *motive*. This motive may be enlarged by repetitive or developmental methods into a more extended unit — a *theme*. The various typical designs represented by such conventionalized forms as the canon, fugue, rondo, and sonata grow naturally out of the different manners of treatment of the basic thematic material.

From the contrapuntal method, with its characteristic use of imitation and the simultaneous juxtaposition of "independent" melodies, come the *polyphonic* forms; and from the treatment of melodies according to the harmonic method, come the *homophonic* forms.

A representative procedure in the homophonic forms is to take a short musical idea or motive and extend it by repetition or development into an antecedent phrase and then follow this with a consequent phrase, thus producing a sentence or period. The period is next expanded into a double period by repetition of the material already presented, or by the addition of a complementary period of similar dimensions. The double period, in turn, is extended by its repetition, or by the addition of another double period of corresponding

---

[43] For a more extended discussion, see, especially, George S. Dickinson, *The Pattern of Music*, pages 24–53.

proportions. In this alternation of motives, phrases, periods, and double periods — with all the subtleties of theme and variation, similarity and contrast, balance and rhythm — there is a certain periodicity, a rhythm of pattern, called *structural rhythm*.[44]

In the typical, well-crystallized forms, such as the fugue, sonata, or rondo, the basic principles of design are realized in innumerable characteristic ways. The conventional fugue, for example, exhibits a highly unified, closely knit, organic compositional pattern, embodying the principles of *dominance* and *thematic variation, harmony* and *contrast, balance* and *rhythm.*

A few of these relationships may be briefly mentioned; a more detailed study will reveal many others. *Dominance* is exhibited in the relation of the subject to the counter-subject and to the other subsidiary thematic material; in the relation of the central tonality to the auxiliary tonalities; and in the relation of the dominant mood to more transient moods. *Thematic variation* is found in the modifications of the subject through change of mode, stretto, diminution, augmentation, and other conventional permutations; closely related are the concomitant variations in tonality and mood. *Harmony* is displayed in similarities in the various intrinsic orders, thematic materials, and moods. *Contrasts* occur in the relation of subject to countersubject, of sets of entrances to attendant episodes; and among the intrinsic orders with their various factors. *Balance* takes place between the exposition and corresponding subsequent sections, and in numerous compositional elements at similar levels of organizational integration. And, finally, *rhythm* — in a dynamic structural sense as opposed to the static implications of balance — is manifested through the interplay of subject and answer, exposition and counter-exposition; and in more subtle ways,

[44] *Cf.* Dickinson, *op. cit.,* page 28.

perhaps, even in such matters as the swing from pedal point to stretto, and from augmentation to diminution.

Similar analyses may be made of the sonata with its characteristic exploitation of the developmental idea, and of the rondo with its attendant use of repetition and reiteration.[45] In general, it should be noted that the principles of design operate in the relations of corresponding elements of the same dimension and at similar organizational levels. Also, it is important to realize that the generic forms are abstractions of features common to many members of a given class; that they have no particularized existence except as they are embodied in individual compositions; and that their importance derives largely from the significant role they play in the fields of expression or meaning, and value.

Expression, Content, or Meaning

No phase of aesthetic inquiry is more fraught with difficulties, or more conducive to misunderstandings and controversies, than that dealing with the problems of expression, content, or meaning. A large part of the difficulty arises from the ambiguity of terminology and the inaccurate definition of terms. In addition to this difficulty, there is ample room for confusion in the inherent complexity of the problem with its several variable factors.

In general, two main classes of theories may be distinguished, each with its characteristic variations. The first is the theory of so-called *musical autonomy*, which asserts that music is *sui generis* — that its content or meaning is purely musical and cannot be expressed in other than musical terms. The second is the theory known as *musical heteronomy*, which maintains that music expresses a content which is, in its essence, non-musical, that music is primarily the vehicle for

---

[45] For a comprehensive table of design types and forms, with a significant characterization of each, see Dickinson, *op. cit.*, pages 44 f.

the communication of a reality existing independently of its embodiment in music.[46]   There can be little doubt that there are elements of truth in both viewpoints, and that they are complementary rather than contradictory ways of interpreting the significance of the musical experience.

MUSIC AS AUTONOMOUS ART

There is considerable evidence, in the literature on both musical aesthetics and the psychology of music, that most musicians and the more musical laymen regard music as essentially *autonomous*.[47]   This means, substantially, that the musician looks upon the musical thematic material as his subject matter; and upon this material as it is elaborated into a compositional pattern, as the content.   This musical content is what is being expressed in the music; it is the meaning of music.   The grasping of this content or meaning of music is a matter of perceptual intuition, supported by cognitive insight and rational intellectual processes.   The attention of the musician is directed toward the tonal-rhythmic structure, whether complex or simple.   Emotional overtones, moods — whatever emotive-conative [48] states are associated with the music — are not ordinarily at the focal point of the attention.

Musical values must be felt, rather than arrived at by intellectual processes; and feeling is in the emotional, intuitive, rather than in the intellectual, rational, dimension.   But, for this reason, to characterize music as the language of the emotions is likely to be ambiguous and misleading.   From

---

[46] See C. C. Pratt, *The Meaning of Music*, pages 205–215.   For an attempt at a systematization of the various views in the German literature on musical aesthetics, see Felix M. Gatz, *Musik-Ästhetik in ihren Hauptrichtungen*, pages 11–50.

[47] See, for example, Gatz, *op. cit.*, pages 14–20; and Max Schoen, *The Psychology of Music*, pages 127–142.

[48] Conation, according to Greene (*op. cit.*, page 46), includes "all dynamic tendencies and processes, such as wishing, willing, and striving, at various stages of conscious reflection."

the viewpoint of musical autonomy, the essential emotional content of music can be expressed only in terms of the tonal-rhythmic structure of music; it has no existence apart from its specific musical expression. All attempts to express this content in words are foredoomed to failure; at best, words can only suggest the general character or mood of the music.

Music as Heteronomous Art

There are many varieties of *heteronomous* doctrines, but one of the most plausible is that the moods or affective states expressed in music constitute, or through their expression become, the essential content of music. This idea has been recently expressed by Greene, who refers to [49]

those emotive-conative associations which, prior to composition, constitute the composer's secondary raw material, and which reappear in the composition as the work's objective spiritual content.

In a similar vein, Prall writes: [50]

Music expresses the will and the passions of human beings, feelings and emotions being its burden in a variety and precision not possible to words.

It should be noted, however, that this is not quite the same idea Prall expresses in another passage, when he writes: "What works of art express is simply the determinate beauty they specify." [51] Hanslick cites some twenty authors who, in one way or another, regard the emotions as the content of music; [52] and Hanslick contends against this view. Although it is not within the scope of the present work to enter into any extensive discussion of the problem, a brief consideration of some of the fundamental issues can scarcely be omitted.

---

[49] *Op. cit.*, page 335.
[50] *Aesthetic Judgment*, page 216.
[51] *Op. cit.*, page 226.
[52] Eduard Hanslick, *The Beautiful in Music*, pages 28–31.

TYPES OF EXPRESSION

Expression can take place in several fairly distinct ways. First, there is the type of expression that occurs when facial expression indicates state of mind, or when tone of voice reflects feeling. A classical statement says that it is but a step from highly-inflected emotional speech to musical melody. Insofar as this type of expression exists in music, there seems to be some organic-causal connection between what is expressed and the expression of it. It must be an expression of this kind that Riemann refers to when he speaks of ascending pitches, crescendos, and accelerandos as positive expressions of the will; and of descending pitches, diminuendos, and ritardandos as negative.[53] In vocal music, direct expression of the type described is attained in various ways, but especially through the use of the portamento and related devices.

A second type of expression is that of language in which a word is a symbol for a meaning; there need be no organic-causal connection between the word and its meaning. Of course, words may become expressive in the first sense by the way in which they are delivered. The use of bugle calls in the army illustrates this type of expression musically. Santayana's use of the term *expression* falls into the same category, insofar as he means by expression *the quality acquired by objects through association.*[54] Expression in this sense has a wide application in music — for every tone quality, every motive, melody, or harmony, is sure to awaken some reverberation of previous experiences. The associations aroused may be either musical or nonmusical.

A third type of expression is that which takes place through imitation. Characteristic of the representative arts, this mode of communication conveys its message through the direct re-

---

[53] *Grundriss der Musikwissenschaft*, pages 66–68.
[54] *Op. cit.*, page 193.

semblance between the thing represented and the representation of it. In painting, a landscape or a portrait is depicted through imitation. In music, this mode of expression finds a limited application in such instances as the direct imitation of the sounds of nature — for example, the call of the cuckoo. The imitation in these examples takes place in the same sense modality; visible objects are imitated in visual representations, and auditory phenomena in auditory representations.

It is also possible to work, not only across different sense modalities, but also from subjective or mental states to objective or physical phenomena; that is, certain states of mind may be suggested, if not directly imitated, through auditory or visual media. How auditory patterns can suggest mental states is a problem for psychology which is probably best answered in terms of certain factors common to the different orders of reality or experience. C. C. Pratt, for example, has suggested the idea of movement as an important factor common to tonal-rhythmic patterns and emotional states.[55] Thus, a fourth way in which expression may take place is by analogy or suggestion. The imitation is not so direct or complete as in the third type, and Gatz[56] calls this type of expression *analogically imitative* representation.

Music may be expressive in any or all of the foregoing ways. For example, an ascending figure may depict an intensification of an emotion — a "positive expression of the will" (type one); it may be a signal or a sign with a conventional meaning, or a meaning acquired by association (type two); it may be some natural sound (type three); or it may simply suggest a mood by analogy (type four).

More specifically, the ascending skip of the octave may be the pitches in which Herbert Spencer intoned the word

---

[55] In this connection, read the section on "Dynamism" in Pratt's *The Meaning of Music*, pages 221–237.

[56] *Op. cit.*, page 26. *Cf.* Hanslick, *op. cit.*, page 53.

"Mary" when he called his maid for the third time after receiving no response on two previous tries. The same figure
might serve as a signal for a Boy Scout troop to mean "Let's
go!"; it might be used to imitate a bird call, "Bob-white"; or
it might be used as Strauss uses it in the beginning of the well-
known horn theme in *Don Juan*, to express the idea he is trying to introduce at that point in the composition.

Types one and four are related, in that they both deal
with the expression of emotion; they differ, in that the former
refers to a more or less involuntary or reflex expression of an
emotion by an individual, whereas the latter refers to a studied
and stylized kind of expression. Modes of expression characteristic of the second and third types are by no means devoid
of possibilities for the expression of emotion; for both sym-
bolic communication of the second type and directly imitative communication of the third type may be heavily charged
with emotional overtones.

In view of the great potential capacities of music for the
expression of emotion in the ways indicated, it is not surprising that music should be regarded as "the language of
the emotions." But this is not a particularly fitting expression,
because it says both too much and too little: too much, as it
implies that music is the only art that expresses an emotional
content; and too little, as it fails to indicate specifically the
particular sense in which music may be regarded as expressing emotion.

All art has an emotional content in the sense that the intrinsic values are emotionally felt or directly intuited. All
the arts differ, not so much in the nature of their ultimate content — their emotive-conative states as expressed in the various
media — as in the type of expression employed. We should
not be confused by the fact that music and architecture, as
abstract arts, do not have objective subject matter comparable
to a landscape in painting, or a human figure in sculpture.

The landscape and the human body as represented in the respective arts do not become the contents of these arts; they are merely the factors these arts use, according to their characteristic imitative techniques, for the expression of the felt qualities, emotive-conative states, or perceptual intuitions [57] that constitute the real content of all art.

Thus the *autonomy-heteronomy* problem resolves itself into a matter of attitude. As far as the artist is concerned, he is dealing, primarily, with the melodic-harmonic structure in all its richness of felt qualities or emotional overtones. The psychologist or aesthetician may call his themes or melodies emotions, but to him they are concrete tonal-rhythmic realities. The composer may be motivated in his work by moods or emotions arising from his own experience, or suggested by a program or a text; but as he sets to work, these all become transfigured and lost in the specific tonal material of his art so that his attention is focused on the music rather than on anything else. The further consideration of the problem leads directly to the discussion of *value*.

VALUE

Rather than a real property of an object, *value* is a relational property attributed to the object by virtue of a relationship with an organism into which the object may come.[58] In the broadest sense, *aesthetic value*, according to Lee,[59]

is a property attributed to an object by virtue of the fact that it may be perceptually apprehended with pleasure or displeasure.

It is a value arising from interest in the perceptual aspects of phenomena, when these aspects are "regarded not as the sign of meaning or of fact, but only in their own nature." [60]

---

[57] Cf. Lee, *op. cit.*, especially page 45.
[58] Cf. Lee, *op. cit.*, page 85.
[59] *Op. cit.*, page 88.
[60] Lee, *op. cit.*, pages 87 f.

The measure of the aesthetic value of a work of art is *the pleasure arising in the aesthetic experience*. Perceptual grasp, empathic response, sensuous agreeableness, and emotion are among the factors that may operate to enhance the pleasure of the aesthetic experience. But not all pleasure can be regarded as aesthetic; the distinction must be made in terms of the aesthetic attitude. On this basis we may distinguish between direct values attributed to material and form, and indirect or derived values attributed to expression and function.

In music, the material values are those of the intrinsic orders as they may be discovered in the tones themselves. The most obvious of these values is that of *tone quality*.

As the materials of music are organized into patterns or designs of more or less complexity, these values merge into formal values. The appreciation of formal values on the various levels and in the several dimensions of formal organization is of primary importance to the musician. The spread and depth of this appreciation is the natural result of extensive technical training and experience in music. Therefore, technical training in music is the surest way to the fullest appreciation of music. The mere listening to music and to lectures about music, unaccompanied by technical instruction, can at best lead to a more or less superficial apprehension of intrinsic musical values.[61]

Although it is difficult to make a sharp distinction between *direct*, and *indirect* or *derived*, *values*, within certain areas the differences are clear. *Expressiveness*, in the sense of Santayana — as those associations that accrue to an object by reason of past experiences — is clearly a derived value.[62] In general, intellectual, moral, and functional aspects of a work of art, insofar as they affect the aesthetic experience in the

---

[61] In this connection, read David W. Prall, *Aesthetic Analysis*, pages 203 f.

[62] See Santayana, *op. cit.*, pages 193 and 195, and Lee, *op. cit.*, pages 101–122. Lee's discussion of derived value is fundamental and should be carefully studied.

perception of aesthetic value, may be classed as derived aesthetic values.

The nature of an experience changes with the attitude of the individual. For example, in a church service, as long as a person's attention is directed toward the religious values of the experience, his experience is predominantly religious. But, perhaps, in the course of the service his attention may turn to the intrinsic values of the music; religious values may become secondary to aesthetic values, and the experience may become aesthetic rather than religious. Conversely, at a concert the attention may shift from purely musical values to religious values, and the experience may become religious rather than aesthetic. The aesthetic values of the experience are not entirely lost; they merely become secondary, indirect, or derived. Similar examples may be construed for intellectual and practical aspects of experience.

In functional music, such as religious, dance, or patriotic music, the appropriateness of the music to the occasion becomes important (though still secondary), as a criterion of aesthetic value. The role of expression in the problem of aesthetic value, as interpreted by Greene, can probably best be discussed in the light of Bullough's analysis of the aesthetic experience. If the attention of the individual is directed toward emotive-conative states as the content of the music, and, if the individual is conscious of emotive-conative states aroused within himself, rather than lost in the contemplation of these qualities as attributed to the work of art — the aesthetic experience (if, indeed, it can be called an aesthetic experience at all) is of the lowest type. But, if these qualities are attributed to the work of art, they may acquire important, though secondary or derived, aesthetic value.

Wherever music is connected with something not music (music with words, program music, opera, music and dance), as in functional music — the effectiveness with which the music accomplishes its various tasks becomes an important, though still secondary, criterion of aesthetic value. The values derived from any nonmusical content that may be associated with the music itself must be regarded as essentially indirect. The intrinsic musical value is likely to decrease as the nonmusical element is increasingly emphasized. Hence the fallacy, for example, of Wagner's dream of a super-art based upon the combination of music, drama, and dance.[63]

TASTE [64]

If the expression *de gustibus non est disputandum* is taken to mean *there is no disputing about tastes,* in the sense that because the expression of preference among aesthetic values is individual there can be no rational justification of taste — the statement is false. Fundamental criteria of good taste may be established upon a frame of reference that includes variable factors, but there can be no doubt that such normative criteria do exist and function, within limits, on all levels of artistic activity.

Artistic sensitivity to the materials of art in their intrinsic orders, and at least to the simpler structural units in musical design, is a fundamental factor that can be approximately determined in the frame of reference. A second factor is a certain level of training and experience in the technique of music. And, finally — a third factor — a degree of orientation in the essentially nonmusical background enriches the musical experience through the perception of derived values. Tastes are individual, but they can be compared in terms of this multiple frame of reference.

---

[63] See, for example, Guido Adler, *Richard Wagner,* pages 169 f. Second Edition. Munich: Drei Masken Verlag, 1923.

For a further discussion of aesthetic value, see Lee, *op. cit.,* pages 5–8, 67–122, *et passim.*

[64] In connection with this section, the student should read Lee's chapter on "Taste," *op. cit.,* pages 123–146.

Native sensitiveness to intrinsic musical values is the first condition and basis of musical taste. Through musical experience the individual develops a consciousness of various formal and technical types which constitute standards of taste. The types referred to include a wide variety of factors, from such relatively simple concepts as *tone quality*, *scales, intonation, chord progressions*, and *cadence structures*, to such complex and composite concepts as the various *techniques of performance and composition, interpretation, form*, and *style*.

The type tends to be an idealization superior to the average. For example, an oboe player's conception of a fine oboe tone is an idealization superior in quality to the average tone he has heard. As a result of training and experience he develops an idea of what the tone of an oboe should be; this concept of the type, then, constitutes the standard which he attempts to attain in his own playing, and with reference to which he judges any oboe tone he may hear. A similar process of reasoning may be applied to types at all levels of complexity. In general, the greater the natural artistic sensitivity, and the broader the training and experience, the more refined will be the taste.

The statement made above, with respect to the conditioning of taste by the third factor, may be amplified by pointing out briefly some of the ways in which a liberal education may enhance the apprehension of value by increasing the spread and depth of derived aesthetic values. Assuming, always, that the individual meets the first two requirements — *artistic sensitivity* and *training and experience in the art* — the person who has a good background in musicology, history, languages, literature, philosophy, and the like is much more likely to attain a full apprehension of indirect or derived values. Knowledge of a composer's life, the circumstances under which a composition was written, the sociocultural background, and innumerable other related, though non-musical, details makes possible the development of more complex and significant standards of taste.

The operation of the psychological law of *habituation* prevents the establishment of rigid, unchanging standards of musical value. In accordance with this law, the concept of a variable frame of reference allows for, and explains, changes in taste during the processes of history, and differences of taste in any particular period.

CRITICISM

Criticism implies evaluation. It is based upon appreciation but is not identical with it. The critical evaluation of a work of art implies more than the mere appreciation of aesthetic values; it requires a justification of the evaluative judgment through pointing out potential aesthetic values. Hence, criticism is not merely evaluation, but justification through intelligent description and comparison.

Criticism, an intellectual process, normally leads to an enhanced appreciation of aesthetic values. Comprehensive criticism, which is largely technical in character, finds its basic criteria in the fundamental aesthetic principles of design, and must be oriented to a systematic and historical frame of reference. To fulfill his function adequately, the critic must be sensitive to artistic values in the medium with which he is dealing; he must have a broad experience, fortified by technical training in the systematic and historical aspects of the art he is criticising; he must have an insight into the fundamental problems of philosophy as he relates the art to manifold sociocultural phenomena; and, finally, he must have a command of language adequate to the expression of his ideas.

A detailed account of all the implications of the foregoing discussion of artistic criticism would provide ample material for a separate treatise; for present purposes we must be content with this very brief treatment of the subject.

APPLIED MUSICAL AESTHETICS

Musical criticism is one of the important fields of applied musical aesthetics; [65] another is that of *musical theory* in the narrow sense.[66] Further reflection leads to the conclusion that, in a sense, all phases of musical activity — especially composition, performance, and listening to music — are branches of applied musical aesthetics. Certainly, individual and collective insight into the fundamental problems of musical aesthetics has far-reaching consequences at all levels and in all aspects of musical practice; just as, conversely, a wide experience in musical practice affords the empirical basis for the theory of musical aesthetics.

BIBLIOGRAPHY

Anschütz, Georg, *Abriss der Musikästhetik*. Leipzig: Breitkopf & Härtel, 1930.

Bullough, Edward, " 'Psychical Distance' as a Factor in Art and an Aesthetic Principle," *The British Journal of Psychology*, Vol. V (1912), pages 87–118.

Calvocoressi, Michel D., *The Principles and Methods of Musical Criticism*. New and Enlarged Edition. London: Oxford University Press, 1931.

Chandler, Albert R., *Beauty and Human Nature*. New York: D. Appleton-Century Company, Inc., 1934.

————, and Edward N. Barnhart, *A Bibliography of Psychological and Experimental Aesthetics*. Berkeley, California: The University of California Press, 1938.

Croce, Benedetto, *Aesthetic: As Science of Expression and General Linguistic* (Tr. from the Italian by Douglas Ainslie). Second Edition. London: Macmillan & Co., Ltd., 1922.

---

[65] Cf. Lee, *op. cit.*, pages 191–196.

[66] Riemann, for example, defines music theory as a branch of technical instruction as applied musical aesthetics. (*Grundriss der Musikwissenschaft*, page 15.)

Dewey, John, *Art as Experience*. New York: Minton, Balch & Company, 1934.

Dickinson, George S., *The Pattern of Music*. Poughkeepsie, New York: Vassar College, 1939.

Eastman, Max, *Enjoyment of Poetry*. New York: Charles Scribner's Sons, 1913.

Gatz, Felix M., *Musik-Ästhetik in ihren Hauptrichtungen*. Stuttgart: Ferdinand Enke, 1929.

Gilbert, Katharine E., and Helmut Kuhn, *A History of Esthetics*. New York: The Macmillan Company, 1939.

Greene, Theodore M., *The Arts and the Art of Criticism*. Princeton: Princeton University Press, 1940.

Gurney, Edmund, *The Power of Sound*. London: Smith, Elder, & Co., 1880.

Hammond, William A., *A Bibliography of Aesthetics and of the Philosophy of the Fine Arts from 1900 to 1932*. Revised and Enlarged Edition. (First published as a supplement to the May, 1933 issue of the *Philosophical Review*). New York: Longmans, Green & Company, 1934.

Hanslick, Eduard, *The Beautiful in Music* (Tr. from the Seventh Edition, Leipzig, 1885, by Gustav Cohen). New York: H. W. Gray Company, Inc., 1891. (First Edition, 1854.)

Lalo, Charles, *Esquisse d'une esthétique musicale scientifique*. Paris: Félix Alcan, 1908.

Lee, Harold N., *Perception and Aesthetic Value*. New York: Prentice-Hall, Inc., 1938.

Ogden, C. K., and I. A. Richards, *The Meaning of Meaning*. New York: Harcourt, Brace & Company, 1936.

Ogden, Robert M., *The Psychology of Art*. New York: Charles Scribner's Sons, 1938.

Parker, DeWitt H., *The Analysis of Art*. New Haven: Yale Univ. Press, 1926.

————, *The Principles of Aesthetics*. Boston: Silver, Burdett and Company, 1920.

Pepper, Stephen C., *Aesthetic Quality*. New York: Charles Scribner's Sons, 1937.

Prall, David W., *Aesthetic Analysis*. New York: Thomas Y. Crowell Company, 1936.

————, *Aesthetic Judgment*. New York: Thomas Y. Crowell Company, 1929.

Pratt, Carroll C., *The Meaning of Music: A Study in Psychological Aesthetics*. New York: McGraw-Hill Book Company, Inc., 1931.

Puffer, Ethel D., *The Psychology of Beauty*. Boston: Houghton Mifflin Company, 1905.

Rader, Melvin M. (Editor), *A Modern Book of Esthetics*. New York: Henry Holt & Company, 1935.

Reid, Louis A., *A Study in Aesthetics*. London: George Allen & Unwin, Ltd., and Macmillan & Co., Ltd., 1931.

Riemann, Hugo, *Catechism of Musical Aesthetics* (Tr. by H. Bewerunge). London: Augener & Co., 1895.

————, *Die Elemente der musikalischen Aesthetik*. Berlin: W. Spemann, 1900.

Santayana, George, *The Sense of Beauty*. New York: Charles Scribner's Sons, 1896.

Schmitz, Eugen, *Musikästhetik*. Second Edition. Leipzig: Breitkopf & Härtel, 1925.

Schoen, Max, *Art and Beauty*. New York: The Macmillan Company, 1932.

Schole, Heinrich, *Tonpsychologie und Musikästhetik*. Göttingen: Vandenhoeck & Ruprecht, 1930.

Sorantin, Erich, *The Problem of Musical Expression*. Nashville: Marshall & Bruce Company, 1932.

Stieglitz, Olga, *Einführung in die Musikästhetik*. Stuttgart: J. G. Cotta'sche Buchhandlung Nachfolger, 1912.

Torossian, Aram, *A Guide to Aesthetics*. Stanford University, California: Stanford University Press, 1937.

Woods, Elizabeth Robinson, *Music and Meaning*. Cambridge: Harvard University Press, 1932.

CHAPTER V

THE THEORY OF MUSIC THEORY

THE TERM "THEORY," AS USED IN THE STUDY OF MUSIC, is applied specifically to courses in notation, sight-singing, dictation, harmony, counterpoint, and the like, as distinguished from courses in applied music and in the history of music. In this specific sense the term is used in this chapter. The theoretical knowledge imparted in these courses is presented "ready-made," so to speak; that is, students are told how scales are constructed, how intervals are named and classified, and similar facts. Such courses, intended to give the student basic knowledge which may properly be called theoretical, actually develop certain skills in the manipulation of the materials of music. In this latter effect, they are really courses in one type of applied music.

It is the business of musicology to supply the best available information in these fields. The branch of musicology we call *the theory of music theory* includes not only the theory of what is ordinarily known as *elementary theory of music*, but also *the theory of harmony, the theory of counterpoint*, and so on. In the scope of the theory of music theory lie such tasks as the accurate definition of the technical terms used in theoretical instruction, the formulation of general principles underlying the various branches of music theory, and numerous other tasks in the discovery, verification, and organization of technical knowledge in music.

[155]

Questions of the organization of materials for teaching purposes and of the methods involved in teaching fall, rather, under the head of *musical pedagogy*. The teacher's chief responsibility is to have a clear conception of what the student needs to know, and how he can most effectively impart this knowledge to the student.

THEORY AND PRACTICE

The foregoing discussion suggests that the concern of a class in music theory, so-called, is not so much theoretical as it is practical, and quite properly so. The place for theorizing, except, perhaps, for passing mention, is in advanced courses in theory or in the graduate seminar. For example, it is one thing to know how the conventional cadences of a given musical style are formed, and how to handle the musical materials to produce similar results, but it is quite another to investigate and understand the how's and why's of ca-.dences. To understand the theory of cadences, the musicologist must investigate many factors. He must comprehend the physical acoustical basis of tonal relations, the findings of psychophysiology, and any aesthetic principles involved. Furthermore, he will need to know the history of the cadence, from the comparatively simple procedures of purely melodic music to the complicated harmonic structures of the modernists. From the mass of material these and other sources yield, the investigator may get enough insight into the nature and function of the cadence to formulate the principles that govern its use in any given style. Essentially, the same is true of other similar details and problems of music theory. Only the results of the musicologist's research, organized for teaching purposes, go into the textbooks.

The distinction between the theory of music abstractly considered and the theory of music as a practical subject of instruction is further evident in the literature of books on music. Compare, for example, the works of Yasser[1] and Shirlaw[2] with any textbook of music theory, and the difference will be immediately apparent. The works named are theoretical, whereas the textbook is practical.

ELEMENTARY THEORY

It is neither possible to distinguish absolutely among the various phases of musical theory, nor necessary to do so. Nevertheless, for purposes of discussion certain rough distinctions are very convenient. We shall, therefore, consider the subject matter of the present chapter under the headings *elementary theory, melody, rhythm, harmony, counterpoint, instrumentation and orchestration,* and *form.*

Elementary theory concerns what are commonly known as the rudiments of music, such as scales, intervals, rhythm and meter, the definition of terms, and the fundamentals of notation. Music theory, in working out its definitions and formulating its theories about these matters, approaches its task from both a systematic and a historical viewpoint. It accepts what the auxiliary sciences of acoustics, psychophysiology, and aesthetics have to contribute and, in the light of historical developments, translates the data into the technical terms of music.

Consider, for example, *scales.* Acoustical and mathematical sciences give us certain information concerning the physical basis of tonal relations. Some musicologists, on the one hand, attach great importance to what acoustics tells us about the nature of music; but, on the other hand, others belittle the importance of acoustical knowledge, even denying that it has anything at all to do with music.

Without extended discussion of the question, we may conclude, for example, that no matter how far the practice of

---

[1] Joseph Yasser, *A Theory of Evolving Tonality.*
[2] Matthew Shirlaw, *The Theory of Harmony.*

music may depart from the tunings of the overtone series, the presence of overtones in every tonal complex is an acoustic fact which necessarily affects the total situation. Departures from the tunings of the overtone series, and from the tunings mathematically based on them, have ample justification and explanation on psychophysiological, aesthetic, and artistic grounds; but the physical basis is still a factor not to be ignored. Thus, it is not strictly true to say that [8]

> Scales are arbitrary conventions, man-made affairs, agreed upon and adopted by nations or groups who have made music, varying among different peoples in different periods.

On the other hand, it is just as inadequate to say that any purely natural scale exists. Because the scales used in music are complex — both systematic and historical in character — any adequate explanation of scales must itself be complex, taking into consideration as far as possible all the conditioning factors, both systematic and historical. One can begin his investigation of scales from any one of many starting points, but, before he is through, he will need to view them from a number of other points if he is to arrive at a valid and comprehensive conception of their nature and significance. Therefore, following our general procedure in the present work, we begin the study of scales from the starting point of acoustics.

Psychophysiology has contributed to our knowledge of scales the fact that tones are perceived as having breadth. This fact allows for certain deviations from the mathematical-physical norms basic to tonal relations in general. The nature of tonal sensation and perception sets such limitations as, for example, the number of scale degrees which can be effectively used within the octave. These and many similar facts partly determine the scales of music.

---

[8] Marion Bauer, "Scales," *The International Cyclopedia of Music and Musicians*, pages 1621 f.

Since aesthetic theory regards scales from still another view-point, what aesthetics has to say about them is likewise important for a full comprehension of the theory of scales. Aesthetically, the musical scale, whatever its physical and psychological bases, represents a fundamental principle of order in the tonal dimension of pitch. Without scales as a means of organizing the tonal material of music with respect to pitch, music as an art would be inconceivable.

Music theory approaches the study of scales in diverse ways. It attempts to interpret and evaluate the musical significance of all that the auxiliary sciences contribute to our knowledge of the subject. It studies actual music to see which scales are used. It considers such related matters as interval structure, cadences, and tonality. It considers what comparative musicology says about the scales used in non-European and primitive musical systems. And, also, it makes a careful investigation and study of the history of scales. With the knowledge and insight gained from all these various sources, it defines the various kinds of scales, explains the use of key signatures, solves problems of notation, and evolves its systematic theory of scales.

What has been said about scales applies, with necessary changes, to the other items under the heading of elementary theory. Among these other topics are *notation, time and time signatures, intervals,* and *ornaments.*

MELODY

Acoustically, a *melody* may be just a succession of tones; psychologically, a form of emotional response; aesthetically, one of the ways tonal materials are given artistic form; but in the theory of music theory, melody is something of all these — even though the theorist may express it simply as "a well-ordered succession of tones." In other words, when the theorist develops his theory of melody, he considers *the nature of tonal relations* as expounded by acoustical science, *emotional coherence* and the like as worked out by the psychologist, *aesthetic principles of design*, and whatever other light the auxiliary sciences shed upon the nature of melody. In addition, he makes an extensive systematic and historical study of the melodies in the folk and art music of the world. Gradually he analyzes and describes the melodic structure of the principal style-species and style-periods in the technical terms of music. Eventually he may formulate the general principles that seem fundamental to each musical style. An excellent example of this kind of work occurs in the section on *melody* in Knud Jeppesen's *The Style of Palestrina and the Dissonance*.[4] Another significant study of melody is Robert Lach's study of *melodic ornamentation*.[5] Lach, instead of selecting one composer or style-period and studying the various aspects of the melodic structure, chooses one significant feature of melodic structure and investigates it through a long period of time.

Obviously, systematic and historical study of the theory of melody lies outside the scope of the present book, but a brief discussion of some pertinent problems may be appropriate.

To the question, "What is a melody, anyway?", we must answer that it is a number of different things. In a song, it is the succession of tones in the vocal part, as distinguished from the accompaniment of the piano. But the psychologist is probably not referring to melody in this sense when he says: "A sequence of tones constitutes a melody when it is apprehended in terms of a unified and single response"[6] — for this sequence of tones may be too long to be apprehended in the manner indicated. In a symphony, the complex part called

---

[4] Pages 43–76.
[5] *Studien zur Entwickelungsgeschichte der ornamentalen Melopöie. Beiträge zur Geschichte der Melodie.*
[6] Mursell, *Psychology of Music*, page 104.

melody is likely to consist of many diverse elements — for instance, a melodic structure made up of a principal theme and certain subordinate themes. At a given time we may say the melody — that is, the principal melody — is in the first horn, while the violins have a subordinate melody, and other instruments may have other auxiliary melodies. When taken together in this way, the melodies constitute a contrapuntal structure. The part played by the horn may be distinguished as a *theme*, meaning, ordinarily, a significant melodic element variously developed in the course of the composition; or it may simply be designated a *motive*, a still smaller unit in the melodic structure.

Tune and *melody*, though similar, should not be confused. A tune is only one kind of melody. A hymn tune, for example, is a melody; but, even in a simple choral setting by Bach, the bass may be melodic to such an extent that we can properly speak of the *melody* of the bass. In the more elaborate choral settings of the Bach cantatas, much more florid and significant melodies are interwoven in the instrumental parts. But these melodies are not *tunes*. Perhaps a *tune* may be defined as "a melody one tends to remember and whistle or hum."

It becomes apparent, then, that the generic term *melody* covers a wide variety of related meanings, from a very vague "any temporal succession of tones" to "a closely knit, well-defined, characteristic, organic, tonal-rhythmic pattern, thought of as a single line." A prelude of Bach made up most obviously of a succession of figured chords may outline a melody with the succession of top notes of the harmonic complex. And, of course, there are countless other ways of outlining a melodic contour, even in a very complicated harmonic structure. In its broadest sense, *melody* seems to include anything from the lalling of an infant to the most sophisticated theme of a symphony.

Music theory must suspect the psychologist of musical nescience who suggests that "melody is not a sequence of tones at all," but rather "a total contour of tonal movement"; that "Melody always may be, and in its essence always is, entirely independent of harmony"; and that "A melody need have no definite unified tonal structure." [7] Some elements of psychological truth may lie in these and similar statements, applied to melody in the vague general sense. When applied to melody as treated in music theory, however, they have little meaning: for *melody*, to the musician, is certainly a succession of tones; it is related to harmony in every legitimate sense of the term; and it does have definite unified tonal structure.

Generalizations about the nature of melody may be exceedingly useful, if room is allowed for exceptions; but it is probably impossible to formulate a principle governing melody in general, or melody "in the vague." The most fruitful way of studying the theory of melody is undoubtedly that already suggested: studying particular melodies from various style-periods and style-species. The principles found in each of these may point toward still more sweeping generalizations, but there are innumerable difficulties because many of the principles that apply to the music of Palestrina, for example, do not apply to the music of Beethoven or Schoenberg. In the various epochs different frames of reference, scalic systems, and other fundamental conceptions have prevailed. Similarly, in the various style-species, different melodic principles prevail. Instrumental melodies differ in important respects from vocal melodies; religious melodies are not the same as secular melodies; in an opera, soprano melodies may exhibit characteristic differences from bass melodies; and, even in operatic melodies for soprano, numerous stylistic distinctions may be made — for example,

---

[7] Mursell, *op. cit.*, pages 101 ff.

between coloratura arias and songs of more dramatic type, such as the recitative.

Obviously, the field of melody affords unlimited opportunities for further systematic and historical investigation and speculation.

RHYTHM

The physical basis of *rhythm* is a pattern of occurrence and recurrence of stress and duration elements. Physical science provides the means of obtaining objective records of all the measurable quantities involved. These are chiefly *duration, intensity,* and *rate of occurrence,* which, taken together, give the pattern.

Physiology and psychology reveal that though we hear sound, we can only feel rhythm. They show something of the relations among the perception of rhythm, kinesthetic sensations, and bodily motions. They indicate the closeness of the relation between these kinesthetic sensations and emotive-conative states; how judgments of what is relatively fast or slow are formed; and how temporal successions of stresses or durations, or of combinations of the two, are perceived as a pattern. Aesthetics suggests that "the apprehension of rhythmical patterns is the fundamental principle of the perceptual grasp of temporal objects." [8] Thus, aesthetically, rhythm is the chief form-giving principle for the temporal arts. It is the background upon which are deployed the complex tonal factors *frequency* (pitch), *intensity* (loudness, stress), *wave form* (quality), and *duration,* which combine into the higher units of *motive, cadence, tonality,* and the like, and culminate in the whole tonal-rhythmic pattern we call *music.*

What the theorist learns from the systematic sciences about

---

[8] Harold N. Lee, *Perception and Aesthetic Value,* page 57. New York: Prentice-Hall, Inc., 1938.

the nature and function of rhythm in music, he supplements from historical studies. Each historical style-period and style-species exhibits its own peculiar rhythmic characteristics. For example, in some periods and styles the duration accent is a more prominent feature, but in others the stress accent comes to the fore; in some, a strict metric measure dominates, but in others, metric freedom is found; in some, rhythmic patterns are regular and symmetrical, but in others, irregular and more or less unsymmetrical.

In the light of the various systematic and historical data, the musical theorist attempts to formulate his definitions and the general principles of rhythmical procedure; and in terms of these general principles he tries to solve innumerable specific problems of rhythm. Though it is hard to give a comprehensive formal definition of rhythm, its general meaning is clear. It underlies the patterned temporal structure of music. In the current music of Western Europe the durational elements of time are regulated by an elaborate metric system — with all its apparatus of time signatures, note values, measures set off with bar lines, tempo indications, and the like. The time signatures provide certain basic metrical schemes which serve as standards of reference — temporal units — in terms of which the rhythmical patterns of music are worked out.

The accentual system to effect the rhythmical results desired includes several different types of accent. Of these the *stress* accent is the most obvious. It is produced chiefly by means of regulating the intensity (loudness) of tones. The *duration* accent is made by an appropriate arrangement of long and short note (duration) values. Another type of accent, less obvious but of considerable importance, is one which may be called the *perceptual* accent. This is an accentual effect produced when, in the course of a phrase, a rest occurs on a strong beat. A similar effect is often produced by a syncopation, that is, when no note is "struck" on the strong beat. The so-called *subjective* accent is one "read into" a perfectly even series of pulses.

Several other technical terms used in connection with rhythm may be mentioned in passing. *Microrhythm* is the rhythm of the individual parts, as distinguished from *macrorhythm*, which is the rhythm of the whole.[9] *Polyrhythm* signifies the combination of different rhythms in the different voice parts, presumably implying the simultaneous use of different meter signatures. *Multirhythm* is used to indicate frequent changes of meter signature.[10] Further details concerning the theory of rhythm must be left to special works on the subject. The importance of the study of rhythm can scarcely be overemphasized, as it is the principle governing the patterned temporal structure of music.

Harmony and Counterpoint Contrasted

Harmony is ordinarily defined as *the art which deals with the simultaneous combination of tones into chords,* and *counterpoint,* as *the art of combining independent melodies simultaneously.* Frequently, harmony is referred to as the vertical aspect of music; counterpoint, as the horizontal or linear. But such definitions are suggestive rather than comprehensive. Each term is used in several different shades of meaning.

In the broadest sense, *harmony* refers to (1) the theory of tonal relations in general, perhaps because the standard of reference is the harmonic series of nature. In another sense, harmony means (2) the theory of simultaneous sounds, or combinations of sounds or chords. And in still a third sense, harmony concerns (3) the principles governing chord pro-

---

[9] See Knud Jeppesen, *op. cit.,* pages 24 ff.
[10] See Marion Bauer, "Rhythm," *The International Cyclopedia of Music and Musicians,* page 1544.

gressions. Taking harmony in the first sense, it seems that, insofar as a melody is a succession of tones selected according to some such principle of tonal relations as a scale, even an unaccompanied melody has harmonic implications — is founded upon harmonic principles. In the same sense, counterpoint is likewise harmonically grounded and, in the other senses, exhibits the additional harmonic characteristic of simultaneous combinations of tones, and often produces the effect of chords in progression.

In the first sense, the problems of ancient Greek music were partly harmonic. The Greek word ἁρμονία (*joint, proportion, concord*) was applied to the system of scales we call the *octave species.*

Harmony in the second sense became a factor in the history of music when musicians began to sing in octaves, and in fourths and fifths. According to this view, the *magadizing* of the Greeks involved an incipient harmonic problem, as did the selection of the intervals for the early *strict organum.* From then to the present, harmony in this sense has existed, and the classification of chords according to their objective structure has come to be one of its chief tasks.

The third meaning that has become attached to the word *harmony* emphasizes the interrelationship of chords and the principles governing their logical progression. This refers especially to the peculiar significance a chord has because of its relation to the musical context in which it occurs — commonly called the *chord function.* In musical history the functional, or organic, nature of chords in progressions probably became most apparent in the cadence structures, and is closely connected, if not in the last analysis almost identical, with the idea of tonality.

Counterpoint, as suggested, is usually defined as *the simultaneous association of independent melodies.* The word, coming into use about the fourteenth century, is derived from

the Latin expression *punctus contra punctum.* The inde-
pendence of the melodies in counterpoint, however, is chiefly
a rhythmic individuality and a distinction among melodic
progressions. As each part is harmonically conditioned by
every other part, it is not accurate to say that in the contrapuntal period musical composition was purely linear and
that the vertical combinations were accidental. From the
viewpoint of harmony as vertical structure, the principles
governing the association of melodies in counterpoint are
expressed in terms of consonances, which are permitted to
occur freely, and of dissonances, which are subjected to certain restrictions. The point emphasized in sixteenth-century
counterpoint is that the succeeding simultaneous combinations
of tones were not thought of as harmonic *progressions* in the
modern sense. They were simply regarded as vertical combinations of intervals, and were arranged according to the
principles of dissonance treatment — or, stating it another
way — of consonance. Throughout the period, however, the
functional character of the chords in the cadence structures
becomes increasingly apparent.

When, in the harmonic period, we speak of chord progression and of the various qualities desired in good voice leading, we are looking in the direction of counterpoint, especially if we try to make the various parts "interesting." If
an inner part wanders back and forth between two or three
notes and has nothing significant to say in a melodic sense,
or if a bass simply skips up and down from the root of one
chord to that of another, the result may be harmony, but
hardly counterpoint — certainly not good counterpoint.

The ideal for harmonic writing would be to have a good
melodic line in the bass, and more and more of melodic interest in the inner parts; but when this ideal is fully achieved,
a composition turns out to be good contrapuntal writing,
such as the Bach chorales. In counterpoint almost the reverse

is true. We must conclude, then, that to some extent the harmonic problem is present in all contrapuntal writing, and contrariwise the contrapuntal problem is implicit in all harmonic writing. Harmony and counterpoint may be considered just different ways of looking at the same phenomenon.

HARMONY

Auxiliary sciences make many contributions to the theory of *harmony:* acoustics contributes the mathematical and physical basis of tonal relations; physiology and psychology show how chords and chord progressions are perceived; aesthetics formulates the principles of design and related matters; and history records the musical theories and practices of the past. When the contributions of the systematic sciences are applied to the data supplied by historical science, the most comprehensive theory of harmony may be worked out. Studies in harmony that include rigorous application of scientific methods, critical analysis of the basic problems of harmony, and insight into the artistic implications may lead to formulation of the principles governing harmonic procedure in general and certain musical styles in particular. The broader the generalization, the less specific meaning it is likely to have; and yet the details of harmonic procedure point toward a generality of some kind between the extremes of too much abstraction and too much particularization.

The main problems of harmonic theory concern classification and use. A primary classification of the materials of harmony yields *essential* and *nonessential, chordal* and *decorative.* Chordal classification is based upon the direct, objective structure of simultaneous combinations of tones, but it is necessarily modified and extended by functional considerations. Criteria for the classification of chords are the number of tones present, the formal structure, and the function. The problems in the detailed execution of the theory are many and complex. Only a few typical problems can be mentioned.

The simultaneous combinations of tones are grouped into essential combinations called *chords*, and nonessential combinations regarded as purely decorative, or passing, elements; or in complex combinations certain tones are determined to constitute the chord, and the superfluous tones are called *nonchordal, added,* or *decorative* tones of one type or another. The criteria for deciding what is a chord and what is not are (1) the harmonic relationship among the tones, or simply (2) whether or not a given tonal combination has the characteristics of a chordal entity. If a combination of three tones can be reduced to a series of superimposed thirds, it is a chord; but if it cannot, some other grounds must be found for its inclusion, or it is likely to be classed, not as a chord, but as a fortuitous combination.

Chords, we have said, are classified according to (1) the number of tones in the combination, (2) structure, and (3) function. The basic unit under (1) is the *triad* or combination of three tones; but combinations of four, five, and sometimes more notes are also recognized as chordal entities. Two-note combinations are ordinarily not called *chords*, but simply *intervals*. The name of a chord having four tones might logically be *tetrad*, but in conventional theory it is normally called a *chord of the seventh*, or perhaps a *chord of the added sixth*. A five-note chord is the ordinary *chord of the ninth*, which might logically be called a *pentad* — especially in modern music, where it is not always a chord of the ninth.[11]

According to (2), *structure*, the principal means of classi-

---

[11] It might be desirable if the suffix *-ad*, used to form collective numerals or the names of aggregates, were used consistently. Thus *monad, dyad, triad, tetrad, pentad,* and so forth would designate the various types.

fication in conventional theory is the possibility of reducing the combination to an "original" position of superimposed thirds. In terms of this idea and the principle of the identity of the octave, other combinations are brought in as inversions of chords. But, of course, still other schemes are logically possible and have been used to some extent — such as, for example, the chords conceived as superimposed fourths.[12]   In terms of structure, the chords, especially triads, are further classed as *major, minor, altered*, and so on, according to the details of their formation.

According to (3), *function*, triads are further distinguished as *tonic, supertonic, mediant*, and so on; and, in addition, certain chords — such as that of the *added sixth*, the *cadential six-four*, and the first inversion of the *mediant triad* — are shifted from their purely structural class because of changes in function in the particular context in which they occur. Other questions of function concern such matters as *modulation, cadence, modal harmony, polytonality*, and *atonality*.

Theorists have devoted much effort to working out such problems as the explanation of harmonic relationship, derivation of the major and minor triads, the theory of inversion, and theories of modulation.

In harmonic relationship (harmony in the first sense), the basis for determining the relationship between tones is the mathematical-acoustical formulas expressing the ratios of the frequencies, with modifications and extensions of proportions allowable for psychophysiological reasons in the nature of tonal perception. With these modifications, the simplicity of the ratio is the chief factor, so that the octave represents the closest relation, the fifth the next, and so on. The interval of the second, melodically a very natural interval, represents a more distant relationship (9/8 or 16/15) than the third (5/4 or 6/5), but psychological reasons, such as ease

---

[12] See Arnold Schoenberg, *Harmonielehre*, Third Edition, pages 478–492.

of singing, may raise other questions about the nearness of relationship. The determination of the interval relationship considered with the idea of tonality lays the foundation for the concepts of harmony in the second (structural) and third (functional) meanings.

The problem of the minor triad is a classic example of a theoretical difficulty. Zarlino tried to explain the relationship by his well-known theory of harmonic and arithmetic proportions. The major triad is derived from the divisions of a string, called *harmonic proportion,* and the minor triad from the multiples of a string, called *arithmetical proportion.* Rameau brought forward the idea of chord generation from the overtone series to account for the major triad, but encountered difficulties with the minor triad because, of course, it does not occur in this series, at least not in any prominent relation to the generator. To explain the minor triad he wavered between Zarlino's theory and one of double generators. According to the latter theory, the fifth of the triad is the unifying factor, in that it is the fifth harmonic (reduced to the major third) of the third of the triad, and the third tone in the harmonic series generated by the root of the chord (reduced to the fifth). Riemann developed the idea that an *undertone* series exists objectively, while Helmholtz favored the view that the minor third is simply added to the perfect fifth of the overtone series, overpowering the weak fifth partial (major third) with a stronger tone. But the physical presence of the fifth partial lays the foundation for the somewhat dissonant effect of the minor chord. This and similar difficulties have led many theorists to abandon reference to the overtone series and to adopt an empirical method of simply building up chords by superimposition of thirds, but the actual presence of the overtone series still remains an acoustic fact that conditions every chord.

The theory of chord inversion represents a concept of

tonal relations that has dominated musical theory and practice since the time of Rameau. Based on the principle of the identity of the octave, this important concept has acoustical support — in the case of the major triad — in the fact that the configurations of tones in the first and second inversions of triads are actually present in the overtone structure, and that the different tones point to a common generator, which is not sounded. Fletcher's experiments with filtering out lower partials without changing the pitch of given tones provide further evidence supporting the theory of the inversion, especially of the major triad. Additional grounds for the theory of chord inversion are found in the functional similarity of inversions to the fundamental triads; that is, the first inversion of the tonic triad still is psychologically felt to be tonic in character, in most, if not all, instances.

Working against the concept of inversion is the acoustical fact that, for example, the third of a chord placed low in the bass produces overtones sufficiently prominent to dissonate noticeably with the chord fifth and the inverted root. This fact undoubtedly helps to cause the cadential six-four chord to be felt functionally as a dominant chord.

The inversion of the minor chord can be justified, partly by analogy, and partly on the basis of functional relationship. Here again the acoustic role of the actual bass is important, even causing certain chords to be reclassified. For example, the first inversion of the supertonic triad may be classed, not as a supertonic chord at all, but as a subdominant chord with substituted sixth. Space will not permit a further elaboration of this idea, but the student should investigate the problem of the added-sixth chord in this light.

The foregoing are a few of the countless problems that the theory of harmony has to solve with the various methods of science. Simple solutions are not always possible, but neither are they for countless other human problems. Certainly, in spite of the scoffers, without the work of the theorists of all ages, the masterpieces of musical composition could never have been produced. Every composer has his conception of the theory of harmony, and creates in terms of that conception, whether or not it is scientifically defensible. Although bad theory can produce good results, sound theory affords the most reliable basis for sound practice.

COUNTERPOINT

Counterpoint has been defined as *the combination of melodies*, and, in general, the distinction between counterpoint and harmony is sufficiently obvious to warrant the continued differentiation of these terms, and, especially, to emphasize two fundamentally different ways of looking at the texture of musical compositions. As we examine the meanings of the two terms closely, we find enough overlapping to conclude that, at least in certain cases, they are simply two ways of looking at the same thing. Under these circumstances, many of the findings of the systematic and historical sciences referred to — in connection with the theory of harmony, in general, and with the theory of scales, melody, rhythm, and so on, in particular — find significant application in the theory of counterpoint. Hence, it is not necessary to review those findings; but we should not overlook the fact, for example, that every contrapuntal problem has its harmonic implication in some sense or other. Counterpoint does not exist *in vacuo*, but is always just one aspect of, or one of the many possible ways of looking at, the tonal-rhythmic complex.

In a very narrow sense, the term *counterpoint* designates the melodic part which is added to a given melody or *cantus firmus*. It is also applied to the simultaneous combination of two or more independent melodic voice parts. In this sense, it is practically synonymous with the term *polyphony*, which implies "many voices," each having its own individual rhythmic or melodic contour, while the whole produces an acceptable harmonic effect. Opposed to this term are the words *homophony* and *monody*, which refer to music in which one part has the principal melodic interest, for which the other parts merely supply harmonic background.

If we scrutinize the apparent melodic freedom of the individual parts in a contrapuntal composition, we find that the freedom is, in a sense, illusory; for the "freedom" of each part is conditioned by its relation to the other parts individually and collectively. Thus, harmonic factors are present in every contrapuntal or polyphonic composition.

In comparing the polyphonic music of the sixteenth century with the homophonic music of the seventeenth, with respect to melodic freedom, we are led to the somewhat surprising conclusion that the melodies of the latter have greater freedom than those of the former.[13] Apparently, what happens in homophonic music is that the melodic freedom of the accompanying voices is sacrificed to enhance the melodic value of the principal voice. Nevertheless, the individual voices in the accompaniment may and often do have melodic significance.

Without doubt, the problems of counterpoint have been most successfully investigated through the study of the music of particular style-periods, such as those represented by Palestrina and Bach.

Knud Jeppesen's study of the polyphonic vocal style of the sixteenth century is a good example of the application of systematic and historical methods to the fundamental problems of the theory of counterpoint.[14] Formulating his fun-

---

[13] For an interesting and suggestive discussion of this matter, see John Redfield, *Music: A Science and an Art*, pages 93 f. New York: Alfred A. Knopf, Inc., 1928; see also Ernst Kurth, *Grundlagen des linearen Kontrapunkts*, Second Edition, pages 123 *et passim*.
[14] *The Style of Palestrina and the Dissonance;* and *Counterpoint: The Polyphonic Vocal Style of the Sixteenth Century.*

damental problem in terms of the treatment of the dissonance, Jeppesen considers not only the most important psycho-physiological and aesthetic factors, but also the significant historical implications of the situation, and works out such a comprehensive exposition of the material as to throw the basic problems of contrapuntal theory into sharp relief and to indicate how the composers of the period solved them. *The Style of Palestrina and the Dissonance* presents the original research, while *Counterpoint* is an attempt to translate the findings into a textbook.

Comparison of these works of Jeppesen with the conventional books dealing with *strict counterpoint,* so-called, will reveal many striking differences in viewpoint and methods. The latter works are inadequate, chiefly because they attempt what is probably an impossible task: to state in terms of the particular a theory of counterpoint-in-general, without a standard of reference sufficiently well-crystallized for such treatment.

In other words, counterpoint in the various historical style-periods and style-species has been conceived in terms of quite different fundamental premises, different points of view, so that principles which are significant and meaningful when applied to one style are simply not applicable to another. For example, whereas the polyphonic vocal composition of the sixteenth century is based upon a modal system in which the conception of tonality is relatively undeveloped, the contrapuntal music of the early eighteenth century is based upon a well-defined conception of tonality expressed in terms of the major and minor modes. In these terms alone, not considering numerous other shifts of viewpoint, it is obvious that the detailed statement of contrapuntal theory must vary from one style to the other.[15]

---

[15] A more comprehensive discussion of these matters is in Jeppesen's *The Style of Palestrina and the Dissonance*, pages 3 ff. *et passim,* and in his

The works of Bach afford an excellent starting point for the investigation of counterpoint based upon the major and minor scalic system. Bach's most contrapuntal writings are so interpenetrated with the sense of tonality and all that it implies, especially for harmony, that they afford an almost entirely different approach to the theory of counterpoint. Here the harmonic, modulatory basis is presupposed; the rhythmical background is fundamentally different from that of Palestrina; the conception of melody, the treatment of the dissonance is much freer; the formal organization of the works is more organic harmonically; and the use of instruments as a means of performance is a factor determining style almost, if not entirely, missing in Palestrina.

Although much work has been done in this field, much more needs to be done before we can base a definitive statement of the theory of counterpoint upon the works of Bach. A most significant approach to the study of the style of Bach would be the detailed investigation of his treatment of the dissonance. Koechlin's study of passing notes [16] affords a most suggestive and promising beginning in this direction.

The theories of more modern contrapuntal practice have spread out in many directions. The general trend of modern development seems toward greater elaboration of the melodic, rhythmic, and tonal resources toward the limits of comprehensibility, particularly in the treatment of the dissonance. In Bach's counterpoint, the limit was set by the psychological capacity to grasp the underlying harmonic implications in terms of prevailing concepts of tonality, in spite of rhythmical, melodic, and dissonant complexities. One example that may be cited in passing to show changing concepts of con-

Counterpoint, pages x ff. et passim, as well as in Kurth's Grundlagen des linearen Kontrapunkts, pages 123, 143, et passim. Cf. also Glen Haydon, "Music Research and Modal Counterpoint," Yearbook of the Music Educators National Conference, Twenty-Seventh Year (1934), pages 217–222.

[16] Charles Koechlin, Étude sur les notes de passage.

trapuntal theory is the so-called *dissonant counterpoint*. The idea of this theory is to reverse the conventional rules of counterpoint so that dissonances may occur freely, and to introduce consonances carefully, as nonessential or passing material. Major sevenths and minor seconds and ninths would be the principal intervals; minor sevenths and major seconds and ninths would come next, and so on. Twenty-five years ago such a theory would have sounded very strange indeed, but today it approximates a statement of the theory of some dissonant composers.[17]

INSTRUMENTATION AND ORCHESTRATION

The terms *instrumentation* and *orchestration* are used, in general, to designate that phase of technical work in music that deals with scoring music for instrumental ensembles, particularly for band and orchestra. In a somewhat narrower sense, *instrumentation* is sometimes applied to the study and investigation of such matters as range and transposition of the various instruments, their tone quality, relative facility of execution, and adaptability; *orchestration*, to the process of combining different instruments in a musical score.

The theory of instrumentation and orchestration leans heavily upon the systematic auxiliary sciences — especially upon the science of acoustics, which contributes much important information. Acoustics provides information about such items as the construction of instruments, their mechanical and acoustical properties, problems of intonation, and dynamic resources. Such knowledge is of obvious importance in the various details of orchestration, such as tonal balance, tone color, potential mechanical limits in speed of execution, and control of pitch, loudness, and quality.

Psychophysiology yields data that have significant bearings on the theory of orchestration. Among the psychological

---

[17] See Henry Cowell, *New Musical Resources*, pages 35 ff.

topics investigated are tone production and control; and the perception of tonal values, such as pitch, loudness, and quality. And, of course, the science of aesthetics plays an important role in the formulation of basic principles of orchestration; it regards orchestration as important in the design of a composition.

The history of orchestration, the analysis of musical scores, experimental investigations, and many related activities — all carried on in the light of their systematic-historical and style-formative implications — afford the basis for a comprehensive theory of instrumentation and orchestration. Up to the time of Rimsky-Korsakov, the theory of orchestration rested upon an almost purely empirical basis. Rimsky-Korsakov made a definite attempt to apply the laws of acoustics to the problems of orchestration, but in spite of his efforts remarkably little application of these laws has been made.

Though acoustics (through the investigation of the overtone structure of tones) has added greatly to the understanding of the problems of orchestral color, and though improvements in the manufacture of instruments have enlarged the resources in innumerable ways, most investigations of the technique of orchestration have been made in terms of empirical, trial-and-error methods. That is to say, regardless of what the systematic sciences have contributed, the theory of orchestration has been, and probably will continue to be, studied mainly in analytical, historical, and style-critical studies.

Recent developments in radio and sound film are effecting changes in the field of orchestration. For example, the difficulties of assigning definite relative dynamic values to the different instruments have seemed almost insurmountable; but new scientific means of measuring loudness, masking effect, and the like simplify the problems. The idea that if a cornet is given an arbitrary rating of 60 units as compared with 10 for a flute, six flutes would effect a balance of tone,[18] is obviously erroneous in the light of more recent research in the field of the psychology of loudness. The implication that six flutes sound six times as loud is entirely wrong. Let us hope that someone, in the near future, will have the interest, imagination, and ability to investigate such problems anew, and to place the theory of orchestration on a firmer foundation.

FORM

Research in musical *form* has been devoted mainly to investigation of the works of the masters. Treatises on form ordinarily follow a semi-historical, semi-systematic procedure, analyzing and describing the various formal types of musical composition and attempting to set up what might be called theories of musical form. The general theory of musical form has to do with formulation of the principles governing the structure of music.

All the studies in the fields of music theory already discussed contribute to the general theory of form. The structural unit around which the elementary ideas of form are built up is the motive. The characteristics of a motive may be studied in terms of *melody*, or, more particularly, of the absolute and relative pitch of tones involved; in terms of *rhythm*, or, more particularly, of the absolute or relative duration of the tones; in terms of *dynamics*, or, more particularly, of the absolute and relative loudness of the tones; and in terms of *tonal qualities*. In the investigation of musical form, the task of the investigator is to make detailed application of the findings of the systematic sciences to hypothetical or historical musical style-species.

In a narrower sense, the theory of form concerns the theory

---

[18] See Arthur A. Clappé, *The Principles of Wind-Band Transcription*, page 23.

of the various specific types of musical form as crystallized in the thinking and practice of musicians through the ages. Here the work of the theorist is to so analyze and describe the significant details of the structural design of specific compositions as to formulate a conception of the abstract types constituting the principal formal categories. The effective execution of the task depends largely upon the theorist's ability to grasp the implications of aesthetic laws of designs as they apply in detail to the structure of music.

Study, investigation, and thought concerning the problems of musical form are intimately related to the highest activities of the composer, performer, and critic. Aesthetics itself, as Prall says,[19] is theory, and the application of aesthetics to the theory of form may lead to further theory; but such theory, intelligently applied, yields discriminating musical experience of the highest type. That lack of space and other considerations have necessitated a somewhat cursory treatment of the subject in the present work — a treatment wholly incommensurable with its importance — should not cause anyone to underestimate the value and significance of musical *form*. All studies in the field of music theory are or may be pointed in the direction of the theory of musical form, which thus becomes the crowning achievement, or climax, of theoretical endeavor in music.

BIBLIOGRAPHY

Much of the basic material relating to the theory of music theory is in the works on acoustics, psychophysiology, and aesthetics listed in the bibliographies to the preceding chapters. Many of the following references are primarily textbooks, but the introductions frequently contain observations on the theory of music theory; further theoretical implications are implicit in the organization of the material and especially in the definitions of terms. The works of Riemann, Shirlaw, and Yasser are for the

---

[19] David Prall, *Aesthetic Analysis*, page 204.

most part not textbooks but rather discussions of theoretical problems from both historical and theoretical viewpoints.

Many of these works, such as those of Riemann, Watt, and Arnold, contain extensive bibliographical material. Riemann's *Grundriss der Musikwissenschaft* contains an extensive list of German theoretical works; his *Geschichte der Musiktheorie* contains a list of the more important historical works pertaining to music theory. Additional references are given in the bibliographies of Aber, Scholes, *The International Cyclopedia of Music and Musicians*, and the National Association of Schools of Music.

The student should also consult the articles on "melody," "tonality," "harmony," "counterpoint," and the like in *The Encyclopaedia Britannica* (especially the Eleventh Edition) and in the principal musical lexicons and dictionaries. The various musicological journals, books of proceedings, and *Festschrifts* likewise contain innumerable articles pertinent to the theory of music theory.

Harmony

Arnold, F. T., *The Art of Accompaniment from a Thorough-Bass*. London: Oxford University Press, 1931.

Casella, Alfredo, *The Evolution of Music Throughout the History of the Perfect Cadence*. London: J. & W. Chester, Ltd., 1924.

Chevaillier, Lucien, "Les Théories harmoniques," *Encyclopédie de la musique et dictionnaire du conservatoire*, Part II, Vol. I, pages 519–590.

Dickinson, George S., *The Growth of Expression in Harmony* (Fundamentals of Musical Art, Vol. IV). New York: The Caxton Institute, Incorporated, 1927.

Foote, Arthur, *Modulation and Related Harmonic Questions*. Boston: The Arthur P. Schmidt Company, 1919.

Hauptmann, Moritz, *The Nature of Harmony and Metre*. (Tr. & ed. by W. E. Heathcote.) Second Edition. London: Swan Sonnenschein & Co., 1893.

Hindemith, Paul, *Unterweisung im Tonsatz*. Mainz: B. Schott's Söhne, 1937.

Hull, A. Eaglefield, *Modern Harmony*. London: Augener, Ltd., 1915.

Kinkeldey, Otto, "The Harmonic Sense: Its Evolution and Its Destiny," *Volume of Proceedings of the Music Teachers National Association*, Eighteenth Series (1923), pages 9-26.

Kitson, C. H., *The Evolution of Harmony*. Second Edition. Oxford: The Clarendon Press, 1924. (First Edition, 1914.)

Koechlin, Charles, *Étude sur le choral d'école d'après J. S. Bach*. Paris: Heugel et Cie., 1929.

———, *Étude sur les notes de passage*. Paris: Le Monde Musicale, 1922.

———, "Évolution de l'harmonie," *Encyclopédie de la musique et dictionnaire du conservatoire*, Part II, Vol. I, pages 591-760.

Kolinski, M., *Konsonanz als Grundlage einer neuen Akkordlehre*. Brünn: Rudolf M. Rohrer, 1936.

Kurth, Ernst, *Romantische Harmonik und ihre Krise in Wagners "Tristan."* Third Edition. Berlin: Max Hesse, 1923.

Lach, Robert, *Studien zur Entwickelungsgeschichte der ornamentalen Melopöie: Beiträge zur Geschichte der Melodie*. Leipzig: C. F. Kahnt Nachfolger, 1913.

Lenormand, René, *A Study of Modern Harmony*. (Tr. by H. Antcliffe.) Boston: The Boston Music Co., 1915.

Louis, Rudolph, and Ludwig Thuille, *Harmonielehre*. Eighth Edition. Stuttgart: Carl Grüninger Nachf. Ernst Klett, 1913. (First Edition, 1907.)

MacPherson, Charles, *A Short History of Harmony*. London: Kegan Paul, Trench, Trubner & Co., 1917.

Miller, Horace A., *New Harmonic Devices*. Philadelphia: Oliver Ditson Company, Inc., 1930.

Montnacher, J., *Problem des Accordes der neapolitanischen Sexte mit propagandistischem Nachwort*. Leipzig: Fritz Schuberth, Jr., n.d.

Oettingen, Arthur von, *Das duale Harmoniesystem*. Leipzig: Siegel, 1913.

———, *Harmoniesystem in dualer Entwickelung*. Dorpat: W. Gläser, 1866.

Piston, Walter, *Harmony*. New York: W. W. Norton & Company, Inc., 1941.

———, *Principles of Harmonic Analysis*. Boston: E. C. Schirmer Music Co., 1933.

Riemann, Hugo, *Geschichte der Musiktheorie im IX.–XIX. Jahrhundert*. Second Edition. Leipzig: Max Hesse, 1920. (First Edition, 1898.)

Schenker, Heinrich, *Neue musikalische Theorien und Phantasien*. Part I: *Harmonielehre*. Vienna: Universal-Edition, A. G., 1906.

Schoenberg, Arnold, *Harmonielehre*. Third Edition. Vienna: Universal-Edition, A. G., 1922.

Shirlaw, Matthew, *The Theory of Harmony*. London: Novello & Company, Ltd., 1917.

Yasser, Joseph, *Mediaeval Quartel Harmony*. New York: American Library of Musicology, 1938.

————, "A Revised Conception of Tonality," *Volume of Proceedings of the Music Teachers National Association*, Thirtieth Series (1935), pages 100–121.

————, *A Theory of Evolving Tonality*. New York: American Library of Musicology, 1932.

Ziehn, Bernhard, *Harmonie- und Modulationslehre*. Berlin: R. Sulzer, 1887.

————, *Manual of Harmony*. Milwaukee: Wm. A. Kaun Music Co., 1907.

Zulauf, Max, *Die Harmonik J. S. Bachs*. Bern: Stämpfli & Cie., 1927.

Counterpoint and Fugue

Bellermann, Heinrich, *Der Contrapunkt*. Berlin: Julius Springer, 1887.

Cools, Eugène, "Le Contrepoint," *Encyclopédie de la musique et dictionnaire du conservatoire*, Part II, Vol. V, pages 2719–2750.

Gedalge, André, *Traité de la fugue*. Paris: Enoch & Cie., 1901.

Haydon, Glen, *The Evolution of the Six-Four Chord: A Chapter in the History of Dissonance Treatment*. Berkeley: University of California Press, 1933.

————, "Music Research and Modal Counterpoint," *Yearbook of the Music Educators National Conference*, Twenty-Seventh Year (1934), pages 217–222.

Hohn, Wilhelm, *Der Kontrapunkt Palestrinas und seiner Zeitgenossen*. Regensburg: F. Pustet, 1918.

Jeppesen, Knud, *Counterpoint: The Polyphonic Vocal Style of the Sixteenth Century*. (English translation by Glen Haydon.) New York: Prentice-Hall, Inc., 1939.

————, *The Style of Palestrina and the Dissonance*. (English translation by Margaret W. Hamerik.) London: Oxford University Press, 1927.

Krenek, Ernst, *Studies in Counterpoint Based on the Twelve-Tone Technique*. New York: G. Schirmer, Inc., 1940.

Kurth, Ernst, *Grundlagen des linearen Kontrapunkts*. Second Edition. Berlin: Max Hesse, 1922.

Merritt, Arthur Tillman, *Sixteenth-Century Polyphony*. Cambridge: Harvard University Press, 1939.

Morris, R. O., *Contrapuntal Technique in the Sixteenth Century*. Oxford: The Clarendon Press, 1922.

Müller-Blattau, Joseph M., *Grundzüge einer Geschichte der Fuge*. Second Revised Editon. Kassel: Bärenreiter, 1931.

Porter, Quincy, *A Study of Sixteenth Century Counterpoint*. Mimeographed. Boston: New England Conservatory of Music, 1939.

Schenker, Heinrich, *Neue musikalische Theorien und Phantasien*. Part II: *Kontrapunkt*. 2 vols. Vienna: Universal-Edition, A. G., 1910, 1922.

Schwebsch, Erich, *Joh. Seb. Bach und die Kunst der Fuge*. Stuttgart: Orient-Occident-Verlag, 1931.

INSTRUMENTATION AND ORCHESTRATION

Carse, Adam, *The History of Orchestration*. New York: E. P. Dutton, 1925.

Clappé, Arthur A., *The Principles of Wind-Band Transcription*. New York: Carl Fischer, Inc., 1921.

Coerne, Louis Adolphe, *The Evolution of Modern Orchestration*. New York: The Macmillan Company, 1908.

Forsyth, Cecil, *Orchestration*. London: Macmillan & Co., Ltd., 1914.

Pierné, Gabriel, and Henry Woollett, "Histoire de l'orchestration," *Encyclopédie de la musique et dictionnaire du conservatoire*, Part II, Vol. IV, pages 2215–2286, 2445–2718.

Rimsky-Korsakow, Nicolas, *Principles of Orchestration*. English translation by Edward Agate. New York: E. F. Kalmus Orchestra Scores, Inc., 1922. (Original Edition, 1891.)

Soyer, A., "De l'Orchestration militaire et de son histoire," *Encyclopédie de la musique et dictionnaire du conservatoire*, Part II, Vol. IV, pages 2135–2214.

Wellesz, Egon, *Die neue Instrumentation*. 2 vols. Berlin: Max Hesse, 1928–29.

FORM AND COMPOSITION

Cowell, Henry, *New Musical Resources*. New York: Alfred A. Knopf, Inc., 1930.

Ferand, Ernst, *Die Improvisation in der Musik: Eine entwicklungsgeschichtliche und psychologische Untersuchung*. Zürich: Rhein-Verlag, 1938.

Hadow, W. H., *Sonata Form*. London: Novello & Company, Ltd., 1896.

Harburger, Walter, *Grundriss des musikalischen Formvermögens.*
Munich: Ernst Reinhardt, 1912.

Indy, Vincent d', and Auguste Sérieyx, *Cours de composition
musicale.* Two Volumes in Three Parts. Paris: A. Durand
et Fils, 1897–1933.

Lach, Robert, *Das Konstruktionsprinzip der Wiederholung in
Musik, Sprache und Literatur.* Akademie der Wissenschaften in Wien, philosophisch-historische Klasse, Sitzungs-
berichte, 201. Band, 2. Abhandlung. Vienna: Hölder-
Pichler-Tempsky, A. G., 1925.

Leichtentritt, Hugo, *Musikalische Formenlehre.* Third Edition,
Revised and Enlarged. Suppl. Vol. to the Second Edition
(1920). Leipzig: Breitkopf & Härtel, 1927. (First Edition,
1907.)

Prout, Ebenezer, *Musical Form.* London: Augener & Co., 1893.

Riemann, Hugo, *Grosse Kompositionslehre.* 3 vols. Berlin: W.
Spemann, 1902, 1903, 1913.

Stöhr, Richard, *Formenlehre der Musik.* Revised Edition by
Hans Gál and Alfred Orel. Leipzig: Fr. Kistner & C. F. W.
Siegel, 1933.

Straeten, E. van der, *A Handbook of Musical Form.* London:
Wm. Reeves, Bookseller, Ltd., n.d.

Tobel, Rudolf von, *Die Formenwelt der klassischen Instrumental-
musik.* Bern: Paul Haupt, 1935.

Chapter VI

MUSICAL PEDAGOGY

MUSICAL KNOWLEDGE, SKILL, AND INSIGHT ARE NOT IN-
herited characteristics, but are acquired. *Musical
pedagogy*, or music education, concerns the processes through
which musical knowledge, skill, and insight are acquired.
Research in musical pedagogy applies to the problems of
music education methods of thinking that have revealed what
is known about music through acoustics, psychophysiology,
aesthetics, and other related fields of study.

Contributions of Psychology to Music Education

The auxiliary science that contributes most directly to
musical pedagogy is psychology. What general psychology
teaches about the educative process is applied to the specific
problems of music education. Performance on an instrument
is studied as *sensorimotor learning*. The psychological laws
of learning can be applied to piano playing as well as to hand-
writing. For a rough definition in psychological terms, the
learning process is the process of acquiring the ability to make
the correct response to a given stimulus. Five steps may be
distinguished in the process: mental set or adjustment; selection of the correct response; elimination of the unsuccessful
act; fixation of learned responses; and integration of the separate acts into a unified whole.[1]

---

[1] A. M. Jordan, *Educational Psychology*, pages 80 ff.

The right *mental set* means a desire to improve. To stimulate this desire the teacher should see that the pupil is provided with adequate immediate goals as well as ultimate goals. *Selecting the correct response* and *eliminating the unsuccessful act* constitute the crux of the learning process. The pupil comes to his task with a large number of movements at his disposal. The average teacher usually attacks the problem of selecting right movements in a more or less haphazard, trial-and-error manner; but only through analysis and understanding of good and bad movements can the teacher help him select appropriate movements and eliminate inappropriate ones.

The next step is the *fixation of correct habits*. Though mere mechanical repetition does not help much, repetitions carefully spaced and thoughtfully carried out produce great improvement in fixation. Other factors in fixation of habits are vividness and configuration. Other things being equal, if an experience is made more vivid, fixation will come sooner and be more lasting. Likewise, if the pupil grasps something of the significance of a note as an element in a melodic pattern or as a constituent of a chord, fixation will result more quickly. These facts suggest the importance of thoughtful study and analysis away from the instrument.

The performance of a very simple piece of music involves a number of separate acts. The stimulus is each note on the printed page, and the response in piano playing is the striking of the right key. Learning, however, is not merely the simple formation of connections between stimuli and responses, but is also the process of organizing the connections themselves into an integrated habit. The performance of a piece of music requires a concentration of interdependent habits. This *integration of the separate steps into an entity* is the last of the five in the process of learning.

Psychology has also made important contributions in the

field of tests and measurements to educational theory and practice in music. General intelligence tests, aptitude tests, and achievement or accomplishment tests, if intelligently applied and interpreted, constitute valuable aids to music education. They can adequately measure factual knowledge, and partially measure aptitude and skill; though elusive factors like the will to do, mental imagery, and various emotional responses are not fully susceptible to accurate measurement.[2] These tests and measurements are probably most useful when they define the progress of pupils so exactly that the pupils can perceive clearly their immediate goals.

The foregoing discussion suggests two of the many ways in which psychology may assist music education. Problems of attention, interest, discipline, arrangement of material in a particular subject, individual differences — these are a few of the many problems which psychology helps to solve. Indeed, many other sciences — biology, physiology, sociology, history, aesthetics, and philosophy — make significant contributions to education; but detailed discussion of these contributions must be left to the more technical works on the subject.[3]

GENERAL THEORY OF TEACHING

Though it is difficult to define concisely the principles of teaching, we can easily state some major considerations in any attempted general theory of teaching. First, the teacher must have some conception of the general function of education and of the basic aims and objectives of teaching. It is the task of the philosophy of education to discover and give expression to these functions, aims, and objectives. Out of

---

[2] For a survey of the field, see Jacob Kwalwasser, *Tests and Measurements in Music* and articles in more recent technical journals.

[3] See, for example, Herman H. Horne, *The Philosophy of Education,* and in connection with music education, see especially Will Earhart, *The Meaning and Teaching of Music.*

many diverse and often conflicting conceptions of education, two fairly well-defined views emerge. One view is that the function of education is to bring the pupil up to the standards of the society in which he lives. The educational program that serves this purpose is designed chiefly in terms of what it is essential for the child to know. A second view is that the function of education is to develop the child in aptitudes most satisfying to him, but at the same time valuable to society. This conception of education motivates the so-called "child-centered" school. The science and philosophy of education, to reconcile these two views, must set up an educational philosophy combining the positive features in each view and eliminating the negative.

Second, in the development of the general principles of teaching, the teacher must select and organize the subject matter. It is the function of the musicologist as a scholar to supply the best available data with respect to content; and, as a student of education — after study of both the nature and needs of the child and the psychological theory of the learning process — to organize the material into effective study units and projects.

Third, the teacher must motivate or stimulate learning through the selection of learning activities in harmony with the pupils' needs, interests, and capacities. Probably the most significant progress in this stimulation has been made on the elementary school level.[4] With allowance for differences in the various cases, similar applications need to be worked out through the whole program of music education.

Fourth, the teacher must select teaching procedures in terms of the predominating type of learning. For directing the acquisition of skills and habits, basic factors in teaching

---

[4] See, for example, Lillian M. Fox and L. Thomas Hopkins, *Creative School Music*.

procedure are motor activity, associative learning, and practice or drill. To direct the acquisition of general patterns of conduct, the teacher must encourage economical study habits adapted to various types of learning, acceptable patterns of social-moral conduct, and taste and appreciation in art. To direct the acquisition and utilization of knowledge, he must include the use of the laboratory, of textbooks and collateral material, of developmental methods involving reflective thinking and problem-solving, of reviews to attain larger units of thought, and related methods to develop skill in the expression and application of knowledge.

Fifth, the teacher must make effective use of the class period. Important factors are the assignment, recitation procedures (lectures, discussions, questions, reports, and so forth), and adjustments for individual differences.

Sixth, he must measure the results of teaching, through written examinations, true-false tests, multiple-response tests, and standardized tests, together with various performance tests in applied music.

Finally, he must plan instruction. Planning ordinarily means working out effective lesson plans.[5]

Curriculum Studies

The study of the curriculum in music presents a twofold problem: first, the place of music in the curriculum as a whole, and second, the special curriculum in music. One makes an unrewarded search in current books on the philosophy of education for an adequate statement of the significance of the arts in education. The place assigned to music and arts in the curriculum depends upon the prevailing philosophy of

---

[5] The foregoing discussion of the general theory of teaching is based chiefly on Samuel A. Kruse, *A Critical Analysis of Teaching as a Basic Course in Teacher-Training Curricula.* Of special significance is his analysis of the meaning of the terms *principle, theory, doctrine, law,* and *rule,* pages 134 ff.

education. Dewey, speaking of literature and the fine arts in the course of study, stresses appreciation: [6]

> This enhancement of the qualities which make any ordinary experience appealing, appropriable — capable of full assimilation — and enjoyable, constitutes the prime function of literature, music, drawing, painting, etc., in education. . . . They are not luxuries of education, but emphatic expressions of that which makes any education worth while.

Perhaps the most comprehensive statement of the significance of music in the curriculum that has appeared is in James L. Mursell's *Human Values in Music Education.* Mursell interprets the values of music in terms of a social philosophy of education. He treats of the value of music as an individual experience, a social opportunity, an agency for growth, and a moral force. In attempting to determine the place of music in the general curriculum, Mursell places first the fundamental masteries (oral and written speech, reading, and elementary arithmetic); second, the social sciences; and next, on the arguments presented, music.

Similar analyses need to be made concerning the place of music in the curriculum of secondary schools, colleges, and universities, so that a clearer idea of the place of music in the curriculum may be derived. The musicologist, vitally interested in music education, would do well to devote some attention to these problems. Although educational theorists have nearly all neglected the arts in general and music in particular, the subjects have always been implied in the philosophy and practice of education. Music has been an important educational subject since the time of the Greeks. Recognition of the place of music in the curriculum is found in the courses of study of schools and universities throughout the history of Western Europe, and as late as 1927 we find evidence of the growing consciousness of the value of music

---

[6] John Dewey, *Democracy and Education,* pages 278 f.

in a resolution passed by the superintendents of schools of the United States.[7]

We are rightly coming to regard music, art, and similar subjects as fundamental in the education of American children. We recommend that they be given everywhere equal consideration and support with other basic subjects.

The problems confronting the maker of the specific curricula in music are numerous and complex. Determinative factors include the amount of time allotted to music; the equipment and facilities available; the age, interest, and capacity of the pupils individually and collectively; the amount of time to be spent on creative work, on performance, and on appreciation; the qualifications of the teacher; and financial resources. These and numerous other factors make the problem of curriculum building one of the most difficult of all. And yet, the importance of an effective curriculum from the kindergarten through the university can scarcely be overemphasized. Tradition, experience, scientific methods, artistic insight, philosophical perspective, and pedagogical studies of all kinds afford the basis for such solutions as we have achieved. In spite of innumerable conflicts of opinion over both theory and practice, signs of growing agreement among the specialists with regard to the fundamentals of curricular procedure show that definite progress is being made.

The curriculum problem is clarified when we consider that it raises the question, not so much, *What has been?* or *What is?*, or even *What will be?*, but rather, *What should be?* Because the answer to this question essentially involves a judgment, one is not to conclude that such a judgment will be mere opinion; it should be, instead, a considered decision based upon objective data and the results of scientific investigation.

[7] Department of Superintendence, Official Report, page 318. National Education Association, Washington, D. C., 1927. Quoted by John K. Norton and Margaret A. Norton in *Foundations of Curriculum Building*, pages 406 f.

The determination of the ultimate objectives of a curriculum is based upon philosophical investigation and requires the use of philosophical, among other, methods.[8]

INDIVIDUAL INSTRUCTION

Learning, says current educational theory, comes primarily through experience. Experience, involving an organism and its environment, is composed of the interplay of these two elements. The organism does something to its environment, and the environment, in turn, does something to the organism. It is through the individual's perception of the relation between the action and reaction that the value of experience as a learning process arises. The discernment of the relation is *thought*, and thought is essential to learning. By a trial-and-error method we may stumble upon just the right action to produce the desired effect. If we remember only this connection and apply it mechanically, the thinking is not on a very high level. But, if we can discover the specific relation between the action and the result, the thinking becomes significant: it leads to purposive behavior.

In an attempt to make the meaning of the discussion more explicit, let us, for example, apply this analysis of experience and thinking to the problem of learning to play the piano. Striking a key, the pupil immediately hears a tone; striking another key, he hears a tone of different pitch; then, going back to the first key and striking it harder, he hears a louder tone. He learns, too, that when he holds the key down after the impact of the finger, the tone rings on for a time; but when he raises his finger, the tone ceases. Continuing his experiments, he soon discovers that, by striking the keys in proper succession, he can produce a tune. To the extent that he' discerns the relations between his actions and the

---

[8] For a discussion of these methods, see Walter S. Monroe and Max D. Engelhart, *The Scientific Study of Educational Problems*, pages 411–435.

results, he is thinking; the learning process is effectively going on.

Working with the pupil, the teacher will unobtrusively direct his activities to make the experience as meaningful as possible. As the muscle-joint movements become more and more automatic through repetition, the whole process gradually becomes mechanized. This fact suggests both a danger and an advantage. If the eye simply takes in the notes on the printed page of music, and the muscles respond automatically, the performance may become mechanical; that is, the action may be divorced from meaning. But if the performer, freed from conscious thought about the mechanics of playing, can devote his whole conscious attention to the musical significance of the sounds he is producing, mechanization of the motor responses is a distinct advantage. When the performer's mechanization is not adequate for the technical demands of the composition, he must again actively attend to the muscle-joint responses until, through thoughtful repetition, a high degree of mechanization is attained. Since, in mechanical repetition, very little if any learning takes place, "blind" or aimless practice is futile.

The note on the page of music is a symbol which, for the performer, signifies an action with its attendant effect. The note thus becomes identified with the reality it symbolizes, but notes in isolation are not musical ideas. A motive or a phrase can be considered the least common denominator of a musical idea. Therefore, the pupil, who seeks the musical meaning of a composition, should work with motives or phrases. Melodic, harmonic, and formal analysis done intelligently — not as an end in itself but as a means to more significant musical values — is an invaluable aid to learning. To make a fairly simple and reliable check on whether or not the performer is thinking musically, we find out whether he can play his composition just about as readily a tone higher

or lower.   Of course, if the transposition also is done mechanically, as it may be, the test shows little of value, except the
performer's facility in transposition.

The thinking that stops at the note on the printed page,
or at the impact of the finger upon the key, or at the isolated
tones is not on a very high level.   Effective thinking discerns something of the relation between the organism and
its environment; it makes possible action with meaning, or
with an end in view.   Learning to play the piano becomes
more than the acquisition of a skill or of knowledge as these
are directed toward the discernment of the meaningful relations of the music.   In these terms we can say, with Dewey,
that "thinking is method, the method of intelligent experience
in the course which it takes." [9]

Private instruction in music, like teaching in general, requires artistic methods somewhat like those of the creative
artist in any field.   Artistic methods at their best, however,
imply a background based upon broad scientific methods.
That is to say, the teacher should have an insight into the
fundamental principles of the learning process, a knowledge
of the nature of music, an understanding of the technique of
the particular instrument he is teaching, and a conception of
the materials and methods most effective in teaching.   Around
tone production, technique, and *interpretation* he must organize the details of materials and methods needed in the
teaching situation.   Tone production requires the establishment of a high ideal of quality; technique demands a knowledge of how to apply the principles involved in setting up
the proper sensorimotor responses through intelligently applied drill; interpretation implies the ability to focus the attention of the pupil on the musical ends to be attained.

Analysis and correction of faults; tests of the adaptability of

---

[9] John Dewey, *Democracy and Education: An Introduction to the Philosophy of Education,* page 180.

the pupil to the instrument, and of motor control; ear training; analysis of the music; special fingerings, and other matters pertaining to the technique of the instrument; the use of practice methods and lesson plans; the development of incentives — these are a few of the many special problems that confront the teacher. Though he need not be a researcher, he should have enough understanding of scientific methodology to enable him to adapt the fruits of research to his special needs.

Effective investigations in this field may include examination of special problems: physical, physiological, psychological, aesthetic, music-technical or music-theoretical, historical, philosophical, and specifically educational. This increased complexity confronts the teacher engaged in individual instruction; for music today leans heavily upon modern science, which often illuminates educational problems.[10] The teacher must at least be able to assimilate for his own uses the results of scientific investigation. He is in a strategic position to make original contributions of his own. The opportunities for the music teacher as researcher, countless and challenging, are at the same time opportunities for the improvement of individual instruction.

GROUP INSTRUCTION

What has been said about individual instruction in music applies, with a few changes, to group instruction. The teaching and learning are most effective when the whole process is conceived and executed with an awareness of what kind of experience is educational. Intelligent musicianship suggests the direction of the various activities. All work should

---

[10] For example, see Douglas Stanley, *The Science of Voice: An Application of the Laws of Acoustics, Anatomy, Physiology and Psychology to the Problems of Vocal Technic, Including Sections on Music and Interpretation, Acoustics, etc.* (3rd ed. revised and enlarged.) New York: Carl Fischer, Inc., 1939.

point the individual toward an enriched aesthetic experience, with drill and mechanics used as means, not as ends. The allowance to be made for the age level of the various groups especially affects matters like the means of motivating the work, the kind of direct sensory appeal that can be made, the nature of the rhythmic response, the associations and imagery, the approach to structure and form, the mental and emotional attitudes, and the selection and use of materials. The role of the teacher should be that of a guide in a cooperative venture.

Consequently, the progressive tendency in preschool and elementary grades is toward the child-centered school [11] in which the interests of the child give the direction, and creative self-expression is the watchword.[12] According to its philosophy of education, the creative music program is built around the activity of the organism in its environment — as in song interpretation, rhythmic activity, creative expression through song and dance, music reading, instrumental experience, appreciation, and the like. Stress always is laid upon the activities in which the child normally engages. The child thus helps in planning the musical project, and as a result acquires his knowledge and skills as aids in the completion of the project. The child, then, has a richer aesthetic experience because it grows directly out of his own activities.

Musical activities in the junior and senior high schools tend to become more and more specialized in separate organizations such as glee clubs, *a cappella* choirs, and various instrumental classes. Since instruction for all these groups on different levels aims at a richer musical experience, knowledge and technique should be attained, not as ends in themselves, but as means to a significant aesthetic life. The opportuni-

[11] For example, see Harold Rugg and Ann Shumaker, *The Child-Centered School.*

[12] For a more extended discussion of this topic, see Lillian M. Fox and L. Thomas Hopkins, *Creative School Music.*

ties for further research in every phase of the work should be persistently grasped.

Teaching methods in musical organizations on the college level — band, orchestra, and glee club — should be reviewed in the light of the best modern philosophies of education. Many valuable opportunities for excellent educational results are probably sacrificed to display and show. Though the fundamental fault is usually in the system, directors of the organizations are often partly to blame. The little time allotted for rehearsal periods usually makes it impossible for the director to pay much attention to improving the individual's technical handling of an instrument. Members of these groups either have prior ability to play or sing, or must acquire this ability, for the most part, outside the group; for attention in rehearsals is paid chiefly to matters of ensemble and interpretation. But the effective teacher will emphasize at all times the musical values of the experience, quite apart from display.

Study, experiment, and analysis of instructional problems on various levels constitute a real challenge to the musicologist, who can make the fruits of his researches available in clinics and various educational publications. Class instruction in history, theory, and applied music also affords great opportunities for the application of scientific methodology to innumerable problems. What and how to teach, how to interrelate the work of the various classes to produce unified educational results of a high order — these and many other questions call for the best answers musicology has to offer.

It is unfortunate that musicology has often been thought of as having little to do with these vital matters. However, with viewpoints rapidly changing in America, musicology is no longer to be regarded as a highly-specialized, musty study of abstruse matters only, but is to be considered an aggressive discipline concerned with all problems relating to musical theory and practice. The recent survey of college music by Randall Thompson,[13] a constructive step in the right direction, points the way, and should be followed up by special studies of the problems in this field.

MATERIALS AND METHODS OF TEACHING [14]

Since we have considered the problems of musical pedagogy in terms of individual and class instruction on various levels, let us now consider these problems in terms of content. There will, of course, be much overlapping, which the complexity of the situation makes inevitable. Yet each field has characteristic problems that may, to some extent, be isolated and investigated separately. The teacher should always remember that the instruction period, whether for an individual or a group, presents an opportunity for musical growth; he should not lose sight of true ends by burying himself in technical details. He must stress joy of participation and educational values in music, never mere exhibitionism, although the values of public performance should not be overlooked.

VOCAL MUSIC

Only a few of the many problems in vocal music can be mentioned. Modern research methods promise to render valuable aid in technique. The oscillograph, high-speed photography of the vocal cords, and other mechanical means of objective investigation, if intelligently used, may lay the foundations for improved methods of voice production. The singer himself need not do research in these matters; yet, from a study of the results of scientific investigations, he

---

[13] *College Music: An Investigation for the Association of American Colleges.*

[14] For further discussion and extensive bibliographies concerning this and many of the remaining topics in this chapter, see Peter W. Dykema and Karl W. Gehrkens, *The Teaching and Administration of High School Music.*

can avoid some of the confusing and erroneous theories expressed in literature on the subject.

Singing is an art, and there is no danger that the application of scientific methods to the study of voice production will ever reduce it to a science. Instead, objective methods, intelligently used, may further the art. Evidence shows that proper breathing, voice production, and tone quality — not ultimate ends in themselves — may be better attained by attention to artistic interpretation than by too much mechanical drill; mechanics as well as reading can probably best be taught in an incidental way in the course of studying worth-while music.

For vocal work, there is an abundance of excellent material — in folk music, in Gregorian chant, in polyphonic music of the sixteenth century, in art songs, and in all kinds of part songs — available for solo voice, unison chanting, or any of the many possible combinations of men's, women's, or children's voices. The study should always, if possible, be in terms of organic musical ideas, the smallest unit of which is the musical *phrase* or *motive*. The teacher must keep constantly in mind the development of a fine feeling for tone quality, pitch, rhythm, and phrase, so that the pupil, always having some more or less vivid concept of the goal toward which he is working, can enjoy the experience.

Much emphasis has been placed on a full musical experience, with technique belittled as an aim. One can easily undervalue technique. Good tone quality, which may be achieved by practice with the use of mechanical exercises, is desirable; but no one thinks it the ultimate aim of singing. The danger of placing too much stress on the so-called ultimate aims is that one is likely to forget that a single tone may yield aesthetic pleasure, and that technical excellence may also be the source of aesthetic enjoyment. Of course, if one practices only to produce a good tone, or to perfect a technique, he scarcely realizes the full values of a musical experience. Yet there is probably much more satisfaction in the aesthetic surface of the tones themselves than we commonly suspect. The aesthetic satisfaction that comes to either performer or listener from a mastery of technique is always legitimate and never valueless, though the highest values arise when appreciation of the formal and expressive values of the music is added to pleasure in tone and technique.

There are many obvious opportunities for musicology in the teaching of vocal music. In countless ways, from the study of the vibrato to the discovery and publication of unknown musical compositions hidden away in dusty archives, the labors of musical researchers and scholars have been and will continue to be of inestimable value. Knowledge of musical history — of the various style-periods and style-species — assists the teacher in the selection of suitable material; knowledge of acoustics helps him to make effective use of auditoriums and classrooms; knowledge of physiology makes possible the most effective use of the organism; knowledge of psychology aids in the details of method; knowledge of aesthetics is indispensable in interpretation; knowledge of philosophy may provide bases for perspective of the work as a whole. The teacher may bring all these disciplines to bear upon the problems of vocal music.

INSTRUMENTAL MUSIC

Much of what has been said concerning the materials and methods of teaching vocal music applies equally well to instrumental. Motivation of the class or rehearsal, differentiation between immediate and ultimate aims, selection of interesting and worth-while music, study in terms of phrase units rather than isolated notes, effective use of drill, and achievement of expressive tone quality, accurate rhythmical response, and artistic dynamic effects — these are but a few of the many aspects of instrumental teaching that present problems for research.

A number of factors in the selection of an instrument for study may be investigated scientifically. Acoustical and physical factors include the size and structure of the instrument, the means of producing the tone, the means of controlling the pitch, executive potentialities, dynamic resources, and tonal qualities. Anatomical and physiopsychological factors take into account the size and structure of the body (thickness of the lips, alignment of the teeth, size of the hand, shape of the fingers, and the like), characteristics of the sensory organs, and sensorimotor responses. Aesthetic factors are the tastes of individuals for the looks of instruments, tone quality, and technical possibilities.

Elementary Musicianship

Courses in *elementary musicianship* deal with sight singing, dictation, and the rudiments of musical notation. Much of what has been said concerning materials and methods of teaching applies in this field. In addition, many special problems warrant the careful attention of the musicologist. Some of these concern the scientific analysis of the behavior of the whole organism in the activity of sight singing: the use of movable or fixed do, or of numbers or other symbols to designate interval or tonal relation as aids to musical thinking; the role of bodily movements (motor activity) in dealing with the rhythmical problems; and the problems of singing intervals which are isolated or which depart from the tonality as compared to the singing of musically significant phrases.

Many of the above-mentioned problems are pertinent in dictation; and there are other problems such as the empathic character of tonal perception and the nature of chordal perception. For study of some of these problems, the use of statistical methods may be helpful, such as the keeping of records of typical errors as a guide to where to place the emphasis in teaching and practice.[15]

HARMONY

In *harmony*, as in the other classes of music instruction we have discussed, there are two distinct types of literature. The one, theoretical, is of the research type, and the other, practical, of the textbook type. These two types frequently overlap in the same work; for even the most practical textbook, whether the author is conscious of it or not, assumes or postulates a theoretical basis. The preparation of suitable textbooks in harmony, an important research task in itself, compels the writer to treat of the results of research and speculation concerning the fundamental principles of harmonic theory, the organization of the materials in the light of peculiar teaching needs and of sound pedagogical procedure, and the scientific checking of teaching methods.

Moreover, materials and methods well-adapted for conservatory teaching may be ill-adapted for use in the classroom of a liberal arts college; approaches in individual instruction or in the teaching of small groups differ materially from those in instruction of classes of twenty or more students. Introductory courses in harmony should probably carry the subtitle "A Study of Harmonic Practices from Bach to Wagner" in the effort to define standards of reference. More advanced courses could well treat of more recent harmonic procedures. Each of the topics studied in a course in harmony suggests a subject for research: cadences, modulation, ornamental notes, chord structure and classification, systems of figuring chords, and so on. Randall Thompson's survey

---

[15] For a more detailed discussion of the fundamental problems in this field, see Otto Ortmann, *Problems in the Elements of Ear-Dictation*, Research Studies in Music, Department of Research of the Conservatory of Music, edited by Otto Ortmann, Number 2. Baltimore: Peabody Conservatory of Music, Department of Research, October, 1934.

of college music raises many questions in the teaching of music theory which call for careful critical and scientific investigation.

Among the many teachers of harmony must be a number with sufficient training in scientific methodology to prosecute their investigations with significant results. This does not mean that every teacher should be a researcher. Teaching is an art, and many of our finest teachers doubtless know little of the methods of scientific investigation; but those who do have interest and ability in research can render invaluable assistance to the teaching of harmony.

COUNTERPOINT

The materials and methods of teaching *counterpoint* have been the subject of much thoughtful study and investigation, especially during recent years. The most valuable work in this field has been that of Knud Jeppesen. Following suggestive beginnings by Franz Nekes,[16] Wilhelm Hohn,[17] Peter Griesbacher,[18] and R. O. Morris,[19] Jeppesen's basic studies of the polyphonic vocal style of the sixteenth century [20] culminated in a textbook on counterpoint [21] which affords an excellent example of the application of musicological methods to the teaching of that subject.

Among problems needing further study are special questions like the use of the species and the C–clefs, and more

---

[16] In a criticism of Haller's *Kompositionslehre* appearing in the *Gregorius-blatt*, 1891–1893.

[17] *Der Kontrapunkt Palestrinas und seiner Zeitgenossen: Eine Kontra-punktlehre mit praktischen Aufgaben.*

[18] *Kirchenmusikalische Stilistik und Formenlehre.* 4 vols., 1912–1916. (Cited in Jeppesen, *The Style of Palestrina and the Dissonance*, page 6.)

[19] *Contrapuntal Technique in the Sixteenth Century.*

[20] *The Style of Palestrina and the Dissonance.*

[21] *Counterpoint: The Polyphonic Vocal Style of the Sixteenth Century.* See also Arthur T. Merritt, *Sixteenth-Century Polyphony: A Basis for the Study of Counterpoint;* Quincy Porter, *A Study of Sixteenth Century Counterpoint.*

general questions like the relation of the Palestrina counterpoint to that of Bach or Schoenberg. The theory back of
the use of the species in teaching counterpoint is that of pro-
ceeding in easy stages from the simple to the complex, from
the known to the unknown. The criticism of this theory
by modern psychology has been that learning does not proceed by a nicely graded sequence of habit building, and that
mental growth follows no strictly logical order.

Though the questions involved in whole learning as opposed to part learning have not been settled, several issues
are clear. Experiments do not show that whole learning is
under all circumstances superior to part learning. Rather,
where meanings involving broad relationships are involved,
a partial application of the principle of whole learning is
probably more advantageous, at least to show the general
drift and to discover the points at which difficulties may
arise.[22]

In the study of counterpoint, then, it would seem consistent
with psychological theory to proceed somewhat as follows:
Begin with the study of the music of the period in question;
perform it, listen to it, analyze it, and even try to write in the
style. As this is done, the details of the technique can be
presented advantageously through the medium of the species.
These should be used with discretion, certainly not as an
end, but only as a means. In studying the contrapuntal style
of the sixteenth century the writing of motets should be attempted at a very early stage in the work, even while the work
in the species is continued. The relation of the particular
technical detail to the larger aspects of the music should be
kept constantly in mind. The size of the unit of study necessarily depends upon such factors as the maturity and musical
background of the student, and the complexity of the material to be mastered. In short, the study of the whole is

[22] Read Woodworth, *Psychology*, pages 270 f.

most valuable for gaining understanding and meaning; the study by parts — using reasonable units, meaningful in themselves — for the development of techniques.

Since no method *as method* will ever insure best results, intelligent application becomes imperative for effective learning. The study of counterpoint in the sixteenth-century style need never become a fetish, for it is only one of several significant ways of approaching counterpoint. Other approaches — particularly that of tonal counterpoint as exemplified in the music of Bach and his successors, and even atonal counterpoint as exemplified in the works of Schoenberg and other modern composers — should not be neglected. Working out details of these other approaches remains an important concern of musicology.

INSTRUMENTATION AND ORCHESTRATION

Problems in the materials and methods of teaching *instrumentation* and *orchestration* are similar, in many ways, to those in the other branches of theoretical study. The project method, which has been successfully adapted to work in this field by Arthur Heacox,[23] seems in accord with the psychological theory of learning. Units of reasonable size are selected for detailed investigation and study; technical details are introduced as incidental to the central problem; and, to gain meaning and reality, activity is motivated by maintaining a close relation to actual music.

FORM, ANALYSIS, AND COMPOSITION

The teaching of *form, analysis,* and *composition* affords further opportunities for musicological research. Fundamental aims in such courses need to be critically examined.

---

[23] Arthur E. Heacox, *Project Lessons in Orchestration.* Boston: Oliver Ditson Company, Inc., 1928.

The great diversity of titles used is indicative of the confusion that exists.[24]

Here are some typical questions that arise in connection with these subjects. Is the aim to make composers of students? Can composition really be taught? What is the value of trying to compose if one has no intention of trying to become a composer? How can analysis be made most meaningful? How much time should be devoted to harmonic analysis? How much to each of the typical forms? How can eurythmics be used in teaching composition? These, and countless similar questions, afford suitable problems for musicological investigation.

Musical style-criticism, too, is a field of musicological research closely related to work in analysis and composition. Critical studies of the styles of various composers afford valuable material for the student of composition, whether he be composer, theorist, or performer.

Conducting

The materials and methods of teaching *conducting* grow out of the nature of the art. Most fundamental musical knowledge and understanding is acquired through other studies in practical and theoretical fields. Knowledge of the auxiliary sciences — acoustics, psychology, and aesthetics; of the various branches of theory — elementary musicianship, harmony, counterpoint, form and analysis, instrumentation and orchestration; and of musical history, together with skill in performance on one or more instruments, may be presupposed. The technique of the baton should, therefore, constitute the principal topic for study, though supplementary work in score reading, interpretation, and the art of conducting a rehearsal ordinarily call for special attention. The mechanical aspects of time beating, cueing, control of dy-

---

[24] See Randall Thompson, *College Music*, page 36 *et passim*.

namic effects, and the like may perfectly well be studied by objective means; the more elusive factors of imagination, personality, enthusiasm, and the like are less susceptible of scientific investigation. The general pedagogical principles involved in the teaching of conducting are similar to those in teaching most other musical subjects.

History

Learning in the field of *history* is more difficult than in other fields, for, though the same general principles are applicable, a sense of temporal perspective is always necessary, which ordinarily appears very slowly in the average child. Connections between present and past events must be made before effective learning can take place. A study of the lives of interesting men affords one of the most valuable means of establishing the concept of an orderly sequence of events. These facts suggest reasons why formal study of the history of music is not usually begun before the pupil reaches college, and why the lives of great musicians constitute a large part of what children learn about the history of music.

The content of the history of music is supplied by the musicologist. It is of two sorts — the body of factual information concerning music, and the musical monuments themselves. The materials contained in research publications of all kinds are sifted and evaluated for organization into textbooks suitable for instruction purposes. Illustrative materials — scores, records, pictures — are sought out and made available for use in teaching. These are but a few of the many ways in which musicology concerns teaching music history.

Musicology concerns also the methods of teaching. The ideal course would require a happy balance between the emphasis placed, first, upon factual matter and its interpretation, and second, upon the study of the music itself in its historical implications and significance. The factual aspects of musical history are illuminated through the study of the music of various style-species and style-periods; the understanding of music is enhanced by a knowledge of pertinent historical facts. Some of the problems of musicology in relation to the teaching of the history of music concern how much emphasis to place upon lecturing, discussions, reports, playing of illustrations in class or at special audition periods; whether to follow the chronological or reverse chronological method; and how to develop suitable tests, true-false quizzes, and comprehensive examinations.

The *Gestalt* theory of learning is especially applicable to the teaching of history. According to this theory, the whole cannot become meaningful by a mere consideration of the parts, because it determines the meaning of the parts; an element considered in isolation cannot have the significance it has when placed in its proper setting. The date 1770, though without meaning when isolated, becomes significant when properly oriented to the pattern of the history of music in the eighteenth century. As a student gains a perception of the relationships between facts through seeing them in a broad background, the study of history becomes an important factor in his intellectual development. The *Gestalt* theory of learning as applied to history implies the reasoned grasp of trends and movements instead of mere memorization of names and dates in relative isolation, and the perception of the relationships between sequential style-epochs, between simultaneous style-species, between music and other arts, and between music and social, economic, cultural, and religious settings.

First should come extensive rather than intensive work in reading about music, in study of scores, in performance of music, and in listening to music. Factual details should be

[209]

mastered incidentally but meaningfully. Courses in the general history of music should be organized around reasonably large topics, units, or problems. Oral and written reports, essays and free discussions, even debates on disputed points — in short, any approach that encourages an active rather than a passive attitude, that promotes research, self-expression, and appreciation — should be employed. Insofar as learning history invokes interpretation, judgment, or thinking, thought-provoking questions should aid the student to view history as a whole. Mere fact-finding questions should be used with discretion.

The history of music should be taught for comprehension, understanding, and the development of intelligent musicianship. The enthusiastic, resourceful teacher will find ways and means of adapting progressive procedure to the immediate situation. He will overlook nothing in his efforts to develop an adequate supply of books, records, scores, and other materials essential to the successful prosecution of his work.

APPRECIATION

Appreciation implies insight, a critical estimate, or evaluation, and in this sense it should be a factor in all music instruction. Unless connections are seen between any particular activity in music and related activities, there can hardly be effective learning. Proper emphasis on appreciation — which involves not only emotional response but also understanding or comprehension, with attendant enjoyment — prevents a wasteful emphasis on drill and habit formation.

The basic distinction between animal training and human learning is in *appreciation*. This concept of appreciation should enable the teacher to take advantage of the *Gestalt* theory of learning, the principle of learning by the whole, while not sacrificing the values of the analytical approach.

One of the important tasks of the musicologist is to collaborate with the educator in discovering the most effective materials and methods of teaching appreciation. Phonograph records, scores, books, maps, pictures, charts, and sound films constitute the most obvious materials. The work of a great many specialists is involved in the selection, preparation, and use of these materials. The countless problems and numerous debatable questions connected with the teaching of appreciation challenge the best efforts of musicology.[25]

TEACHER TRAINING

Training music teachers presents so many difficulties that, in spite of the importance of the subject, it can be treated only in part here. Though there are many differences of opinion as to procedure in the training of teachers, there can be little disagreement on one or two general principles: The prospective teacher should be thoroughly trained as a musician, and he should be taught the fundamentals of educational procedure. The chief point of dissension seems to be how much of the comparatively small amount of available time should be devoted to each of the two aspects of the subject. The general curriculum in music is devoted to the end of intelligent musicianship; courses in education are designed to produce intelligent teachers. Instruction in the philosophy and history of education, in general educational psychology, and in other related subjects is perhaps less directly the concern of musical pedagogy than are courses in materials and methods of teaching music and in practice teaching. The musicologist interested in the problems of music education can make definite contributions to these fields by the application of scientific methodology.

---

[25] For what is probably the most comprehensive study of these questions and problems, see Percy A. Scholes, *Music Appreciation: Its History and Technics.*

RESEARCH

The teaching of musical *research* is a responsibility of the graduate school. If the preparatory work of the student has been carried on in such a way as to encourage independent thinking, if the student has a reasonable command of the basic techniques — languages, literature, history, philosophy, and sciences (especially psychology) — the transition to work on the graduate level should be easy and natural.

Though a certain amount of the graduate work may be carried on advantageously by the lecture and discussion method, the central core of study should be done in seminars and courses devoted to special studies in which the professor and student work together, with the student assuming as much initiative as possible. Creative imagination is essential for successful graduate work; but this cannot be taught in research work any more than in composition. Yet the resourceful teacher will find ways of encouraging original thinking. The mechanics of research procedure, which can be taught, should be regarded as incidental rather than ultimate objectives.

The materials and methods used in teaching research vary with the student, the teacher, the library and other facilities, and the conception of the ultimate goal to be attained. The musicologist as teacher must study the problems involved with a view to the development of the most effective materials and methods. A representative collection of books and scores that includes fundamental reference works and bibliographical aids, and laboratory equipment if experimental investigations are contemplated, are minimum requirements. Through modern means of photographic reproduction, rare and expensive materials such as books, scores, manuscripts, and other documents are much more readily accessible than they formerly were, so that it is possible for an institution with limited resources to do creditable work in the graduate field.

In the early stages of graduate training, research exercises of modest scope will give the student experience in discovering, evaluating, and defining the problem; in applying typical research procedures used in experimental research, survey, historical research, prognostic research, and philosophical analysis; in making a bibliography; in collecting, analyzing, and classifying data; and in the final report of investigations. The subjects chosen for investigation should be serious, properly oriented to the general field of musicology, and provocative of thought. Mere accumulation of data is of little value unless motivated by a significant idea. The master's thesis need not be a contribution to knowledge, though it should be a genuine test of the student's ability to do creative research while maintaining an objective attitude. The doctor's dissertation, however, must be a real contribution to knowledge.

In assisting the graduate student in his program of research, the adviser in charge of the work should carefully weigh the student's special interests and educational background. He should guide the student in his work so as to avoid unnecessary waste of time and energy. To this end he should see that the problem is a significant one, carefully defined and delimited, susceptible to scientific treatment, and within the student's capacity. Though he should be ready to give counsel as needed at all stages of the work, the adviser should take care not to deprive the student of the main responsibility for the work. By precept and example he may stimulate the student and guide him to a successful completion of his task.

BIBLIOGRAPHY

The following bibliography contains chiefly general literature on education and musical pedagogy; for the extensive literature on special subjects see the bibliographies contained in the works cited and in the lists of books on music of the National Association of Schools of Music, Percy Scholes, *The International Cyclopedia of Music*, and Riemann's *Grundriss der Musikwissenschaft*. The research bulletins, the yearbooks, and the journal of the Music Educators National Conference and the volumes of proceedings of the Music Teachers National Association contain important material on all phases of music education.

Demiashkevich, Michael, *An Introduction to the Philosophy of Education*. New York: American Book Company, 1935.

Dewey, John, *Democracy and Education: An Introduction to the Philosophy of Education*. New York: The Macmillan Company, 1937. (First Edition, 1916.)

Dykema, Peter W., and Karl W. Gehrkens, *The Teaching and Administration of High School Music*. Boston: C. C. Birchard & Company, 1941.

Earhart, Will, *The Meaning and Teaching of Music*. New York: M. Witmark & Sons, 1935.

Fitzpatrick, Edward A. (Editor), *Readings in the Philosophy of Education*. New York: D. Appleton-Century Company, Inc., 1936.

Fox, Lillian Mohr, and L. Thomas Hopkins, *Creative School Music*. New York: Silver, Burdett & Company, 1936.

Handbuch der Musikerziehung. Edited by Ernst Bücken. Potsdam: Akademische Verlagsgesellschaft Athenaion, m.b.H., 1931.

Horne, Herman H., *The Democratic Philosophy of Education*. New York: The Macmillan Company, 1932.

———, *The Philosophy of Education*. New York: The Macmillan Company, 1910.

Jordan, A. M., *Educational Psychology*. New York: Henry Holt & Company, Inc., 1933.

Krusé, Samuel Andrew, *A Critical Analysis of Principles of Teaching as a Basic Course in Teacher-Training Curricula*. Nashville: George Peabody College for Teachers, 1929.

Kuehner, Quincy A., *A Philosophy of Education*. New York: Prentice-Hall, Inc., 1936.

Kwalwasser, Jacob, *Problems in Public School Music*. New York: M. Witmark & Sons, 1932.

———, *Tests and Measurements in Music*. Boston: C. C. Birchard & Company, 1927.

Mersmann, Hans, *Das Musikseminar*. Leipzig: Quelle & Meyer, 1931.

Monroe, Walter S., and Max D. Engelhart, *The Scientific Study of Educational Problems.* New York: The Macmillan Company, 1936.

Mursell, James L., *Human Values in Music Education.* New York: Silver, Burdett & Company, 1934.

————, *Principles of Musical Education.* New York: The Macmillan Company, 1927.

————, and Mabel Glenn, *The Psychology of School Music Teaching.* New York: Silver, Burdett & Company, 1931.

Norton, John K., and Margaret A. Norton, *Foundations of Curriculum Building.* Boston: Ginn and Company, 1936.

Rugg, Harold, and Ann Shumaker, *The Child-Centered School: An Appraisal of the New Education.* Yonkers-on-Hudson, New York: World Book Company, 1928.

Saucier, W. A., *Introduction to Modern Views of Education.* Boston: Ginn and Company, 1937.

Scholes, Percy A., *Music Appreciation: Its History and Technics.* Edited for American Readers by Will Earhart. New York: M. Witmark & Sons, 1936.

Seymour, Harriet Ayer, *The Philosophy of Music.* New York: Harper & Brothers, 1920.

Thompson, Randall, *College Music: An Investigation for the Association of American Colleges.* New York: The Macmillan Company, 1935.

Thorn, Alice G., *Music for Young Children.* New York: Charles Scribner's Sons, 1929.

Van de Wall, Willem, *Music in Institutions.* New York: Russell Sage Foundation, 1936.

Whitney, Frederick Lamson, *Methods in Educational Research.* New York: D. Appleton-Century Company, Inc., 1931.

CHAPTER VII

COMPARATIVE MUSICOLOGY: FOLK MUSIC AND NON–EUROPEAN MUSICAL SYSTEMS[1]

O F THE MANY WAYS OF STUDYING OUR ART MUSIC SYS-tematically, one of the most enlightening is to com-pare it with folk music and non-European musical systems that have grown up more or less independently. Largely because of the predominance of the comparative viewpoint in the study of these other musical systems, this field has com-monly been called *comparative musicology*. The term is not entirely satisfactory, however, for the comparative method is frequently used in the other fields of musicology, and studies in this field are often not directly comparative. But, if used with discretion, the term *comparative musicology* may be legitimately employed as a convenient and significant rubric for a large and important field of musicological knowledge and research.

The comparative viewpoint is exemplified by Alexander John Ellis' work in the study of the extra-European scales. After many years of study of the musical scale from acous-tical, psychological, and historical viewpoints, Ellis, in about 1880, became interested in the comparative study of other scalic systems. With the aid of a series of tuning forks of

---

[1] As a general background for this chapter read A. L. Kroeber, *Anthro-pology*, Chapter I, "Scope and Character of Anthropology," Chapter IX, "Parallels," and Chapters XIV and XVI, "The Growth of Civilization."

accurately determined pitch, he attempted to determine the actual frequencies of tones produced on native instruments, and to indicate the comparative values of the interval relations in terms of *cents* — the hundredths of an equal semitone.[2] The titles of his first papers in this field, read before the Society of Arts in 1885, indicate the comparative viewpoint: "Tonometrical Observations on Some Existing Non-Harmonic Scales"[3] and "On the Musical Scales of Various Nations."[4] Ellis' studies were based on other researches which were comparative only by implication.[5] The methodological importance of Ellis' work was that he consciously employed comparison, and that he applied objective, scientific methods. For this reason Hornbostel, Lach, and others have regarded him as the founder of comparative musicology.

In 1885 Guido Adler, recognizing the subject as a division of musicology, defined its task as *the comparison of the musical works — especially the folksongs — of the various peoples of the earth for ethnographical purposes, and the classification of them according to their various forms.*[6] In 1905 E. M. von Hornbostel read a paper on the problems of comparative musicology before the Viennese chapter of the International Musicological Society,[7] and in 1924 Robert Lach published the first book devoted to the problems and methods of comparative musicology.[8] During all this time countless monographs appeared. George Herzog's more recent sur-

---

[2] See the article on Ellis by A. J. Hipkins in *Grove's Dictionary of Music and Musicians.*

[3] *Proceedings of the Royal Society of London,* Vol. XXXVII (1884), pages 368-385.

[4] *Journal of the Society of Arts,* Vol. XXXIII (1885), pages 485-517.

[5] For example, those by Jan P. Land, Eli Smith, and Rajah Tagore. See A. J. Ellis, "Non-Harmonic Scales," in an appendix to Hermann L. F. Helmholtz, *On the Sensations of Tone,* pages 514-527.

[6] "Umfang, Methode und Ziel der Musikwissenschaft," *Vierteljahrsschrift für Musikwissenschaft,* Vol. I (1885), page 14.

[7] "Die Probleme der vergleichenden Musikwissenschaft," *Zeitschrift der internationalen Musikgesellschaft,* Vol. VII (1905), pages 85-97.

[8] *Die vergleichende Musikwissenschaft, ihre Methoden und Probleme.*

vey [9] of research in primitive and folk music in the United States indicates a growing interest in the field all over the world, and especially in America.

The use of the term *comparative musicology* to designate a particular field of inquiry should not be taken to mean that this field is the only one that makes use of comparative methods in its work. In general, comparison is one of the favorite methods of all scientific investigation, whether systematic or historical. Further, the comparative method is based upon fundamental investigations that are themselves descriptive, analytic, experimental, speculative, and historical. There are so many different musical systems in the various cultural divisions of the world that the organization of the systematic and historical knowledge about the music of any one of them may involve the whole apparatus of musicological research. In fact, from a certain viewpoint, what we, as members of Western European culture, regard as the field of musicology, may be only one division of musicology conceived on a world-wide basis. Such a view is maintained by Charles Seeger.[10] However, since we are concerned with our own musical cultural inheritance, comparative musicology, as defined, must be regarded as but one division of general musicology.

Divisions of the Field

Although a sharp delimitation of the various fields of comparative musicology is difficult to make, the main subdivisions of the subject are fairly clear. Non-European musical systems and folk music constitute the chief subjects of study; the songs of birds and phylogenetic-ontogenetic parallels are subordinate topics. The extra-European systems are further

---

[9] *Research in Primitive and Folk Music in the United States.*
[10] See "Music and Musicology," *Encyclopaedia of the Social Sciences,* Vol. II, pages 244–250.

distinguished in terms of cultural level and geographical distribution. As applied to musical systems, the term *primitive* is used in two senses; it may refer either to ancient or prehistoric music, or to music of a low cultural level. It is in the latter sense that primitive music is chiefly studied in comparative musicology. The music of the American Indians, the African Negroes, and many native peoples throughout the world may be classed as primitive if it is representative of a low degree of culture. Other musical systems studied are those of highly civilized peoples such as the Chinese, Japanese, and Indians. Folk music is usually studied in terms of national or racial distinctions and in terms of style-species or type.

AUXILIARY SCIENCES

Anthropology, ethnology, cultural history, and related sciences are in many ways closely allied to comparative musicology. Most, if not all, of the music studied in comparative musicology is transmitted by oral tradition without the aid of written notation; [11] hence, the importance of having accurate transcriptions — especially phonograph records — of the music as performed. The foregoing fact also suggests the reason why comparative musicology concerns itself so much with the collection, transcription, and preservation of the music with which it deals, and why its historical scope is limited in many ways. But, just as anthropology "rests upon biological and underlies purely historical science," [12] so comparative musicology depends upon the natural and contributes to the historical sciences that deal with music. Acoustics, physiology, and psychology make important contributions to comparative musicology, as do aesthetics, history, comparative philology, and the theory of music theory.

---

[11] Concerning this point see, for example, Robert Lachmann, *Die Musik der aussereuropäischen Natur- und Kulturvölker*, page 1.

[12] A. L. Kroeber, *Anthropology*, page 10.

Equipment

The scientific study of music from the viewpoint of comparative musicology depends upon the possibility of obtaining objective records of the music. Ellis' studies were based upon experiments with instruments, in which the *tonometer* [13] was used to compare the tones produced. The invention of the *phonograph* provided an instrument that has become the chief apparatus of the researcher in comparative musicology. The modern *electrical recorder*, using aluminum or acetate disks with microphone and amplifier, is in general use today. The *sound film* offers many advantages, but the costs have prevented its extensive use. *Phonophotography* provides a means of obtaining an accurate objective record of pitch variations and other details of the performance of a song.[14]

In addition to apparatus for collecting and transcribing music, the researcher needs laboratory facilities for experimental and practical work, a library for reference work, and archives for the preservation of his collections.

Collecting Material

One of the first problems of the researcher in comparative musicology is the collection of material or data. This generally involves the making of phonograph or sound-film recordings of the music to be studied, in as large quantities as possible. In doing this, the worker must keep careful notes about the authenticity of the music, the conditions under which the recordings are made, and other details that have a bearing on the validity of the investigation. The direct transcription of a song into musical notation, while not gen-

---

[13] See the article on J. H. Scheibler in *Grove's Dictionary of Music and Musicians*.

[14] See Milton Metfessel, *Phonophotography in Folk Music*, and Joseph Tiffin, "Phonophotograph Apparatus," *The Vibrato*, University of Iowa Studies in the Psychology of Music, Vol. I, pages 118–133.

erally satisfactory for objective scientific purposes, may be of some value in "prospecting" work and as a preliminary or tentative step. In certain cases the investigator has gained valuable insights into the music by placing himself under the tutelage of the performer, learning to play or sing the music himself. Important, too, is the collection of instruments and data about their use. Collateral information of a sociocultural nature must also be obtained. Since most primitive, non-European, or folk music is vocal, special attention must be given to the texts. Frequently the assistance of a linguistic specialist is necessary in order to obtain a reliable transcript of both the sung and spoken forms of the text.[15] The failure to follow any of these suggestions may greatly impair the significance of the investigation.

TRANSCRIPTION

The transcription of the music collected on records presents many difficulties, some of which may be insuperable. Our conventional system of notation must be modified by various means such as the use of a system of diacritical markings, omission or special arrangements of bar lines, and the approximate indication of note values carefully checked against a basic pulse-rate indicated by metronomic means.[16] Such an adaptation of the notation gives a record of the music which, however inadequate in many respects, is indispensable for scientific study. The notation may not show many subtleties of performance in pitch and rhythmic variations and the like, but it does afford a basis for description and analysis.[17] From a comparative viewpoint, the attempt to

---

[15] For a more detailed discussion of this particular problem, see George Herzog, *op. cit.*, pages 9 f., 15, *et passim*.

[16] See Otto Abraham and Erich M. von Hornbostel, "Vorschläge für die Transkription exotischer Melodien," *Sammelbände der internationalen Musikgesellschaft*, Vol. XI (1909–10), pages 1–25.

[17] Phonophotography may prove an invaluable aid in transcription. It is too early to predict what role the phonophotograph and the sound film,

transcribe exotic music and folk music accurately into conventional notation is, for the most part, an effort to write down the music of systems that grew up under different conditions, almost entirely without any system of notation, in a notation that had its own peculiar historical development in a particular musical system.

The adequacy with which our notation records the music under investigation is an index to the degree of similarity and difference among the systems. Music which lends itself to our notation must have many elements of similarity; that which practically defies notation must be radically different.

DESCRIPTION AND ANALYSIS

Among the items to be considered in the description and analysis of exotic or folk music are *scale, rhythm, melody, harmony, form*, and *performance* or *interpretation*. The treatment of each of these topics involves certain characteristic problems and techniques, some of which may be mentioned briefly by way of illustration.

SCALES

In general we speak of music only when the tonal materials may be organized in terms of a fairly well-defined scale. The transition from highly inflected speech to a more purely musical utterance is gradual. The more or less indefinite pitches of the sounds of speech become more and more highly inflected until definite pitch distinctions can be made. Robert Lach, in discussing this subject, begins with the primitive cry or *Urschrei* — presumably a long-sustained emotional yell — and outlines the possible development through the portamento and glissando, the various stages of adding a tone above and a tone below with gradually increasing definite-

as objective records, will play in the future of comparative musicology. For a further discussion on this point, see Herzog, *op. cit.*, pages 17 f., and Seashore, *The Psychology of Music*, pages 346 ff.

ness of pitch, to the establishment of the historical scales.[18] In the course of his discussion, Lach mentions intermediate forms between speech and music, such as the *recitative* and related forms in the drama, the *parlando* of the couplet singer, and the "counting out" jingles of children. He makes comparisons with similar phenomena in the speech and music of many nations and primitive peoples. He also refers to the sounds made by animals, and the songs of birds. Finally, he outlines the ontogenetic developments in the growth of the child, suggesting the phylogenetic parallel.

The study of *scale* entails, first, an accurate measurement of the frequency relationships between the tones used. The use of the tonometer, tonoscope, and phonophotographic camera for this purpose involves special technical problems in each case.[19] After the frequencies of the tones have been determined, the next step is their arrangement in serial order. This gives the total number of tones of different frequencies occurring in a given song, the compass or range, and the patterns of interval relations; it gives the scale only in the sense of tonal material arranged in pitch sequence. But such a procedure may or may not produce a significant scale norm comparable to the conventional scales of our art music. *Modulation,* the transfer of motives to different pitch levels, may occur in such a way as to make the systematic arrangement of tones practically meaningless; ornamental notes may be introduced in such a way that, if they are given equal prominence in the scale, they may completely distort the scale pattern; and the absence of anything corresponding to

---

[18] *Op. cit.*, pages 32 ff.

[19] The tonometer is apparently not much used in America. For a discussion of the use of the tonoscope, see Harold M. Williams, "Experimental Studies in the Use of the Tonoscope," *Psychological Monographs*, Vol. 41 (1931), pages 266–327. The use of the phonophotographic camera is discussed in Metfessel, *op. cit.*, pages 18–46. Abraham and Hornbostel, *loc. cit.*, pages 19–24, explain methods of calculating interval relations in terms of cents.

a tonic or final may cause further difficulty. In simple songs the technique described may give quite satisfactory results, but in more complicated songs other methods must be found.[20]

The word *scale* is used to designate all the tones in a musical system, arranged in order of pitch; it is also used with reference to the system of tones within the octave. Scales, in the latter sense, are classified according to the number of steps or tones within the octave. Thus, there are *pentatonic* or five-tone scales; *heptatonic* or seven-tone scales, of which our ordinary diatonic scale is an example; twelve-tone scales, the so-called *chromatic* scales; the *seventeen-tone* scale of Arabia; and the *twenty-one-tone* scale of India.

A given song does not necessarily use all the tones in the basic scale. Sometimes the scales with a smaller number of tones may be regarded as composed of a certain number of tones selected from a scale of more tones. Thus, our diatonic scale may be regarded as a derivative of the chromatic scale. Or, to express the problem another way, the scale basic to a particular song may be a portion of the scale that in a larger sense is the composite sum of all the scales, or tones, occurring in all the songs of a particular musical system. Hornbostel calls the composite scale the *material* scale (*Materialleiter*), and the scale basic to a particular song, the *use* scale (*Gebrauchsleiter*).[21] Scales of more than seven tones are generally *material* scales, and from them are selected certain tones to make up the *use* scales.

A number of different principles are involved in the determination or selection of tones used in forming the various scales. So-called *natural* principles indicate the relations to the overtone series. The *distance* principle refers to construction of scales with intervals of equal, or nearly equal,

[20] See, for example, Helen H. Roberts, *Form in Primitive Music*, pages 157 ff.
[21] "Die Probleme der vergleichenden Musikwissenschaft," *Zeitschrift der internationalen Musikgesellschaft*, Vol. VII (1905–1906), pages 88 f.

size — for example, by cutting pan pipes of proportional lengths. The *consonance* principle implies a psychological basis. The *nonmusical* principles are, for example, those implied in mathematically calculated interval systems, or those prescribed by religious or superstitious motives, or those derived from some factor in the construction of instruments. The application of many of these principles gives rise to scales with intervallic relations very different from those in occidental music; for a case in point, the equal division of the fifth may produce the so-called neutral third, which is neither major nor minor but between the two.

Extra-European musical systems often show little or no trace of a principle of tonality. Where the feeling of finality is not very definite, the researcher usually makes a tabulation of the frequency of occurrence of the several tones;[22] this tabulation may give a suggestion as to the presence or absence of an idea of finality.

The problem of scale is always important in the description and analysis of exotic music.[23]

RHYTHM

The description and analysis of the rhythmical characteristics of exotic and folk music afford many opportunities for significant comparison. Although much of this music presents no particular problem, some of it offers difficulties that are almost insurmountable. Sometimes non-European musics have greater rhythmic complication than our own music, and often there is an entirely different conception of rhythmic procedure. The dynamic accentuation of the so-called weak beats, the complication of syncopation effects, the almost para-

---

[22] *Cf.* Jan Philip Schinhan, *Die Musik der Papago und Yurok*, pages 74–76.
[23] For a systematic survey of scalic systems, see Erich von Hornbostel, "Musikalische Tonsysteme" in *Handbuch der Physik*, ed. by F. Trendelenburg, Vol. VIII, *Akustik*, pages 425–449.

doxical counter rhythms of percussion instruments against the melodic rhythms — these and other rhythmic differences require careful study if there is to be reasonably accurate description and analysis. Very often the strict metrical system is quite inapplicable. However, extensions and diminutions of melodic phrases, irregularities due to agogic variations, unusual cadence formations, and recitative-like passages do not necessarily signify rhythmical amorphism; for underlying apparent freedom may be a unifying basic pulse that almost eludes detection. As Hornbostel suggests, the relation between rhythm and meter may not offer the key to the rhythmic problem, but, instead, may constitute a problem in itself.[24]

MELODY

The further pursuit of rhythmical investigations leads naturally over into the field of musical architectonics — the elucidation of the formal structure of music — and into the study of *melody* and form in general. The description and analysis of the melodic aspects of music naturally overlap with the consideration of formal design.

Since most exotic and folk music is vocal, the relation between text and melody must receive a good deal of attention in comparative musicology. The melody of speech is musical melody in an embryonic form, but it is extremely important for the meaning of spoken language. Slight changes of inflection may cause complete changes in meaning. Melody and words are often so closely interdependent that they can scarcely be separated. The use of nonsense syllables tends to emphasize the melodic line, whereas the growing need for comprehension of the meaning of the text tends to subordinate the importance of melodic line. A vocalise may be pure mel-

---

[24] For a more detailed discussion of these problems, see Hornbostel, *loc. cit.*, pages 94 f.; Lach, *op. cit.*, pages 84 ff.; and Robert Lachmann, *Die Musik der aussereuropäischen Natur- und Kulturvölker*, pages 9 ff., *et passim*.

ody, whereas the recitative or parlando approaches speech.

The description and analysis of melody may begin with a consideration of the interval. Here some of the factors to be taken into account are size, direction, frequency of occurrence, initial and cadence characteristics, and relation to motive and phrase structure. Other topics that require treatment are motive structure, repetition, sequence, variation and ornament, cadence, rhythmic pattern in a narrow and broad sense, melodic line or contour (including the question of culmination note), dynamic and agogic contours, and expressive qualities. From the analysis and description of these factors in detail, and from a consideration of melody as *Gestalt*, melody may be significantly characterized as to its essential objective and subjective features and implications.

The organization of data about melody through tabulation and systematization according to criteria appropriate to particular situations lays the foundation for the comparative study of melody. Though simplicity of melodic structure with respect to number of tones used, type of motive repetition, and degree of tonal organization may be an index to musico-cultural level, such criteria must be used with circumspection; paucity of tones and the adherence to a limited tonal range may characterize the music of a relatively high cultural level, and extreme complexity bordering on chaos may occur at lower cultural levels.[25]

Homophony, Polyphony, and Heterophony

Some types of exotic and folk music exhibit characteristics more or less closely resembling, or corresponding to, the

---

[25] See Lachmann, *op. cit.*, pages 3 ff.; E. M. von Hornbostel, "Melodie und Skala," *Jahrbuch der Musikbibliothek Peters*, Vol. XIX (1912), pages 11–23; and Marius Schneider, *Geschichte der Mehrstimmigkeit*, pages 15 ff.

For a proposed method of obtaining a graph of duration and pitch values of melodies, see Schinhan, *op. cit.*, pages 77 and 356.

harmonic and contrapuntal aspects of conventional occidental music.

harmonic and contrapuntal aspects of conventional occidental music. Therefore, the study of the relations involved, with distinction between likenesses and differences, constitutes an interesting task for comparative musicology.

It is difficult to make a sharp distinction between *monophonic* music and the beginnings of *homophonic* music; but the transition begins, at least in embryo, whenever men and women, or men and boys, sing together in parallel octaves. This means simply that the same melody is sung at different pitch levels. In this sense, singing in octaves is accidental, and, to some extent, so is singing in fourths and fifths. But, in the latter case, the procedure may be intentional; if so, it may be regarded as a definite art means comparable to the parallel organum. Examples of this type of rudimentary *homophony* or *polyphony*, and even that which involves singing in parallel seconds, are reported among primitive peoples.[26]

A second type of polyphonic or "part" music is the *bourdon* (sometimes *burden*), which involves some kind of a drone bass effect. A simple type of bourdon is the long-sustained tone of the bagpipe, but there are many similar kinds of bourdon obtained in diverse ways. In Africa, India, and China, there are guitars or guitar-like instruments with bourdon strings,[27] and vocal bourdons are also common.[28] The most rudimentary type of bourdon is the percussion accompaniment to both vocal and instrumental music. Perhaps we should classify the bare percussion accompaniment

---

[26] See, for example, Erich M. von Hornbostel, "Ueber Mehrstimmigkeit in der aussereuropäischen Musik," *III. Kongress der internationalen Musikgesellschaft* (1909), pages 298–303; also Lachmann, *op. cit.*, page 13. For a more comprehensive discussion of this and related matters, see Marius Schneider, *Geschichte der Mehrstimmigkeit*, Erster Teil: *Die Naturvölker*.

[27] See, for example, Hornbostel, *loc. cit.*, page 300.

[28] Hornbostel, *loc. cit.*; Schneider, *op. cit.*, pages 22 ff.; Edwin G. Burrows, "Polynesian Part Singing," *Zeitschrift für Vergleichende Musikwissenschaft*, Vol. II (1934), pages 69–76.

to the dance, such as hand clapping or foot stamping, with this type. Hornbostel calls the former the "rhythmized" or "noise" bourdon, and suggests that it may be regarded as the germ of the polyphonic idea.[29]

The bourdon of instruments capable of playing tones of different pitch leads to the introduction of slight decorative motives at points where the principal melody has sustained tones. Such modifications of the bourdon may lead directly to the *ostinato* — the accompaniment of a main melody with a short motive that is constantly repeated.[30] The principal tones of a melody at the interval of the fourth or fifth may afford the basis of an instrumental, or vocal, double bourdon. Thus may be produced perhaps the simplest type of three-part music.

Other forms of polyphonic music grow out of the common practice of antiphonal singing. Two groups or two voices often alternate, and in so doing the second voice may enter before the first has completed the phrase.[31] When the second voice sings the same melody, or a slightly modified version of it, along with the overlapping of entrances, a kind of canon or free imitation occurs. The relation of such phenomena to similar procedures in occidental music affords an interesting opportunity for comparative investigation and speculation.[32]

Heterophony refers to the simultaneous performance or singing of a melody by two or more voices in such a way that, while they do not exactly coincide, they closely resemble each other in basic contour; that is, one voice may be regarded as a melodic variant of the other. It occurs quite naturally when the accompanying instrument, playing the

---

[29] Hornbostel, *loc. cit.*, page 301.
[30] *Ibid.*
[31] Lachmann, *op. cit.*, page 13.
[32] For examples and further discussion, see the references already cited, especially Schneider and Lachmann.

basic melody, does not follow all the incidental ornamental figurations of the voice; or when an instrument, such as a flute, elaborates the simple melodic line of the vocal part.

Instrumental, vocal, and mixed types of heterophony seem to exist quite independently, so that it is not possible to place them in any order of development. Unisons, parallel seconds, and other dissonances both passing and unresolved, occur frequently in such tonal-rhythmic structures; but in all this music there is little or no evidence of a harmonic or contrapuntal structure based upon principles of consonance and dissonance treatment like those that obtain in the music of Western Europe.

In a sense, most exotic music is essentially nonharmonic, or anharmonic;[33] that is, there is little use of harmony in the sense of functional chord progression. But there is extensive use of harmony in the sense of simultaneous combination of sounds of different pitch. Contrapuntal-like imitations, simultaneous combinations of more or less independent melodies, and practices resembling the parallel organum are not unknown to exotic music; but further contrapuntal sophistication is practically, if not entirely, unknown.

Form

The problems of analysis and description of the formal design of folk music and exotic music are probably best approached from the viewpoint of structural rhythm.[34] From this viewpoint a musical composition may be studied as to its degree of conformity to a conception of form as an organic structural-rhythmic growth. The elemental motive may develop into a phrase; the phrase, as an antecedent factor,

---

[33] See Benjamin I. Gilman, "The Science of Exotic Music," *Science*, Vol. XXX (1909), page 533.

[34] See George S. Dickinson, *The Pattern of Music*, pages 24 ff. Poughkeepsie, New York: Vassar College, 1939.

may expand, through the addition of a consequent phrase, into a period; and the period may grow into a larger structural unit which, in turn, may afford the basis for further elaboration into still more extensive forms.

The whole structural-rhythmic pattern is made manifest through the comparison of corresponding units in the design. This pattern may be exhibited in any one or several of the tonal dimensions of duration, pitch, loudness, and quality. Melodic pattern, as a complex of these various elements, affords the most convenient and obvious basis for comparison in most folk and exotic music. From the simple repetition of tones and irregular, relatively amorphous structures of more primitive cultures, to more definitely patterned forms (such as the strophe, canon, rondo, and suite) of higher cultures, the various levels of application of structural-rhythmic principles may be traced. Systems of analysis which have proved significant in the study of the musical styles of conventional occidental music may often be effectively applied with appropriate changes to primitive and folk music.[35]

The diverse musical systems of the various peoples of the world are, of course, based on many different conceptions of tonal relations. The differences of attitude toward our familiar notions of scale, rhythm, melody, cadence, tonality, modulation, sequence, motive, and other details of musical theory and practice, must be taken into account in any description and analysis of musical form. The comparative musicologist must guard against the fallacies of reading into exotic musical systems the musical conceptions of his own experience.

---

[35] See, for example, Jan Philip Schinhan's adaptation of the type of analysis used by Alfred O. Lorenz in his work *Das Geheimnis der Form bei R. Wagner* (Berlin: Max Hesse, 1926) to American Indian music (in *Die Musik der Papago und Yurok*, Dissertation, University of Vienna, 1937) and to folk music in "Spanish Folklore from Tampa, Florida: (No. VI) Folksongs," *Southern Folklore Quarterly*, Vol. III (1939), pages 129–163.

Some of the possible distinctions which should be kept in the description and analysis of musical form are *anharmonic structure* (the absence of our conventional harmonic system of relations); *isotonic scales* (scales based upon tonal distance rather than consonance); *heterophony* (each voice approximating the melody); *neotonality* (one or more tones occurring frequently, but with no clear-cut tonic); *rhythmic complications* (several basically different rhythms at once); unusual melody types (*ethos* determined by religious or superstitious moments); and "scale versus song" (the conception of notes as constituents of familiar sequences of tones rather than as members of a scale). [36]

PERFORMANCE

The description and analysis of performance implies the consideration of such matters as the use of the voice; the technique of the instruments; intonation, tone quality, dynamics, and agogics; and the use of the vibrato and incidental embellishments and portamentos. In addition to the use of what we may loosely call the normal or natural voice, the rendition of exotic and folk music is frequently characterized by the use of the falsetto, of high, pinched, nasal tones, and of harsh chesty and throaty tones.

From the Chinese sheng to the hoedown fiddle, each instrument implies an individual technique of performance which is a legitimate item for description and analysis in comparative musicology. The study of such details as intonation, tone quality, dynamics, and agogics presents many difficulties, but such studies are necessary for the accurate characterization of any musical performance. For the investigation of these and related matters such as the vibrato and portamento, the use of kymographic instruments, phono-

---

[36] See Benjamin I. Gilman, "The Science of Exotic Music," *Science*, Vol. XXX (1909), pages 533 f.

photography, and other visual aids is extremely important for scientific accuracy. But such aids must be used with circumspection, for, as Herzog [37] points out, the more refined the technic, the more the musical phenomena may be distorted, until the researcher may not be able to cope with the difficulties of properly relating the objective data to the realities of the original musical aesthetic experience.

INSTRUMENTS

The study of musical instruments is, in many ways, closely related to the foregoing, chiefly theoretical, problems and to other more general historical and cultural problems. Musical instruments not only furnish data about the technical nature of music, but they also give valuable clues of sociocultural interest.[38]

Before the advent of the phonograph, the comparative study of musical instruments afforded the chief means for the scientific study of various scalic systems. Ellis' investigations were largely devoted to the determination of the pitch of the actual notes produced on native instruments. Since the invention of the phonograph, more attention has been paid to the study of the music itself, with the aid of recordings, and the study of instruments has been somewhat neglected. Curt Sachs and the late E. M. von Hornbostel have been leaders in the scientific study of exotic instruments. They have proposed a system for the classification of instruments, developed technics of study, defined the problems, and done outstanding work in the field. With technical improvements in the apparatus for measuring frequencies, the work of Ellis and others in determining the pitch of scales on instruments of fixed pitch should be carried forward. The various collec-

---

[37] Herzog, *op. cit.*, pages 8 f. and 17 f.
[38] See Herzog, *op. cit.*, pages 12 ff.

tions of instruments afford rich opportunities for further research.[39]

HISTORY

In recent years there is evidence of a tendency to place the beginning of the history of music at a later and later date. Not so many decades ago it was the common practice to devote considerable space to the discussion of extra-European and "pre-Greek" musical systems, which was usually followed by an extensive account of Greek music. Thus, Ambros [40] uses practically the whole first volume of his history of music for this purpose; and Fétis,[41] going even further, devotes almost three complete volumes to similar topics. Riemann,[42] however, chooses to omit the preliminaries and to begin with the music of the Greeks; he suggests that such matters are rather the concern of comparative musicology, whose findings must be interpreted with care by the historian.[43] Nef [44] devotes about a half-dozen pages to the problem of origins and to pre-Greek music, basing his discussion chiefly on the work of comparative musicologists. Adler [45] quite frankly turns his opening chapter over to a comparative musicologist, Robert Lach.[46] Hugo Leichtentritt [47] suggests that, since our knowledge of the music of antiquity is inadequate, and actual musical documents are

---

[39] For a list of the better-known collections of instruments, see *The International Cyclopedia of Music and Musicians*, pages 871 f. Carleton Sprague Smith has suggested how important it is that libraries should maintain collections of old instruments in playing condition ("The Service of the Library to Musicology," *Proceedings of the Music Teachers National Association, Thirty-First Series* (1936), pages 239 f.).

[40] August W. Ambros, *Geschichte der Musik.*

[41] François-J. Fétis, *Histoire générale de la musique* . . .

[42] Hugo Riemann, *Handbuch der Musikgeschichte.*

[43] Riemann, *op. cit.*, pages v f.

[44] Karl Nef, *An Outline of the History of Music.*

[45] Guido Adler, *Handbuch der Musikgeschichte.*

[46] "Die Musik der natur- und orientalischen Kulturvölker," *ibid.*, pages 3–34.

[47] *Music, History, and Ideas*, page 3.

few, the history of music more properly starts with the music of the Christian Church in the later Middle Ages. He does allow one chapter for the discussion of Greek music, but he makes little or no reference to the subject of comparative musicology.

This tendency to place the beginning of the history of music at a later date seems quite logical if we think of the history of music as the history of the music of Western Europe. If *comparative musicology* means the study of extra-European musical systems, it is natural that the study of Chinese, Indian, Arabian, and other musical systems should fall to the lot of comparative musicology. In carrying on its work it is natural, too, that it should become involved in historical investigations. Many of the primitive systems of today have little or no far-reaching historical materials, for the music is transmitted chiefly by oral tradition. Other musical systems, especially those of the more highly civilized peoples of the Far East, have a certain amount of historical data. The sifting of these materials becomes the obvious task of comparative musicology.

When the beginnings of European music are traced back as far as possible, it is natural that questions should arise as to connections with pre-existing musical systems. Studies of such problems necessarily tend to become speculative in character, and comparative musicology has its own characteristic technics for dealing with problems of this complicated type.

The methods of comparison or analogy are applied in many different ways in studying the origin of music. For example, from one point of view, it is thought that, since in the world today are peoples in various stages of cultural development, the comparative study of the different musical systems would suggest ways in which our own musical system may have originated. From another viewpoint, the biological or ontogenetic approach attempts to trace the growth of musical knowledge, skills, and insights in the individual from childhood to maturity, and to work out phylogenetic parallels. And, again, the music of birds offers certain opportunities for speculative comparison.

Although work in these fields presents many difficulties — the pitfalls for the unwary are numerous — the results give us about all we can hope to know about many problems where conventional historical methods are inapplicable. Unduly biased findings may result from overenthusiasm for a particular hypothesis and the mistaking of superficial resemblances for significant similarities — and these tend to invalidate a whole inquiry, since objectivity is imperative for reliable results. But a wrong theory is sometimes better than no theory at all; for, in many fields of scientific investigation, absolutely adequate theories or explanations are ideals to be worked toward, not to be actually attained.

The use of comparison is very common in historical studies within the field of the music of Western Europe. Such comparisons do not come within the scope of comparative musicology as we have defined the subject. Comparison between different style-species and different style-periods, between different composers, and even between different works of the same composer are routine matters in musical history and in musical style-criticism. But, when comparative methods reach over into extra-European musical systems — when, for example, Gregorian music is compared with certain musical procedures in the Orient with respect to notation, performance, decorative features, melodic structure, and tonal systems — we get into the field of comparative musicology.[48]

The comparative method, involving the use of sweeping

---

[48] See, for example, Georg Schünemann, "Ueber die Beziehungen der vergleichenden Musikwissenschaft zur Musikgeschichte," *Archiv für Musikwissenschaft,* Vol. II (1919–1920), **pages** 175–194.

analogies, as exhibited in the works of Lorenz,[49] Spengler,[50] and Sorokin,[51] may or may not involve comparative musicology as we have attempted to define it. Comparative musicology has its characteristic subject matter chiefly in extra-European and folk music; its methods, however, are in common with many systematic and historical researches. It is futile to attempt finely drawn distinctions in such matters. The differences between systematic, historical, and comparative methods in general are perfectly clear, and may perhaps best be regarded as differences in point of view. Certainly there is much overlapping both in method and material.[52]

Different methods may be applied in the study of practically any topic or problem in music. For example, the cadence may be studied systematically, historically, or in terms of comparative musicology. The systematic approach would, presumably, imply an examination of what the systematic sciences might have to contribute to the subject, and an investigation of all types of cadences used in music today. The historical approach would study cadences as they have occurred throughout the history of music. Comparative musicology would examine them in exotic and folk music, in speech, and perhaps in the songs of birds.

In all approaches the comparative method would predominate, actually or implicitly, for any classification or systematization of knowledge involves comparison. Hence, it is not correct to assume that comparative musicology, so-called, has an exclusive claim on the use of comparative

[49] Alfred Lorenz, *Abendländische Musikgeschichte im Rhythmus der Generationen.* Berlin: Max Hesse, 1928.

[50] Oswald Spengler, *The Decline of the West* (tr. by Charles F. Atkinson). 2 vols. New York: Knopf, 1932. (Special Edition, 1939.) Original German Edition, München: C. H. Pecksche Verlagshandlung, 1918.

[51] Pitirim A. Sorokin, *Social and Cultural Dynamics.* Vol. I: *Fluctuation of Forms of Art.* New York: American Book Company, 1937.

[52] See Charles Seeger, "Systematic and Historical Orientations in Musicology," *Bulletin of the American Musicological Society*, No. 1, June, 1926, page 16.

methods. The term is used simply to designate a field of inquiry which deals with the reasonably well-defined subject matter of exotic and folk music, with the general aim of comparing it with occidental art music.

APPLICATIONS

It would far exceed the scope of the present work to attempt even a brief discussion of the innumerable musical systems that fall within the scope of comparative musicology. Nevertheless, it may be helpful to mention some of the more important musical types which constitute fairly well-defined special fields of investigation.

Primitive musics are those of peoples at the lower levels or stages of cultural development. The determination of what constitutes a low cultural level is made on the basis of general ethnological criteria of which music is one factor. Musical systems belonging in this category may be found in many parts of the world. In many cases they exist geographically alongside systems of a higher cultural order. In the United States the outstanding representative of this type of music is that of the American Indian.[53]

Most of the music of civilized man outside Europe and the Americas is to be found in the Orient. The chief cultural divisions are (1) the Far East, or China and Japan; (2) Indo-China, Burma, Polynesia; (3) India; (4) Persia, Arabia, and the Moslem countries of the eastern Mediterranean and northern Africa.[54]

It is almost axiomatic to say that folk music is the basis of all music. We have every reason to suppose that folk music

---

[53] For details concerning the special problems of work in this particular field, see George Herzog, *Research in Primitive and Folk Music in the United States*. A brief discussion of primitive music is to be found in Lachmann, *op. cit.*, Chapter I, "Naturvölker."

[54] For a concise discussion with bibliography, see Arthur Prichard Moor, "Oriental Music" in *The International Cyclopedia of Music and Musicians*. See also Lachmann, *op. cit.*, Chapter II, "Hochkulturen."

flourished long before historical evidence reveals the existence of so-called art music. It has continued to thrive and to exercise an influence on art music throughout the period of recorded history. All the fundamental principles of form, and many of the actual forms of art music are exemplified in folk music. The motive, the phrase, the principle of repetition and contrast, of theme and variation — all these and many other similar principles of musical construction are found in folk music. Both composers and scholars are interested in folk music, though, presumably, for different reasons. Composers look to folk music for inspiration — musical ideas or themes — to be used in their own compositions. Scholars study it for systematic and scientific purposes. This difference in attitude naturally leads to differences in method of treatment. For example, while the composer is often content to jot down a folk melody approximately as he hears it in terms of his own peculiar musical bias, the scholar seeks accurate objective transcriptions of what is actually there.[55]

The study of the songs of birds — long of much interest to ornithologists, composers, and musicologists — has entered a new phase of development with the development of the sound camera and the parabolic microphone. Field trips with modern recording apparatus are producing invaluable objective materials in this field.[56]

The influence of folk and exotic music on the art music of Western Europe is well known. In recent years a number of composers have taken an active part in comparative musicological work. Béla Bartók, Zoltán Kodály, Henry Eichheim, John Powell, Henry Cowell, and Ernest Bloch are a

---

[55] For lists of collections, extensive bibliography, and general discussion of research problems and methods, see Herzog, *op. cit.*, pages 45–97. See also articles on folk music in *The International Cyclopedia of Music and Musicians.*

[56] See Albert R. Brand, "Hunting with a Sound Camera," *Natural History*, Vol. XXXIII (1933), pages 381–394. See also article, "Bird Music," *The Oxford Companion to Music*, pages 97–99.

few of the many composers who have shown a special interest in work in this field and who have made extensive use of exotic and folk materials in their compositions. There seems to be no valid reason why scientific work in exotic and folk music should not contribute to general knowledge of music, and at the same time provide great quantities of inspirational materials for use in musical composition. In this field, as in many other fields of musicological endeavor, experience has conclusively shown that art and science need not be antipathetic.

BIBLIOGRAPHY

Abraham, Otto, and Erich M. von Hornbostel, "Vorschläge für die Transkription exotischer Melodien," *Sammelbände der internationalen Musikgesellschaft*, Vol. XI (1909–1910), pages 1–25.

Brand, Albert R., "Hunting with a Sound Camera," *Natural History*, Vol. XXXIII (1933), pages 381–394.

Burrows, Edwin G., "Polynesian Part-Singing," *Zeitschrift für vergleichende Musikwissenschaft*, Vol. II (1934), pages 69–76.

Burton, Frederick R., *American Primitive Music, with Especial Attention to the Songs of the Ojibways*. New York: Moffat, Gard and Company, 1909.

Ellis, Alexander J., "Non-Harmonic Scales," Hermann L. F. Helmholtz, *On the Sensations of Tone*. Fourth Edition tr. by Alexander J. Ellis, pages 514–527. London: Longmans, Green & Company, 1912.

————, "On the Musical Scales of Various Nations," *Journal of the Society of Arts*, Vol. XXXIII (1885), pages 485–517.

————, "Tonometrical Observations on Some Existing Non-Harmonic Scales," *Proceedings of the Royal Society of London*, Vol. XXXVII (1884), pages 368–385.

Farmer, Henry George, *The Arabian Influence on Musical Theory*. London: Harold Reeves, 1925.

————, *Historical Facts for the Arabian Musical Influence*. London: William Reeves, Bookseller, Ltd., n.d.

————, *Studies in Oriental Musical Instruments*. London: Harold Reeves, 1931.

Garstang, Walter, *Songs of the Birds*. New Edition. London: John Lane, The Bodley Head, Ltd., 1935.

Haraszti, Emile, "Fétis fondateur de la musicologie comparée." *Acta musicologica,* Vol. IV (1932), pages 97–103.

Herzog, George, "Research in Primitive and Folk Music in the United States," *American Council of Learned Societies,* Bulletin No. 24. Washington, 1936.

Hornbostel, Erich M. von, "Melodie und Skala," *Jahrbuch der Musikbibliothek Peters,* Vol. XIX (1912), pages 11–23.

————, "Musikalische Tonsysteme," *Handbuch der Physik,* Vol. VIII, *Akustik,* pages 425–449. Edited by F. Trendelenburg. Berlin: Julius Springer, 1927.

————, "Die Probleme der vergleichenden Musikwissenschaft," *Zeitschrift der internationalen Musikgesellschaft,* Vol. VII (1905–1906), pages 85–97.

————, "Ueber Mehrstimmigkeit in der aussereuropäischen Musik," *III. Kongress der internationalen Musikgesellschaft* (1909), pages 298–303.

Kroeber, A. L., *Anthropology.* New York: Harcourt, Brace & Company, Inc., 1923.

Lach, Robert, *Die vergleichende Musikwissenschaft, ihre Methoden und Probleme.* Vienna: Hölder-Pichler-Tempsky, A. G., 1924.

Lachmann, Robert, *Die Musik der aussereuropäischen Natur- und Kulturvölker.* Wildpark-Potsdam: Akademische Verlagsgesellschaft Athenaion, m. b. H., 1929.

Mersmann, Hans, "Grundlagen einer musikalischen Volksliedforschung," *Archiv für Musikwissenschaft,* Vol. IV (1922), pages 141–154, 289–321; Vol. V (1923), pages 81–135.

Metfessel, Milton, *Phonophotography in Folk Music.* Chapel Hill: University of North Carolina Press, 1928.

Moor, Arthur Prichard, "Oriental Music," *The International Cyclopedia of Music and Musicians,* pages 1322–1332.

Nicholson, E. M., and Ludwig Koch, *More Songs of Wild Birds.* (With gramophone records.) London: H. F. & G. Witherby, Ltd., 1937.

————, *Songs of Wild Birds.* (With gramophone records.) London: H. F. & G. Witherby, Ltd., 1937.

Roberts, Helen H., *Form in Primitive Music.* New York: American Library of Musicology, W. W. Norton & Company, Inc., 1933.

Sachs, Curt, *Geist und Werden der Musikinstrumente.* Berlin: Dietrich Reimer, 1929.

————, *Vergleichende Musikwissenschaft.* Leipzig: Quelle & Meyer, 1930.

Sammelbände für vergleichende Musikwissenschaft, Vol. I. Edited by Carl Stumpf and E. M. von Hornbostel. Munich: Drei Masken Verlag, 1922.

Saunders, Aretas A., *A Guide to Bird Songs*. New York: D. Appleton-Century Company, Inc., 1935.

Schinhan, Jan Philip, *Die Musik der Papago und Yurok*. Dissertation, University of Vienna, 1937.

————, "Spanish Folklore from Tampa, Florida: (No. VI) Folksongs," *Southern Folklore Quarterly*, Vol. III (1939), pages 129–163.

Schneider, Marius, *Geschichte der Mehrstimmigkeit*, Erster Teil: *Die Naturvölker*. Berlin: Julius Bard, G. m. b. H., 1934.

Scholes, Percy A., "Bird Music," *The Oxford Companion to Music*, pages 97–99.

Schünemann, Georg, "Ueber die Beziehungen der vergleichenden Musikwissenschaft zur Musikgeschichte," *Archiv für Musikwissenschaft*, Vol. II (1919–1920), pages 175–194.

Seeger, Charles, "Music and Musicology," *Encyclopaedia of the Social Sciences*, Vol. XI, pages 244–250.

————, "Systematic and Historical Orientations in Musicology," *Bulletin of the American Musicological Society*, No. 1, June, 1936, page 16.

Spencer, Herbert, "On the Origin and Function of Music," *Essays*, Vol. I, pages 210–238. London: Williams and Norgate, 1868.

Strangways, A. H. Fox, *The Music of Hindostan*. Oxford: The Clarendon Press, 1914.

Stumpf, Carl, *Die Anfänge der Musik*. Leipzig: Johann Ambrosius Barth, 1911.

Tiffin, Joseph, "Phonophotograph Apparatus," *The Vibrato*, University of Iowa Studies in the Psychology of Music, Vol. I, pages 118–133. Iowa City: University of Iowa Press, 1932.

Torrefranca, Fausto, "Le Origini della musica," *Rivista musicale italiana*, Vol. XIV (1907), pages 555–594.

Wallaschek, Richard, *Anfänge der Tonkunst*. Leipzig: Johann Ambrosius Barth, 1903.

Wellesz, Egon, "Probleme der musikalischen Orientforschung," *Jahrbuch der Musikbibliothek Peters*, Vol. XXIV (1917), pages 1–18.

Williams, Harold M., "Experimental Studies in the Use of the Tonoscope," *Psychological Monographs*, Vol. XLI (1931), pages 266–327.

Witchell, Charles A., *The Evolution of Bird-Song*. London: A. & C. Black, Ltd., 1896.

Zeitschrift für vergleichende Musikwissenschaft. Berlin: Gesellschaft für vergleichende Musikwissenschaft, 1933–1935.

PART TWO

HISTORICAL MUSICOLOGY

Chapter VIII

THE PHILOSOPHY OF MUSIC HISTORY

THE word "history" is derived from a greek word which originally meant *a learning by inquiry*, or *knowledge or information obtained by inquiry*. From this it came to signify a narration of what one has learned. In ordinary usage today, the term has two essentially different meanings. It is used, in a general way, to designate those things which have happened, that is, the events themselves; or it may refer to the record of events. We speak about the history of music, or the history of opera, without any reference to the written narrative or record; and, in this sense, everything that has happened in the realm of music constitutes the history of music. But, in the second sense, history is the literary presentation of those events which the scholar has been able to establish as facts. Our immediate concern is history as inquiry and statement, as research and interpretation.

History involves two distinct types of activity, each with its own characteristic methods. The one has to do with research, with collecting and establishing the facts; the other concerns the literary presentation, the interpretation and exposition, of the material. Although it would probably be unwise to insist upon too sharp a differentiation of method, one may say that, whereas the methods of historical research are primarily scientific, those of literary presentation tend to be artistic and philosophical. The historian, to be successful in his work, needs to avoid the extremes of either method; for history is neither the mere accumulation of facts, nor the free play of the imagination. The following quotation is pertinent: [1]

> History as it is conceived today may blossom into art, may be crowned with philosophy; but it is primarily and necessarily the solid establishment of facts and the precise exposition of the facts established, a task . . . singularly difficult and delicate; in short, the pursuit and the expression of truth.

At first thought, the task of history may seem to be quite simple — to recount what has happened in the past — but few fields of learning are confronted with more complex problems than that of history. Because the happenings of the past are countless, only a few can be recorded; and of the few which can be substantiated, only a small proportion can be presented in any given history. It is necessary to select from available data those events which are significant. But, in order to distinguish between the significant and the immaterial, one must have some criteria; and from the need for such criteria have come the philosophies of history.

Philosophy as applied to history has various meanings. When we say that philosophies of history have arisen out of the feeling of a need for criteria in historical writing, the philosophy of history would seem to mean a theory of value. For example, suppose that in a certain year ten thousand musical compositions were written. It would scarcely be considered good history to attempt merely to list all these works. Nor would the historian necessarily select the "best" composition for inclusion in his history. Composition A might be regarded as a "better" composition than B, but it might be of less historical importance. A might be in the same style as hundreds of other compositions of a hundred

---

[1] Henri Berr and Lucien Febvre, in the article on "History," *Encyclopaedia of the Social Sciences*, Vol. VII, page 357.

or more years earlier, whereas B, although inferior to A, might be an innovation destined to exercise a profound influence on subsequent compositions and lead toward a revolution in musical style. If it can be established that this fact is true, composition B becomes historically more important than A and should be dealt with accordingly by the historian, whereas A may not even be mentioned.

Therefore, the criteria of historical value are not the same as those of aesthetic value; and the fundamental criterion for historical value is the influence of an event upon subsequent events.

Implicit in the foregoing discussion is the idea that history is concerned chiefly with trends, processes, and sequences of events that involve some kind of causal, organic, or other influential relation or connection among the constituent events or subevents.

In technical writings on the problems of historical methodology, the philosophy of history has come to mean any system of thought which attempts to set up an all-embracing criterion for the interpretation of history. Such systems of thought have been worked out more or less clearly in terms of evolution; of teleology; of cycles, involving growth, maturity, and decay; of pragmatism, in the sense of particular applications to present problems; of mutation, or sudden sporadic changes; of relativism; and of many related theories. Insofar as these systems attempt to interpret history in terms of one general principle, they are called *monistic*.

Opposed to *monism* is historical *pluralism*, which maintains that all events in the large-scale processes of history are not necessarily related, except in a temporal manner. Of course, if the pluralistic theory is correct, a philosophy of history in the narrow sense — the attempt to find the meaning of "the historical process as a whole" — is an impossibility. But, if we take the philosophy of history in a broader sense to include the general theoretical basis for the interpretation of history, then historical pluralism itself represents one viewpoint within the field. The philosophy of history, thus broadly conceived, is intimately related to, if not identical with, historical methodology.

Bernheim distinguishes three principal stages or types of historical methodology: the *reporting* or *narrative method;* the *pedagogical* or *pragmatic method;* and the *evolutionary* or *genetic method.*[2] Each of these methods implies a certain philosophy of history, a certain interpretation of the facts or events of history; and, although they are not entirely distinct from each other, and do not exhaust the possibilities of difference in methodology, they will, nevertheless, serve as points of departure for the discussion of the philosophies of history.

The *reporting* or *narrative method* is presumably the first method used in historical writings. Its aim is simply to recount the facts of history as directly and succinctly as possible. If it has a dominating motive, it is aesthetic rather than didactic or evolutionary in character. In its most primitive form it is not scientific in character, but largely imaginative. Other forms of narrative history are more scientific, insofar as they depend upon annals, genealogies, and other substantial documentary evidence. One would think that

---

[2] Ernst Bernheim, *Lehrbuch der historischen Methode und der Geschichtsphilosophie.* Bernheim's conception of the science of history is based upon the view that there are three types of sciences distinguishable in terms of the attitude of each science toward its material. One science inquires into the nature and interrelation of things as they are. Such a viewpoint is typical of what we have designated as the systematic sciences. Another science is concerned with how things came to be as they are, with their evolution. This is the viewpoint of history. A third science wishes to know the meaning of things in their interrelations among themselves and with the world as a whole, both as they are and as they have come to be what they are. This is the province of philosophy. Obviously there is much overlapping among the sciences thus distinguished; a given inquiry may be classified as systematic, historical, or philosophical, according to which viewpoint predominates in the work.

such methods would be most objective because they have no ulterior motives, no hidden designs. But the questions as to how and why an event took place, and what were the results, almost inevitably arise — so that it becomes next to impossible to give a philosophically disinterested account of an event. The how and why, and the results of an event can only be stated in relative terms; that is, in terms of the bias of the individual, of the period, or of the nation. And it is well known that other individuals, other periods, or other nations may interpret the facts differently. For example, at the beginning of the Christian era, Suetonius wrote: [3]

At that time the Jews, incited by a certain Chrestus, stirred up strife and discontent in Rome and had, therefore, to be expelled.

The Christian historian interprets this situation very differently.

Every historical account is narrative insofar as it attempts to relate events in a temporal sequence. But, when the underlying motivation becomes more obviously tinged with practical considerations of one sort or another, a history may be classed as *pedagogical* or *pragmatic*. Thus, when Thucydides in the fifth century B.C. wrote a history of the Peloponnesian War to be useful as a guide to future events, his method was pragmatic. This method has a moralizing tendency and is, therefore, ethical rather than aesthetic in character. Pragmatic histories in general try to find, in history, lessons valuable for purposes of instruction — usually for instruction with a certain bias, whether nationalistic, religious, racial, or otherwise.

Musical historical writings, from the earliest times down to the present day, usually exhibit some pragmatic tendencies. Calvisius and Praetorius, for example, attempted to relate the

---

[3] Quoted in Egon Friedel, *A Cultural History of the Modern Age*, Vol. I, page 10.

musical practices of the ancients to those of the seventeenth century, presumably for purposes of instruction;[4] and evidence of a pragmatic viewpoint can be found in practically every history of music since that time.[5] But, as music historians became more and more concerned with seeing how things came to be what they were or are in any particular period, the genetic method came to be emphasized.

THE GENETIC METHOD

Taking into consideration both inner relations and external conditions, the *genetic method* tries to understand and interpret the trend of events in continuity as an organic whole. The motivation is, thus, logical rather than aesthetic or pragmatic.

The genetic viewpoint, as described by Bernheim,[6] is based upon three fundamental assumptions. First, it conceives human affairs as having an inner homogeneity and continuity. This is expressed as the inner unity of the human race. Second, it regards human activities as having an inner relationship and interaction among themselves and with the physical conditions. This refers not only to the influence of climate, geography, and race upon the nature and character of a people, but also to the complicated interworkings of art, science, religion, and social relations with their political life. Third, the genetic viewpoint assumes that there is a continuous, unbroken change going on in all human relations. It is essentially a monistic conception of history which allows for the view that particular changes may take place within the continuum of history.

---

[4] See Warren D. Allen, *Philosophies of Music History*, pages 5 ff. See also Guido Adler, *Methode der Musikgeschichte*, page 37.

[5] For a discussion of pragmatism in general histories, see J. B. Black, *The Art of History*, pages 9 ff. See also Wilhelm Bauer, *Einführung in das Studium der Geschichte*, Second Edition, pages 151 f.

[6] Bernheim, *op. cit.*, pages 26 ff.

There are, of course, many different ideas as to the meaning of the theory of evolution as applied to history. In general, however, it should be noted that there is a fundamental difference between the idea of evolution in history and in natural science. And, further, the notion of causality is, in many respects, different in history from what it is in the natural sciences. The natural scientist can study causal relations and the growth or development of a plant under laboratory conditions — repeating experiments, if necessary, almost at will. The historian must base his studies upon available records of the past, and the processes he deals with may not be repeated at will.

From this rather sketchy discussion of the genetic method as applied to historical processes, it is apparent that the idea of evolution must be used with some caution in connection with the history of music. The theory leaves itself open to serious question if it maintains (1) that all music evolves in terms of a single principle of evolution; (2) that cultural trends or processes are strictly analogous to biological relations; or (3) that growth, progress, or development goes on in a gradual, continuous manner without gaps. In spite of all attacks on the genetic theory of history, there can be no doubt of its profound influence on the thinking of historians.

There are many striking analogies and actual interrelationships between cultural and biological processes; yet each particular application to musical history of any detail of the general theory of evolution must be examined critically before it is accepted or rejected. It seems unlikely that any theory can be regarded as embracing the whole truth concerning historical processes. These processes are as complex as life itself, and any explanation of them will undoubtedly be very complex and only relatively adequate. In the end, that theory will be found most valid which em-

[253]

braces in a logical, meaningful system the largest proportion of the total complexity. Extravagant claims for or against the genetic theory must be regarded skeptically until these claims are more fully established or clearly interpreted than they now are.[7]

There is evidence of the genetic viewpoint in music-historical writings at least as early as the eighteenth century.[8] Burney, Martini, Forkel, and Hawkins show signs of this attitude toward historical processes in music, but none of these writers carries the idea of evolution through consistently. In the nineteenth century, Kiesewetter, Ambros, and Fétis, among others, write in the evolutionary vein, and countless special studies appear which are dominated by similar tendencies.[9] Though most of the twentieth-century histories of music show narrative-pragmatic tendencies in one way or another, they are at the same time permeated with the notion of evolution. Even such a writer as Paul Bekker, who discards "the idea of development as misleading" and puts "in its place that of metamorphosis, of transformation," and who claims that "the forms of art never develop, they can only change; that the music of all times is artistically, absolutely, ever the same; . . ."[10] finds it difficult to avoid the implica-

---

[7] For a discussion of some of the ways in which the theory of evolution may be applied in the field of music history, see Oswald Koller, "Die Musik im Lichte der Darwinschen Theorie," *Jahrbuch der Musikbibliothek Peters*, Vol. VII (1900), pages 35–50. For more general criticism and discussion, see Warren D. Allen, *Philosophies of Music History*, pages 261–285, *et passim*.

[8] The specific meaning of the term· *evolution* is so ill-defined that there may be some reason for wanting to discard the term altogether. The author feels, however, that even in its vagueness it is reasonably meaningful and may be safely used even at the risk of vagueness just as we use innumerable abstract terms such as *democracy, truth,* and *liberty*, which are exceedingly difficult to define exactly, though none the less useful and meaningful to express certain generalities.

[9] For further details, see Allen, *op. cit.*; also Guido Adler, *Methode der Musikgeschichte*, pages 37 ff.; and Ernst Bücken, "Grundfragen der Musikgeschichte als Geisteswissenschaft," *Jahrbuch der Musikbibliothek Peters*, Vol. XXXIV (1927), pages 19 ff.

[10] Paul Bekker, *The Story of Music*, page 22.

tions of the theory of evolution. In his chapter on Bach and Handel, for example, he states: [11]

> . . . the eighteenth century produces so many composers of the highest rank that the period immediately preceding it grows dim in comparison.

Bekker does not deny the extraordinary contribution of the theory of evolution, for he says: [12]

> It is clear enough that a causal connection exists between the different stages of development, that each stage is an organic consequence of the preceding stage; . . .

His chief objection is to the idea that "later developments appear necessarily *higher* in the sense of absolute improvement over what went before." [13]

An examination of Allen's *Philosophies of Music History* will reveal the multiplicity of views concerning the history of music that are more or less closely related to the genetic viewpoint, views that employ in one way or another such ideas as growth, development, or progress. These theories regard music as somewhat like an organism — subject to the principles of selection, generation, variation, survival of the fittest, progress, and the like, as these principles are expounded in the biological sciences.

But music is not a biological organism. It is a social phenomenon, and yet there are many things in music that seem to undergo changes comparable to those found in biology. Certain forms, such as the sonata form, seem to have an inception comparable to birth; a growth or development not unlike that of a plant or animal; and a period of decadence or disintegration like old age and death. The typical adherent of the evolutionary doctrine, however, does not think that music as a whole declines, but rather that, in the struggle

---

[11] Bekker, *op. cit.*, page 105.
[12] Bekker, *op. cit.*, page 21.
[13] *Ibid.*

for existence, the better and more perfect is always the victor; that everything living in the world follows the same law; that under the operation of this law, everything of a superior order has evolved from simple, almost imperceptible beginnings, with ever-increasing fullness and complexity; and that, in the future, still more beautiful, better, and more perfect manifestations will continue to evolve.[14]

THE CYCLIC METHOD

Embracing much of the genetic theory, but opposed especially to the idea of constant progress, are the exponents of the *cyclic method*. Many musical, as well as general, historians have made use of the life cycle of birth, growth, and decay in treating of particular long-term processes of history. Only a few, however, have employed the cyclic idea systematically and stressed it to such an extent that it became a fundamental principle governing the organization of the work.

In recent years there have been several notable attempts to interpret musical history directly or indirectly in these terms, according to one principle or another of determining the duration and nature of the cycle. Spengler's[15] cyclic theory is an organismic philosophy of history based upon the assumption of a strict and necessary organic succession in the processes of history. He divides the history of man into four analogous cycles of approximately 1000 years each; and music as one of the cultural elements is interpreted historically in terms of his basic theory.[16]

Lorenz[17] has proposed a cyclic theory of music history,

---

[14] See, for example, Oswald Koller, *op. cit.*, pages 49 f. For further examples, see Allen, *op. cit.*, pages 253 ff.

[15] Oswald Spengler, *The Decline of the West.*

[16] For a discussion of Spengler's views in relation to musical history, and an introduction to the literature pertaining to the Spengler controversy, see Arthur Mendel, "Spengler's Quarrel with the Methods of Music History," *The Musical Quarterly*, Vol. XX (1934), pages 131–171.

[17] Alfred Lorenz, *Abendländische Musikgeschichte im Rhythmus der Generationen.*

based upon what he calls the "rhythm of generations," and worked out in terms of periods of dominance of homophonic and polyphonic styles of musical composition. He believes that out of the struggle between the two conceptions of music has come a rhythmical series of periods of growth, now of homophonic music and again of polyphonic music. Lorenz divides the history of music from 410 A.D. to 1910 into five periods: Gregorian song, organum, minnesingers, polyphony, and the classics. Each period consists of approximately 300 years, each century having three generations.[18]

THE THEORY OF FLUCTUATION

Sorokin [19] proposes a philosophy of history which regards the processes of history as not strictly linear or cyclic, but rather what he calls variably or creatively recurrent. According to this theory, the recurrent process patterns may be neither linear nor cyclical but variable. The movement in one link of a process may be unilinear, while in other links it may be oscillating, cyclical, or curvilinear. As Sorokin interprets the variably recurrent conception,[20]

It contains within itself all the varieties of the unicist, cyclical, and linear theories; but it admits each only as one element, only as applying to some processes, to some aspects of historical or sociocultural movements, never to all of them.

Although Sorokin's application of his theory of variably recurrent patterns to the processes of musical history is not convincing in many respects, nevertheless there can be little doubt that his fundamental theory contains much truth.[21]

---

[18] For a brief account of Lorenz's theory, see Allen, *op. cit.*, pages 249 ff.

[19] Pitirim A. Sorokin, *Social and Cultural Dynamics*, Vol. I: *Fluctuation of Forms of Art* (Painting, Sculpture, Architecture, Music, Literature, and Criticism).

[20] *Op. cit.*, page 186.

[21] For further discussion see Glen Haydon, "Sorokin's Theory of Fluctuation of Forms of Music," *Papers Read by Members of the American Musicological Society at the Annual Meeting, Washington, D. C., December 29th and 30th, 1938*, pages 74–83. Printed privately by the Society, 1940.

HISTORICAL RELATIVISM

Various philosophies of history often have so much in common, and the differences among them are so slight, that it is very difficult to draw hard and fast lines of demarcation. A reaction against organismic theories of history has led certain historians in the direction of *historical relativism.* According to this view, any historian inevitably writes in terms of his own time and cultural setting; that is, he is influenced by a particular bias, by certain prejudices, likes and dislikes, and by other similar factors which constitute his "frame of reference." [22]   Maurice Mandelbaum has devoted the greater part of his book, *The Problem of Historical Knowledge: An Answer to Relativism,* to a discussion and criticism of historical relativism.   In simplest terms he holds this viewpoint as maintaining [23]

that no historical work grasps the nature of the past (or present) immediately, that whatever "truth" a historical work contains is relative to the conditioning processes under which it arose and can only be understood with reference to those processes.

One form of relativism tends to deny that historical events in themselves possess continuity and pattern; whatever structure is portrayed in an account of a historical development is a matter of construction or interpretation of actual processes on the part of the historian.   Mandelbaum reviews and criticizes the theories of Croce, Dilthey, and Mannheim as representatives of the relativistic position.   He counters the relativistic theory by pointing out in terms of the correspondence theory of truth [24] that there is a fallacy in maintaining that the

---

[22] See Charles A. Beard, "Written History as an Act of Faith," *American Historical Review,* Vol. XXXIX (1934), pages 219–231; especially pages 220 and 227.   See also Carl L. Becker, *Everyman His Own Historian: Essays on History and Politics,* pages 233–255.

[23] Mandelbaum, *op. cit.,* page 19.

[24] *Op. cit.,* pages 185 ff.

historian's account of an event or historical process is purely a matter of interpretation: the actual facts are "not different in nature from the sum and substance of the historical account itself." [25] They do seem to have a structure and order of their own.

RELEVANCE AND CAUSATION IN HISTORY

In his next two chapters, Mandelbaum contends that the ideas of *relevance* and *causation* are fundamentally applicable to the actual facts of history, and not merely a function of the mind's activity. Two facts are relevant when the one cannot be comprehended without an understanding of the other. "Thus, we cannot understand the fact that water freezes without taking into account the facts of temperature and pressure"; [26] but we may grasp the meaning of the French Revolution without considering Newton's first law of gravitation.

To deal with the relation of relevance to causality, it is necessary to consider the difference between a fact and an event. A fact is the occurrence of a particular event at a particular time; an event is the occurrence itself. Thus, a flash of lightning is an event; *that it occurred* is a fact. [27] The relevance between facts depends upon the causal connection between the events referred to by the facts. The animistic conception of causality, which may be roughly characterized as the notion that a previously existing object somehow produces a thing or a change in its state, is open to serious challenge.

The problem of causality may be more advantageously studied in terms of the relationship between events, an *event* being interpreted as meaning "anything that endures at all." [28]

---

[25] *Op. cit.*, page 200.
[26] *Op. cit.*, page 211.
[27] See Mandelbaum, *op. cit.*, page 212.
[28] Here Mandelbaum (*op. cit.*, page 222) is quoting from C. D. Broad,

But such an entity, possessing either continuity or change in its quality at different moments or stages in its history, has a certain unity — a "unity of pattern" — and a certain complexity, which may be expressed in terms of subevents. Complex events may be spoken of as "strands of history"; and the subevents then become "fibers" in these strands. In these terms, the relation between cause and effect is seen as a relationship in which all those events which are [29] " . . . sufficient and necessary conditions for the existence of a new event or for the existence of a new quality within an already enduring event," are regarded as the cause of any particular event. The relation between cause and effect, the relation between the set of events known as the "determining conditions" of an event, and the event itself, is called the relation of *existential dependence.*

This view of the problem of causality differs from the popular view in that it does not regard the cause and effect relation as a temporal sequence, but maintains that the events in question are contemporaneous although not necessarily coterminous. If the whole set of events constituting the cause of a given event terminated before the inception of the event constituting the effect, no relation of existential dependence could be found.

The function of science, at least in part, is to investigate causal relations in particular situations with a view to establishing scientific laws. The historical enterprise, however, aims not at discovering general laws but at concrete description.[30] Relevance between facts is connected with and depends upon the actual causal relation between the events to which they refer. Mandelbaum seeks the substantiation of this view as necessary to show that the ideal of historical

Scientific Thought, page 54. London: Kegan Paul, Trench, Trubner & Company, Ltd., 1923.
[29] Mandelbaum, *op. cit.,* page 223.
[30] See Mandelbaum, *op. cit.,* pages 236 ff.

objectivity is not an illusory one. It would far exceed the limits of the present work to attempt to trace the arguments for and against such a view.

A discussion of external and internal criticism leads to the conclusion that the former is merely an accessory technique in historical understanding, whereas the latter is an integral part of the historian's synthesis of the facts. The historian, according to Mandelbaum, does not merely select the important facts; he carefully follows where the material leads. Descriptive analysis aims at the discovery of existential dependence, of causal relations between events. In the many cases where this relation is not immediately clear, the historian may formulate a working hypothesis or historical principles which, because they cannot be tested like the laws of the experimental sciences, are much less satisfactory than the laws of the natural sciences. But the seeking out of general principles is the function of sociology and the other theoretical social sciences rather than history, although the two main fields are interdependent. The aim of giving an adequate causal description of any historical event does not entail the description of every detail of relevant subevents. What is to be included is determined by the level of abstraction of the historical subject matter selected for treatment.

HISTORICAL PLURALISM

If we accept the view that the relation of existential dependence may obtain between the events that constitute a certain strand of history, but that the subevents of a given event may not have that relationship, we are tending toward *historical pluralism*. This view, according to Mandelbaum,[31] maintains:

that the grand sweep of events which we call the historical process is made up of an indefinitely large number of components

---

[31] *Op. cit.*, page 274.

which do not form a completely interrelated set. According to this view, whether we take the historical process as a whole or segregate out any particular portion of that process, we shall always find that in themselves all of its components are not related to each other in any save a temporal manner.

The various monistic theories of history tend to regard all events as being somehow related in more than a merely temporal or spatial sense, and tend to regard them from "the single lofty point of view." Organismic theories of history try to embrace all the events of history in one grand process of evolution. But historical pluralism contends that the processes of history consist of many strands, between which there may or may not be pronounced causal connections. Although historical events may fall into epochs, these epochs do not necessarily coincide in various fields. This means that the epochs in political and art history may differ; that, in artistic fields, music, architecture, or painting may have independent epochs; and that, in the field of music, various events and sets of events may independently constitute their respective epochs. All this does not prevent an event in one field from entering as a subevent in another field. There are, for example, many interpenetrations of events in politics and music, in economics and music, in art and music, and in literature and music.

If we think of the goal of the historian as historical understanding, we may conclude that he attempts to reach this goal through descriptive analysis, or through showing the significance of events. With either aim he proceeds by attempting to discover the evidence for existential dependence between events. The success of such an attempt must be judged in relation to the nature of the concrete material with which the historian has to deal. Certain types of events may yield a very specific pattern of existential dependence, whereas others may defy any attempt to discover immediate connections with particular subevents. It is one thing, for example, to discover the events leading to the composition of a particular work for a special occasion; but it is quite another to find the relations of existential dependence between a particular composition and other works of the same genre. For the one purpose, the historian may deal with specific events, whereas, for the other, he may be forced to work in more general terms or at a higher level of abstraction. This by no means signifies that the latter procedure may produce less valid or meaningful results for the purposes of historical understanding.

The history of music may be regarded as consisting of many more or less independent strands of events, lying side by side. The various style-species, instruments, musicians, and geographical and cultural areas represent potential strands of events which may be investigated by the historian. In fact, each category outlined under the heading of systematic musicology represents a stratum of events which may be dealt with historically at different levels of generality. The situation is naturally very complex, for, within any category, each event and a larger or smaller number of its subevents may appear in the context of events of another category. For example, the perfection of an instrument such as the piano may be a factor in the history of acoustics, of psychology, of composition, of performance, or of keyboard music.

The pluralistic viewpoint does not lead to chaos; on the contrary, through seeking out and emphasizing the interpenetration of events, it tends to bring meaningful order out of the complexities of historical processes. In a sense, the temporal process is the basic fact of music, — for that matter, of the universe. The philosopher's question *When is a man?* may seem foolish at first thought. But if we consider whether man is the child, the youth, the adult, or the senescent, we may be forced to the conclusion that he is perhaps all of these, and that at any given time a man is a cross section of his biography.[32]

It is not possible, at the present stage of our knowledge, to state any comprehensive, precise, and ultimately valid philosophy of history. In fact, historical pluralism denies that such a philosophy is possible if the philosophy of history is taken to mean one all-embracing principle in terms of which the processes of history unfold. And yet, the pluralistic view itself constitutes, in a sense, a philosophy of history. It is defined, however, only in general terms. It regards the realities of music history as dynamic rather than static elements.

The idea that the nature of things is revealed only in their relations is not a new one. It dates back at least to the eighteenth century. In more recent times even the physical sciences have begun to "biologize" their concepts, so that material substances are regarded not so much as inert atoms but rather as events somehow expressible mathematically in time-space equations. But description and explanation are two different things; even a relatively adequate descriptive analysis of an event or of a historical process is not the explanation of it, although it may lay the foundation for an explanation. Furthermore, relatively complete descriptive analyses of events may lead, perhaps in terms of the doctrine of probability, to fairly reliable prognostication.

THE THEORY AND PRACTICE OF HISTORIOGRAPHY

The various philosophies of music, methods of musical history, and histories of music have, in spite of differences, much in common. Most histories of music follow the narrative method more or less closely; they usually exhibit, explicitly or implicitly, some pedagogical or pragmatic traits; they gen-

---

[32] See George Boas, *Our New Ways of Thinking*, pages 115–127. New York: Harper & Brothers, 1930.

erally make some use of the ideas of evolution, growth, development, or change — applying them variously to larger or
smaller areas of musical activity; they almost inevitably make
some reference to relativistic principles; and, to the extent
that these various viewpoints are intermixed, they tend
toward the pluralistic philosophy of history. The characterization of a particular history of music as one type or the
other must be made in terms of a judgment as to the dominant
features of the work.[33]

BIBLIOGRAPHY

Adler, Guido, *Methode der Musikgeschichte*. Leipzig: Breitkopf & Härtel, 1919.

Allen, Warren D., *Philosophies of Music History*. New York:
American Book Company, 1939.

Bauer, Wilhelm, *Einführung in das Studium der Geschichte*.
Second Edition. Tübingen: J. C. B. Mohr (Paul Siebeck),
1928.

Beard, Charles A., "Written History as an Act of Faith," *American Historical Review*, Vol. XXXIX (1934), pages 219–231.

Becker, Carl L., *Everyman His Own Historian: Essays on History
and Politics*. New York: F. S. Crofts & Co., 1935.

Bernheim, Ernst, *Lehrbuch der historischen Methode und der
Geschichtsphilosophie*. Third and Fourth Revised Edition.
Leipzig: Duncker and Humbolt, 1903.

Berr, Henri, and Lucien Febvre, "History," *Encyclopaedia of the
Social Sciences*, Vol. VII, pages 357–368.

Black, J. B., *The Art of History*. London: Methuen & Co., Ltd.,
1926.

Broad, C. D., *Scientific Thought*. London: Kegan Paul, Trench,
Trubner & Co., 1923.

Bücken, Ernst, "Grundfragen der Musikgeschichte als Geisteswissenschaft," *Jahrbuch der Musikbibliothek Peters*, Vol.
XXXIV (1927), pages 19–30.

Croce, Benedetto, *Theory and History of Historiography*. (Tr.
by Douglas Ainslie.) London: George G. Harrap & Co.,
Ltd., 1921.

---

[33] For a detailed study of various philosophies of music, particularly as
these are exemplified in the music histories of the past, and a historical account of the histories of music history, see Warren D. Allen, *Philosophies of
Music History*.

Friedel, Egon, *A Cultural History of the Modern Age.* 3 vols. (Tr. by C. F. Atkinson.) New York: Alfred A. Knopf, Inc., 1930–1933.

Koller, Oswald, "Die Musik im Lichte der Darwinschen Theorie," *Jahrbuch der Musikbibliothek Peters,* Vol. VII (1900), pages 35–50.

Lorenz, Alfred, *Abendländische Musikgeschichte im Rhythmus der Generationen.* Second Edition. Berlin: Max Hesse, 1928.

Mandelbaum, Maurice, *The Problem of Historical Knowledge: An Answer to Relativism.* New York: Liveright Publishing Corporation, 1938.

Mendel, Arthur, "Spengler's Quarrel with the Methods of Music History," *The Musical Quarterly,* Vol. XX (1934), pages 131–171.

Sorokin, Pitirim A., *Social and Cultural Dynamics,* Vol. I: *Fluctuation of Forms of Art* (Painting, Sculpture, Architecture, Music, Literature, and Criticism). New York: American Book Company, 1937.

Spengler, Oswald, *The Decline of the West.* New York: Alfred A. Knopf, Inc., 1926 (one-volume edition, 1932; special edition, 1939); translated by Charles F. Atkinson from the original German *Der Untergang des Abendlandes.* 2 vols. Munich: C. H. Beck'sche Verlagsbuchhandlung, 1918, 1922.

Teggart, Frederick J., *The Processes of History.* New Haven: Yale University Press, 1918.

————, *Prolegomena to History.* Berkeley: University of California Press, 1916.

————, *Theory of History.* New Haven: Yale University Press, 1925.

CHAPTER IX

THE SOURCES OF MUSICAL HISTORY

IN GENERAL HISTORICAL RESEARCH TWO MAIN TYPES OF source material are distinguished: *material remains* and *written records*. Both types are found in the history of music, but here the written record is more important, especially if the monuments of music, music in notation, are classed as written records.

Musical instruments constitute the most important class of material remains. Other items include pictures and reliefs, as well as buildings used for musical purposes — temples, concert halls, and opera houses.

The written records include a wide variety of materials such as musical monuments (all music preserved in notation); historical writings of all kinds; general literature; public documents containing vital statistics and other records; private documents, such as letters, diaries, household accounts, and estate records; and newspapers, magazines, and programs. The sources already mentioned are, of course, sometimes supplemented by oral tradition, as in the field of folk music and the Gregorian church music.

Although the sources of information concerning the history of music differ greatly in various periods, musical compositions preserved in some decipherable notation constitute the most important materials for the music of the last thousand years. As we go further back in history, musical monuments

grow less and less common, until we find that we have available only a few fragments of actual music, dating from the time of the ancient Greeks. And even these have not been transcribed into modern notation with complete success, so that we are still unable to know with certainty what the early Greek music may have sounded like. One does not need to go very far into the sources of our knowledge of musical history to realize the importance of the study of musical notation in its historical development.

Historical writings of all sorts constitute important sources for the history of music. Not only do general historical works from the beginnings of literary history contain significant references to music, but from the beginning of the Christian era there is also a special literature of considerable importance for the history of music in such works as Plutarch's *De Musica*.

Most musical writings up to the sixteenth century are devoted to theoretical and practical problems, but since Glareanus in the sixteenth century we find an increasing number of works devoted to historical questions in music. Calvisius' *De Initio et progressu musices* (1600) — the last part of the book *Exercitationes musicae duae* — is regarded as the first chronological history of music.[1] The first part of Michael Praetorius' *Syntagma musicum* (1615) is a historical treatise in Latin, and some of the writings of Athanasius Kircher (1650), Wolfgang Caspar Printz (1690), and Giovanni Andrea Bontempi (1695) are historical, although intermixed with imaginary and legendary material.

More scientific historical writings in music date from the eighteenth century, with the works of Bourdelot-Bonnet

---

[1] Allen, *Philosophies of Music History*, page 8. For further details concerning this and other histories of music, the student should consult the same reference. A briefer statement by the same author is given in the article "Histories of Music" in *The International Cyclopedia of Music and Musicians*.

(1715), F. W. Marpurg (1754–1778), Martini (1757–1781), John Brown (1763), Eximeno (1774), Burney (1776–1789), Hawkins (1776), de la Borde (1780), and Forkel (1788–1801).

The outstanding histories of the nineteenth century are those of Ambros (1862–1878) and Fétis (1869–1876). Later works need not be mentioned here. For the most part, the histories referred to do not go beyond the music of the sixteenth century. The chief historical works for the later periods are the more specialized studies that have appeared in increasing numbers since the middle of the nineteenth century.

In addition to general historical writings and special works on the history of music, all kinds of literature, such as novels, plays, poems, and essays afford source material for the history of music through depicting the life and thought of past epochs in relation to music. Public documents are important because they afford reliable evidence concerning events. Private documents give an insight into the lives and thoughts of individuals. Newspapers and other periodical literature yield material significant for many historical problems. For the early stages of music history, before the development of reliable systems of musical notation, the large number of theoretical writings probably constitutes the chief source of information. This is true particularly of Greek music and, to a large extent, of music throughout the Middle Ages. In later periods, as examples of music in notation become more plentiful, and the notation itself becomes more reliable and decipherable, theoretical works continue to provide important auxiliary material.

Basic work with the sources of musical history entails the application of highly specialized techniques, and requires the assistance of a number of auxiliary sciences. The discovery and use of sources — known in the field of historical methodology as *heuristic* — is, of course, of prime importance in historical research.

Archaeology — the study of the art, architecture, customs, and beliefs of ancient peoples as shown in their monuments, implements, inscriptions, and relics, or the study of the material remains of the historic peoples of antiquity — is the auxiliary science most helpful in studying the history of the music of antiquity from material remains. Among the other auxiliary sciences may be listed *palaeography, diplomatics, epigraphy, philology, bibliography,* and *chronology.* Each of these sciences has its own peculiar problems and techniques. We have already suggested the importance of the historical study of musical notation, which may be called *musical palaeography* or *semeiography.*

After musical manuscripts and documents of historical significance have been discovered and collected in the archives and libraries throughout the world, much work remains to be done before the material is readily available to scholars. Knowledge of the existence and location of manuscripts and publications is disseminated through such mediums as Eitner's *Quellen-Lexikon,* and many manuscripts and early publications need to be edited or re-edited and made available to scholars in general. The various series known as *Monuments of Music (Denkmäler der Tonkunst),* the sets of the complete works of composers, the publications of the English Plainsong and Mediaeval Music Society, and the *Paléographie musicale* of the monks of Solesmes are examples of this sort of work. Other examples are the publications of early theoretical writings such as those edited by Meibom, Gerbert, Coussemaker, and Jan.

The following lists of source materials for study and research in musical history are illustrative of the principal types of bibliographical items; they, of course, lay no claims to completeness.

THE MUSIC OF ANTIQUITY

The sources of information concerning the early history of music are comparatively meager, and yet it is little short of amazing how much historians have been able to piece together concerning the music of antiquity. From a single bas-relief of the Egyptian museum in Cairo, dating from about the beginning of the third millennium B.C., Curt Sachs [2] is able to reconstruct an imaginative but remarkably convincing account of the state of music in the Old Kingdom of Egypt. The relief shows a flutist, a harpist, several singers, and another instrumentalist whom Sachs calls a clarinetist. From such a representation, and from what Egyptologists are able to tell of the general culture of the Old Kingdom, the historian of music can make many reliable deductions.

Martini, writing in the middle of the eighteenth century, depended almost entirely upon Greek and Latin writers for his account of Egyptian music.

In addition to the Bible, Burney refers to Diogenes Laërtius (of about the third century A.D.), Plato (427–347 B.C.), Diodorus Siculus (first century B.C.), Strabo (first century B.C.), Herodotus (c. 484–425 B.C.), Proclus (410–485 A.D.), and others among the early Greek and Latin writers. For his chronology, Burney depends, at least in part, upon Sir Isaac Newton, and indicates in his preface that he is familiar with the works of Bontempi, Martini, Bonnet, de Blainville, Printz, Marpurg, Kircher, and Rousseau. Apparently the only piece of Egyptian sculpture with a representation of a musical instrument on it which Burney examined personally was an obelisk in Rome. He also refers to the accounts of various eighteenth-century Egyptian travelers, but his chief contemporary source of information is a long letter from James Bruce with drawings of two instruments. Burney quotes this

---

[2] *Musik des Altertums,* pages 7 ff. Hermann Ranke gives the date of the relief as about 2650 B.C. (*The Art of Ancient Egypt,* reproduction no. 201.)

letter in full and gives a reproduction of one of the harps. Such are the source materials of Burney's chapter on "The History of Egyptian Music."

By 1861 Ambros writes that — before the French Egyptian expedition of 1798 — excepting a few reports by travelers, the chief sources of information concerning the music of Egypt were the writings of Herodotus, Diodorus, Strabo, and others. He gives special credit to Burney for his discussion of the obelisk in Rome, and mentions the letter of James Bruce, but he stresses the importance of subsequent scientific investigations as affording the most significant insight into the life of ancient Egypt. Of these researches, Ambros makes use, chiefly, of the monumental publications of Rosellini [3] and Lepsius.[4] He further refers to the works of Brugsch, Wilkinson, Röth, Uhlemann, and Duncker — Egyptologists, historians, and philosophers. Ambros likewise makes extensive use of the Greek and Latin writers; apparently, he was thoroughly familiar with the writings of the earlier historians of music. Thus, Ambros includes much of the largely legendary material concerning Egyptian music contained in Burney and others, but he supplements his account with extensive discussions of the source materials found in the publications of Egyptologists.

Engel's chapter on the music of the ancient Egyptians [5] is based upon the same types of sources as the works previously mentioned, and, in addition, upon the study of certain instruments in the British Museum. Engel concludes his discussion with a review of "opinions of some musical historians" in which

---

[3] Ippolito Rosellini (1800–1843), Italian Egyptologist, associate of J. F. Champollion, who edited the *Monumenti dell' Egitto e della Nubia*. Florence: 1832–1840, 10 vol. *fol.* For further details, see article in the *Encyclopaedia Britannica*.

[4] Karl Richard Lepsius (1810–1884), German Egyptologist, who published the *Denkmäler aus Aegypten und Aethiopien*, 12 volumes, completed in 1859.

[5] Carl Engel, *The Music of the Most Ancient Nations*, pages 180–276.

he recommends as the best sources the works of Rosellini, Champollion, and Lepsius. Incidentally, Engel emphasizes the importance of "examining the music of contemporary nations in different stages of civilisation" in order to gain a "clear idea of the gradual development of the art of music . . ."[6]

F.-J. Fétis, in his *Histoire générale de la musique*,[7] bases his discussion of Egyptian music upon essentially the same sources, or, at least, upon the same types of sources as Engel. He is, however, somewhat more daring than most of the other writers in his deductions concerning the tonal system and a possible musical notation.[8] Fétis' account of his attempts to reconstruct the scale of an Egyptian flute preserved in the museum of Florence makes interesting reading, and, even if his findings cannot be regarded as entirely satisfactory, at least his work suggests a possible approach to one aspect of Egyptian music.[9] Further investigations in this field, carried on by Victor Loret, are reported in Lavignac, *Encyclopédie de la musique et dictionnaire du conservatoire*.[10]

In spite of the very considerable body of source material pertaining to Egyptian music, the absence of any examples of the actual music itself makes a complete account of its history impossible. Historians of music can only speculate on the characteristics of the music from the available data concerning the musical instruments and their apparent use. Some attempts have been made to suggest, by the citation of modern Egyptian music,[11] what the music may have sounded like — but these must be regarded as inconclusive.

---

[6] *Op. cit.*, pages 8 ff.
[7] Vol. I, pages 187–315.
[8] For a summary and criticism of Fétis' theory of the Egyptian origin of a system of notation, see Engel, *op. cit.*, pages 271 ff. (Fétis published his views in 1837 in his *Biographie universelle*.)
[9] See *Histoire générale de la musique*, pages 222–249.
[10] Part I, Vol. I, pages 17–22.
[11] See, for example, Engel, *op. cit.*, pages 256 ff.

Material remains, consisting of a few pictorial representations and inscriptions — with occasional references to music, musical instruments, and musicians — constitute the chief sources of our knowledge of the music of the ancient Babylonian-Assyrian civilizations. Jastrow's account of the excavations in the nineteenth century which made these materials available to modern scholars makes fascinating reading for the student of historical sources.[12]

Perhaps the oldest representation of musical instruments is that depicted on an inlaid vase found by E. J. Banks at Bismya in southern Babylonia. Two instruments of the harp or lyre type are shown, one with five strings and the other with seven. The instruments are evidence of the musical culture of the ancient Sumerian civilization, and are thought to date from the fourth millennium B.C.[13]

The excavations of Ernest de Sarzec — begun in 1877 and carried on for more than twenty years at the site of Lagash — uncovered, among other things, a bas-relief in limestone, representing a musician playing a harp of eleven strings.[14]

For examples of how the historian treats such materials, the student should read the discussions of this relief by Virolleaud and Pélagaud;[15] and that by Sachs.[16] Sachs refers to a single example of musical notation for which he proposes a possible solution.[17] Further information about other ar-

---

[12] Morris Jastrow, Jr., *The Civilization of Babylonia and Assyria*, pages 1–62. Philadelphia: J. B. Lippincott Company, 1915. The chapter on "The Decipherment of Cuneiform Scripts" is also interesting and instructive.

[13] See Curt Sachs, *Die Musik der Antike*, page 3; Sachs, *Musik des Altertums*, page 36; and Jastrow, *op. cit.*, plate XVI, fig. 3.

[14] See Jastrow, *op. cit.*, page 44 and plate XLV, fig. 2.

[15] "La musique Assyro-Babylonienne," *Encyclopédie de la musique et dictionnaire du conservatoire*, Part I, Vol. I, page 36.

[16] *Musik des Altertums*, page 38.

[17] *Op. cit.*, pages 40 f. See also Curt Sachs, "Ein babylonischer Hymnus," *Archiv für Musikwissenschaft*, Vol. VII (1925), pages 1–22; Curt Sachs, "The Mystery of the Babylonian Notation," *The Musical Quarterly*, Vol. XXVII (1941), pages 62–69; and Francis W. Galpin, *The Music of the Sumerians, and Their Immediate Successors, the Babylonians, and Assyrians*, pages 42–50.

chaeological discoveries pertaining to the music of this early period (*c.* 3000 B.C.) can be found in the various works of Virolleaud and Pélagaud,[18] and Sachs,[19] which were mentioned.

The sources for the subsequent history of music in the countries already mentioned, in Syria, and in Asia Minor are similar to those previously discussed. The material remains, Biblical writings, and the writings of early Greek authors leave many unsolved problems, but at the same time they constitute a very considerable body of evidence in the history of music.

The following is a representative list of modern writings on the music of antiquity. The histories of music listed in the general bibliography at the end of the book should also be consulted.

Cahen, Abraham, "Hébreux," *Encyclopédie de la musique et dictionnaire du conservatoire*, Part I, Vol. I, pages 67–76. (1910)

Engel, Carl, *The Music of the Most Ancient Nations*. Facsimile of the 1864 edition, with added illustrations. London: William Reeves, Bookseller, Ltd., 1929.

Galpin, Francis W., *The Music of the Sumerians and Their Immediate Successors, the Babylonians, and Assyrians*. Cambridge: The University Press, 1937.

Idelsohn, A. Z., *Jewish Music in Its Historical Development*. New York: Henry Holt & Company, Inc., 1929.

Loret, Victor, "Égypte," *Encyclopédie de la musique et dictionnaire du conservatoire*, Part I, Vol. I, pages 1–34. (1910)

Pélagaud, Fernand, "Syriens et Phrygiens," *Encyclopédie de la musique et dictionnaire du conservatoire*, Part I, Vol. I, pages 49–66. (1910)

Pulver, Jeffrey, "The Music of Ancient Egypt," *Proceedings of the Musical Association*, Vol. XLVIII (1921–1922), pages 29–55.

Ranke, Hermann, *The Art of Ancient Egypt*. New York: Oxford University Press, 1936.

---

[18] *Op. cit.*, pages 37 f.
[19] *Musik des Altertums*, pages 38–41, and *Die Musik der Antike*, pages 2 f.

Sachs, Curt, *Geist und Werden der Musikinstrumente.* Berlin: Dietrich Reimer, 1929.

————, *Musik des Altertums.* Breslau: Ferdinand Hirt, 1924.

————, *Die Musik der Antike.* Wildpark-Potsdam: Akademische Verlagsgesellschaft Athenaion, m.b.H., 1928.

————, *Die Musikinstrumente des alten Agyptens.* Berlin: Karl Curtius, 1921.

Saminsky, Lazare, *Music of the Ghetto and the Bible.* New York: Block Publishing Company, Inc., 1934.

Smith, Hermann, *The World's Earliest Music.* London: William Reeves, Bookseller, Ltd., n.d.

Stainer, John, *The Music of the Bible.* New Edition. New York: H. W. Gray Company, Inc., 1914. (First Edition, 1879)

Virolleaud, Ch., and Fernand Pélagaud, "Assyrie-Chaldée," *Encyclopédie de la musique et dictionnaire du conservatoire.* Part I, Vol. I, pages 35–48. (1910)

THE MUSIC OF ANCIENT GREECE

The sources for the history of music in ancient Greece are much more abundant than for earlier civilizations, and yet, examples of the actual music in notation are very few. Furthermore, the transcription into modern notation of such musical monuments as remain has not been entirely successful. Archaeological investigations have found few musical instruments from ancient Greece, but numerous pictorial representations of them in objects of decorative art. Historical, philosophical, theoretical, and general literary works of all kinds have come down to us in considerable quantities, and each year adds new materials to those already available. Much of this material has been transmitted by very indirect and undependable means, so that innumerable problems have arisen in its interpretation. Only by the most meticulous and patient study and comparison of the various sources has it been possible to work out a fairly comprehensive account of music in the culture of ancient Greece.

Of the extant examples of Greek music, three, attributed

to Mesomedes, were first edited by Vincenzo Galilei in 1581 with Greek musical notation. The problems involved in transcribing and interpreting these hymns of the second century A.D. have occupied the attention of such scholars as Burette, Fr. Bellermann, Westphal, Gevaert, Jan, Reinach, Riemann, and, more recently, Schlesinger and Gombosi.[20] The next publication of a fragment of Greek music is that of the first Pythian Ode of Pindar, in 1650, by Kircher.[21] If this is genuinely the melody of Pindar, it [22] is the oldest example of Greek music, for it is supposed to date from the fifth century B.C.

After the publication — in 1841 by Bellermann — of three short fragments, the next discoveries are the Seikilos inscription, published by W. M. Ramsay in 1883; a fragment of a chorus from Euripides' *Orestes*, published by Carl Wessely in 1892; and two Delphic hymns to Apollo, published by Weil and Reinach in 1893–1894. The subsequent discoveries include several fragments from Contrapollinopolis, found in a Berlin papyrus by Schubart and published in 1918; an early Christian hymn found at Oxyrhynchus, Egypt, and published in 1922 by Arthur S. Hunt and Stuart Jones; and a slight fragment of Greek music, published by Mountford in 1931. The examples cover a period of history extending from the fourth or fifth century B.C. to the third century A.D.

*   *   *

---

[20] For a survey of some of the earlier studies, see Rudolf Westphal, *Die Musik des griechischen Alterthumes*, page 325. Samples of the trend of more recent discussions may be found in Kathleen Schlesinger's *The Greek Aulos*, pages 360 ff.; and Otto J. Gombosi's *Tonarten und Stimmungen der antiken Musik*, pages 131 ff.

[21] Athanasius Kircher, *Musurgia universalis*, Vol. I, pages 541 f. Rome: Corbelletti, 1650.

[22] For a bibliography concerning the controversy over the genuineness of the melody, see Otto Gombosi, "The Melody of Pindar's 'Golden Lyre,'" *The Musical Quarterly*, Vol. XXVI (1940), page 381. Gombosi defends the thesis that the work is a forgery; but compare Schlesinger, *op. cit.*, pages 354 ff.

The following is a summary of data on extant pieces of Greek music.[23]

The First Pythian Ode of Pindar

Fifth century B.C.; original source lost; authenticity doubtful. Given by Athanasius Kircher, *Musurgia universalis*, Vol. I, pages 541 f. (Rome: Corbelletti, 1650); reproduction of page from Kircher, *op. cit.*, given by Gombosi, *The Musical Quarterly*, Vol. XXVI (1940), facing page 382. Transcriptions: Schlesinger, *op. cit.*, page 359; Sachs, *op. cit.*, page 12; Riemann, *Geschichte der Musik*, Vol. I, Part I, page 135; Gevaert, *La Musique de l'antiquité*, Vol. I, page 450; and Ambros, *Geschichte der Musik* (Second Edition, 1880), Vol. I, pages 448 f.

Fragment of Chorus from "Orestes" of Euripides

408 B.C. (Reinach, *op. cit.*, page 175); source — found among the Rainer papyri. First edition: Carl Wessely, *Mitteilungen aus der Sammlung der Papyrus Erzherzog Rainer*, Vol. V, Vienna, 1892 (Reinach, *ibid.*). Transcriptions: Otto Crusius, *Philologus*, Vol. LII (1893), pages 174–200 (facsimile); Sachs, *op. cit.*, pages 17 f. (photographic facsimile); Mountford, *op. cit.*, pages 148 and 169; Reinach, *op. cit.*, pages 175 f.; and Jan, *Musici scriptores graeci, supplementum*, pages 4–7. Further reference: Wessely and Ruelle, *Revue des études grecques*, Vol. V (1892), pages 265–280.

The Cairo Musical Fragment

Circa 250 B.C.; source — a scrap of papyrus in the Cairo Museum. Published by J. F. Mountford, *Journal of Hellenic Studies*, Vol. LI (1931), pages 91–100 and Plate V (transcription and photographic facsimile). Transcriptions: Mountford, "Greek Music: The Cairo Musical Fragment," pages 260 f.; Gombosi, *op. cit.*, pages 127 f.; and C. Del Grande, *Aegyptus, Serie scientifica*, Vol. V (1936), pages 369–382.

The Two Delphic Hymns to Apollo

Second century B.C.; source — marble slabs discovered in the ruins at Delphi. First published: H. Weil and Théodore Reinach,

---

[23] *Cf.* Th. Reinach, *La Musique grecque*, pages 175–208; J. F. Mountford, "Greek Music in the Papyri and Inscriptions"; Gustave Reese, *Music in the Middle Ages*, pages 48 f.; Otto Gombosi, *Tonarten und Stimmungen der antiken Musik*, pages 123–135; R. P. Winnington-Ingram, *Mode in Ancient Greek Music*, pages 30–47; Curt Sachs, *Die Musik der Antike*, pages 12–20; and Kathleen Schlesinger, *The Greek Aulos*, pages 351–370.

Bulletin de correspondance hellénique, Vol. XVII (1893), pages
569–610, with Plates XXI and XXIbis; and Vol. XVIII (1894),
pages 345–389, with Plates XII–XIIbis, XIX–XXIII, and XXV–
XXVII. Transcriptions: Jan, *op. cit.*, pages 8–34; Reinach, *op.
cit.*, pages 177–192; Phillips Barry, *The Musical Quarterly*, Vol.
V (1919), pages 592–597. Further references: Gombosi, *op. cit.*,
pages 122–131; Schlesinger, *op. cit.*, pages 366–370; and Mountford, "Greek Music in the Papyri and Inscriptions," pages 149 f.

The Epitaph of Seikilos

First century A.D.; source – inscription on tombstone found in
Asia Minor. First published by W. M. Ramsay, *Bulletin de correspondance hellénique*, Vol. VII (1883), pages 277–278; musical
notation discovered by Wessely. Photograph of the stone published by Laumonier, *Bulletin de correspondance hellénique*, Vol.
XLVIII (1924), page 507; photographic facsimile, Sachs, *op. cit.*,
page 19. Transcriptions: Sachs, *op. cit.*, page 18; Mountford,
op. cit., page 170; Jan, *op. cit.*, pages 35–39; Reinach, *op. cit.*, page
193. Further references: Philipp Spitta, *Vierteljahrsschrift für
Musikwissenschaft*, Vol. X (1894), pages 103–110; and Mountford, *op. cit.*, pages 147 f.

Four Fragments from Contrapollinopolis, Egypt

Circa 160 A.D.; source – Egyptian papyrus in Berlin museum.
Edited with a photographic facsimile by W. Schubart, *Sitzungs-
berichte der königlich preussischen Akademie der Wissenschaften*
(1918), pages 763–768. Transcriptions: Mountford, *op. cit.*,
pages 173–176; and Reinach, *op. cit.*, pages 202–206. Further
references: A. Thierfelder, *Zeitschrift für Musikwissenschaft*,
Vol. I (1918–1919), pages 217–225; E. Romagnoli, *Rivista
musicale italiana*, Vol. XXVII (1920), pages 274–313.

Three Hymns Attributed to Mesomedes

Second century A.D.; source – preserved in Byzantine manuscripts (see Westphal, *Die Musik des griechischen Alterthumes*,
page 325; and Reinach, *op. cit.*, pages 194 and 196). First edited
by Galilei, *Dialogo della musica antica e della moderna*, Florence,
1581 (music not transcribed). Transcriptions: Jan, *op. cit.*, pages
40–59; Reinach, *op. cit.*, pages 194–201; Sachs, *op. cit.*, pages 13,
16, and 18; Gevaert, *Histoire et théorie de la musique de l'antiquité*, pages 445–449. Further references: Mountford, *op. cit.*,
page 146; and Reinach, *Revue des études grecques*, Vol. IX (1896),
pages 1–22 (facsimile of "Hymn to the Muse").

The Oxyrhynchus Hymn

Third century A.D.; source — papyrus found at Oxyrhynchus, Egypt. Published by Arthur S. Hunt and A. Stuart Jones, *Oxyrhynchus Papyri*, Vol. XV (1922), No. 1786, pages 21–25 and Plate I (transcription and photographic facsimile). Transcriptions: Reinach, *op. cit.*, pages 207 f.; Mountford, *op. cit.*, page 177. Further references: Reinach, *La Revue musicale*, Vol. III (1922), pages 8–25; Mountford, *op. cit.*, page 152.

GREEK AND LATIN WRITINGS ON MUSIC [24]

Pythagoras, sixth century B.C., apparently left no writings concerning music; what is known of his teachings has been transmitted through the writings of later authors. Plato's writings contain numerous references to music, but he can scarcely be regarded as a musical theorist.[25] Archytas of Tarentum, philosopher and mathematician, a contemporary of Plato, is known chiefly through quotations in later writers. Aristotle's references to music are collected in Jan's *Scriptores*.[26] Probably the most important of the early Greek writers on the theory of music is Aristoxenus of Tarentum (born *c.* 354 B.C.) whose chief extant work has been translated by Macran.[27]

After Euclid (third century B.C.), to whom is attributed the *Sectio canonis*, the next important group of writers dates from the second century A.D. Among these authors may be mentioned Plutarch, Aristides Quintilianus, Kleonides, Pausanias, Theon of Smyrna, Nicomachus of Gerasa, Claudius

---

[24] The following discussion and bibliography are based chiefly upon Riemann, *Handbuch der Musikgeschichte*, Vol. I, Part I, pages 10–28; Riemann, *Grundriss der Musikwissenschaft*, pages 123–124. See also Reese, *Music in the Middle Ages*, pages 17–19; and Abert, "Antike," in Adler, *Handbuch der Musikgeschichte*, pages 35–38.

[25] The more important discussions of Plato's references to music are listed in *The International Cyclopedia of Music and Musicians*, page 1421.

[26] Pages 1–35. For a list of subsequent studies of Aristotle's writings, see Riemann, *Handbuch der Musikgeschichte*, Vol. I, Part I, page 12.

[27] Henry S. Macran, *The Harmonics of Aristoxenus*.

Ptolemy, and Gaudentius. Alypius (fourth century A.D.) is noted for giving a complete table of Greek scales in both instrumental and vocal notation. Boethius (*c.* 475–524) wrote a Latin treatise on music in five books which, with the writings of Cassiodorus (*c.* 485–*c.* 580), constituted the chief source of the knowledge of Greek music for the Middle Ages. Pachymeres (1242–*c.* 1310) and Bryennius (*c.* 1320) are important, not only on account of their close relation to earlier writers (especially Ptolemy), but also because of the information they afford concerning the period of transition into the Middle Ages.[28]

The following is a chronological list of the more important Greek and Latin writings on music.

Aristoxenus of Tarentum (b. *c.* 354 B.C.), *The Harmonics.* Edited by Henry S. Macran. Oxford: The Clarendon Press, 1902.

Euclid (*c.* 300 B.C.), *Sectio canonis.* In Jan, *Musici scriptores graeci,* pages 115–166. Tr. by Charles Davy, *Letters . . . ,* pages 269–289. 1787.

Plutarch (50–120 A.D.), *De Musica.* Edited by W. F. Volkmann (Leipzig, 1856), Rudolph Westphal (Breslau, 1865), and Weil and Reinach (Paris, 1900). Tr. by J. H. Bromby, 1882.

Aristides Quintilianus (first–second century A.D.), *De Musica.* Three books on music, edited by Albert Jahn, Leipzig, 1882. For other references see *Hugo Riemanns Musik-Lexikon.* German tr. by Rudolph Schäfke, 1937.

Kleonides (*c.* second century A.D.), *Introductio harmonica.* In Jan, *op. cit.,* pages 179–207.

Pausanias (second century A.D.), *Graeciae descriptio accurata.* German tr. by Schubart. Stuttgart, 1859.

Theon of Smyrna (second century A.D.), *Expositio rerum mathematicarum ad legendum Platonem utilium.* Edited by Ed. Hiller. Leipzig: Teubner, 1878.

Nicomachus of Gerasa (second century A.D.), *Enchiridion* and excerpts from his other writings. In Jan, *op. cit.,* pages 237–282.

---

[28] See Otto Gombosi, "Studien zur Tonartenlehre des frühen Mittelalters II," *Acta musicologica,* Vol. XI (1939), page 29.

Ptolemy (second century A.D.), *Claudii Ptolemaei harmonicorum libri tres.* Edited by John Wallis. Oxford, 1682. (See Forkel, *Allgemeine Litteratur der Musik,* pages 52–53, for table of contents.)

Gaudentius (second century A.D.), *Harmonica introductio.* In Jan, *op. cit.,* pages 327–355.

Porphyry (third century A.D.), *Commentary* on the *Harmonics* of Ptolemy. Edited by John Wallis. Oxford, 1682.

Alypius (fourth century A.D.), *Isagoge Mousike.* In Jan, *op. cit.,* pages 367–406.

Boethius (*c.* 480–524), *De Institutione musica.* Edited by G. Friedlein. Leipzig: Teubner, 1867. German tr. by O. Paul. Leipzig, 1872.

Cassiodorus (*c.* 485–*c.* 580), *De Musica.* In Gerbert, *Scriptores ecclesiastici de musica,* Vol. I, pages 15–19, and R. A. B. Mynors (Editor), *Cassiodori senatoris institutiones,* pages 142–150 (Oxford: The Clarendon Press, 1937).

Pachymeres (1242–*c.*1310), *Quadrivium mathematicum.* Introduction and second part edited by A. J. H. Vincent in *Notices et extraits de la bibliothèque du roi,* Vol. XVI, Part 2. Paris, 1847.

Bryennius (*c.* 1320), *Harmonica.* Edited by John Wallis, in *Opera mathematica,* Vol. III. Oxford, 1699.

Modern Writings on Greek Music

The following list of works on Greek music has been chosen with a view of orienting the student in the wide range of publications on the subject; it makes no claims of completeness. Supplementary material will, of course, be found in the general histories of music and other standard reference works.

Abert, Hermann, "Antike." Revised by Curt Sachs. In Guido Adler, *Handbuch der Musikgeschichte,* pages 35–67.

————, "Der gegenwärtige Stand der Forschung über die antike Musik," *Jahrbuch der Musikbibliothek Peters,* Vol. XXVIII, Part II (1921), pages 21–40.

————, *Die Lehre vom Ethos in der griechischen Musik.* Leipzig: Breitkopf & Härtel, 1899.

————, "Ein neu entdeckter frühchristlicher Hymnus mit antiken Musiknoten," *Zeitschrift für Musikwissenschaft,* Vol. IV (1921–1922), pages 524–529.

————, "Der neue griechische Papyrus mit Musiknoten," *Archiv für Musikwissenschaft*, Vol. I (1919), pages 313–328.

————, "Zu Cassiodor," *Sammelbände der internationalen Musikgesellschaft*, Vol. III (1901–1902), pages 439–453.

Bellermann, Friederich, *Die Hymnen des Dionysios und Mesomedes*. Berlin: Förstner, 1840.

————, *Die Tonleitern und Musiknoten der Griechen*. Berlin: Förstner, 1847.

Coussemaker, E. de, *Scriptorum de musica medii aevi*. 4 vols. Paris: A. Durand, 1864–1876. Facsimile reprint, Milan: Bollettino bibliografico musicale, 1931.

Curtis, J., "Greek Music," *Journal of Hellenic Studies*, Vol. XXXIII (1913), pages 35–47.

Emmanuel, Maurice, "Grèce," *Encyclopédie de la musique et dictionnaire du conservatoire*, Part I, Vol. I, pages 377–537. (1911)

Gerbert, Martin [Martino Gerberto], *Scriptores ecclesiastici de musica sacra potissimum*. 3 vols. Typis San-Blasianis, 1784. Facsimile reprint, Milan: Bollettino bibliografico musicale, 1931.

Gevaert, F. A., *Histoire et théorie de la musique de l'antiquité*. 2 vols. Gand: C. Annoot-Braeckman, 1875, 1881.

————, and J. C. Vollgraff, *Les Problèmes musicaux d'Aristote*. 3 vols. Gand: Hoste, 1903.

Gombosi, Otto, "The Melody of Pindar's 'Golden Lyre,'" *The Musical Quarterly*, Vol. XXVI (1940), pages 381–392.

————, *Tonarten und Stimmungen der antiken Musik*. Kopenhagen: Ejnar Munksgaard, 1939.

Greif, Francisque, "Étude sur la musique antique," *Revue des études grecques*, Vols. XXII–XXIV (1909–1911) and XXVI (1913), pages 89–139, 1–48, 233–286, 273–346.

Guillemin, M., and J. Duchesne, "Sur l'origine asiatique de la cithare grecque," *L'Antiquité classique*, Vol. IV (1935), pages 117–124.

Hornbostel, Erich M. von, "Tonart und Ethos," *Festschrift für Johannes Wolf*, pages 73–78.

Jan, Karl von [Janus Carolus], *Musici scriptores graeci*. Leipzig: Teubner, 1895; *Supplementum: Melodiarum reliquiae*, 1899.

————, "Bericht über griechische Musik und Musiker von 1884–99," *Bursian's Jahresbericht*, Vol. CIV (1900), pages 1–75.

Laloy, Louis, *Aristoxène de Tarente et la musique de l'antiquité*. Paris: Société française d'imprimerie et de librairie, 1904.

Lehman, Günther, *Theorie und Geschichte der griechischen*

Harmonik in der Darstellung durch August Boeckh. Dissertation. Würzburg: Richard Mayr, 1935.

Macran, H. S., *The Harmonics of Aristoxenus.* Oxford: The Clarendon Press, 1902.

Meibom, Marcus [Meibomius], *Antiquae musicae auctores septem.* Amstelodami: apud Ludovicum Elzevirium, 1652.

Monro, D. B., *The Modes of Ancient Greek Music.* Oxford: The Clarendon Press, 1894.

Mountford, J. F., "Greek Music and Its Relation to Modern Times," *Journal of Hellenic Studies,* Vol. XL (1920), pages 13–42.

————, "Greek Music in the Papyri and Inscriptions," in J. U. Powell and E. A. Barber (Editors), *New Chapters in the History of Greek Literature,* Second Series, pages 146–183. Oxford: The Clarendon Press, 1929.

————, "Greek Music: The Cairo Musical Fragment," in J. U. Powell (Editor), *New Chapters in the History of Greek Literature,* Third Series, pages 260–261. Oxford: The Clarendon Press, 1933.

————, "The Music of Pindar's 'Golden Lyre,'" *Classical Philology,* Vol. XXXI (1936), pages 120–136.

————, "A New Fragment of Greek Music in Cairo," *Journal of Hellenic Studies,* Vol. LI (1931), pages 91–100.

Reinach, Théodore, "Un ancêtre de la musique d'église," *La Revue musicale,* Vol. III (July, 1922), pages 8–25.

————, *La Musique grecque.* Paris: Payot, 1926.

Sachs, Curt, "Die griechische Gesangsnotenschrift," *Zeitschrift für Musikwissenschaft,* Vol. VII (1924–1925), pages 1–5.

————, "Die griechische Instrumentalnotenschrift," *Zeitschrift für Musikwissenschaft,* Vol. VI (1923–1924), pages 289–301.

Schlesinger, Kathleen, *The Greek Aulos: A Study of its Mechanism and of its Relation to the Modal System of Ancient Greek Music followed by a Survey of the Greek Harmoniai in Survival or Rebirth in Folk-Music.* London: Methuen & Co., Ltd., 1939.

Thierfelder, Albert, "Ein neuaufgefundener Papyrus mit griechischen Noten," *Zeitschrift für Musikwissenschaft,* Vol. I (1918–1919), pages 217–225.

Torr, Cecil, "Greek Music," *Oxford History of Music, Introductory Volume,* pages 1–32. London: Oxford University Press, 1929.

Westphal, Rudolf, *Die Musik des griechischen Alterthumes.* Leipzig: Veit, 1883.

Williams, C. F. Abdy, *The Aristoxenian Theory of Musical Rhythm*. Cambridge: The University Press, 1911.
Winnington-Ingram, R. P., *Mode in Ancient Greek Music*. Cambridge: The University Press, 1936.

THE MUSIC OF THE EARLY CHRISTIAN CHURCH

The sources for the history of music in the early centuries of the Christian church are, for the most part, literary. Although *neume* notation was known at least by the middle of the eighth century, the earliest extant musical monuments date, except for a few fragments, from the tenth century.[29] The literary sources are discussed in such works as Pierre de Labriolle's *History and Literature of Christianity from Tertullian to Boethius*. Labriolle's bibliographies, placed at the beginning of each chapter, list numerous editions of the basic source materials. The collections of Gerbert and Coussemaker contain the most important extant Latin writings concerning the music of the early Christian era. The libraries in Rome, Milan, London, Paris, St. Gall, Einsiedeln, Karlsruhe, Munich, Bamberg, and other cities, have many of the original musical manuscripts dating from the tenth century on in increasing numbers. Some of the libraries have published catalogues of their manuscripts. The *Paléographie musicale*, of the monks of Solesmes, is a monumental publication of photographic reproductions of such manuscripts.

A representative bibliography, including the more important music collections and facsimiles, as well as books and articles, is given by Gustave Reese in his *Music in the Middle Ages*.[30] Special sections of the bibliography are devoted to Syrian, Byzantine, Armenian, Coptic, Ethiopian, Russian,

---

[29] See Peter Wagner, *Neumenkunde: Palaeographie des liturgischen Gesanges* (Part II of the *Einführung in die Gregorianischen Melodien*), page 101. Second Edition, Leipzig: Breitkopf and Härtel, 1912. For further details see Wagner's chapter on the earliest Latin neumes, *op. cit.*, pages 95–114.

[30] Pages 431–445.

Ambrosian, Mozarabic, and Gallican, as well as Gregorian chant. The headings of the sections devoted to the Gregorian chant are indicative of some of the more specialized aspects of research in this field: "The History," "The Notation of Intervals," "The Notation of Rhythm," "The Modes," "The Forms of Gregorian Chant and of Some Outgrowths." For further discussion of the sources and additional bibliography, see Kretzschmar,[31] Schiedermair,[32] Riemann,[33] Suñol,[34] Ursprung,[35] and Robertson.[36]

Secular Monody of the Middle Ages

The sources for the history of music in the early Middle Ages do not compare in quantity or quality with those related to the church music of the period. References to secular music occur in the writings of Tacitus (first century A.D.), Tertullian (second–third century A.D.), Augustine (fourth century A.D.), and others on through the Middle Ages; and musical manuscripts, lacking in the earlier periods, become increasingly plentiful from the ninth to eleventh centuries on.

Reese's two chapters on the "Secular Monody," with the accompanying bibliographies, provide an excellent survey of the basic source materials.[37] For further commentary and bibliographies, see Riemann,[38] Schiedermair,[39] Kretzschmar,[40] and Nef.[41]

---

[31] *Einführung in die Musikgeschichte*, pages 34–42.
[32] *Einführung in das Studium der Musikgeschichte*, pages 18–20.
[33] *Grundriss der Musikwissenschaft*, pages 126–132.
[34] Dom Grégoire Suñol, *Introduction à la paléographie musicale grégorienne*, pages 611–613. Paris: Desclée et Cie., 1935.
[35] Otto Ursprung, *Die katholische Kirchenmusik*, pages 6, 14, 22, *et passim*. Potsdam: Akademische Verlagsgesellschaft Athenaion, m.b.H., 1931.
[36] Alec Robertson, *The Interpretation of Plainchant*, pages 110–113. London: Oxford University Press, 1937.
[37] Gustave Reese, *op. cit.*, pages 198–248 and 445–451.
[38] *Op. cit.*, pages 132–136.
[39] *Op. cit.*, pages 21–23.
[40] *Op. cit.*, pages 35–43.
[41] *An Outline of the History of Music*, pages 27, 31, 37 f., *et passim*.

Polyphonic Music through the Sixteenth Century

In the absence of reliable documentary evidence, speculation plays an important role in the discussions of the earlier
stages of the *organum*. Literary references to the simultaneous singing of tones of different pitch are rare before the
Carolingian times, and the few that have been discovered
give little unequivocal information.[42] From the ninth century on, however, theoretical writings become more plentiful and clear. Many of these are available in the monumental collections of Martin Gerbert[43] and Charles-E.-H.de
Coussemaker.[44]

The number of musical monuments increases from the
twelfth to thirteenth centuries on, until, in the sixteenth century, great quantities of music in notation are available.
The problems of the decipherment of the musical notation
of part-music, which, in the earlier periods, make impossible
definitive transcriptions, gradually become more simple until in the later periods, when the publication of entirely reliable editions of the music becomes possible. The transition was one from a period in which the symbols of notation
represented no definite duration-values, through a period in
which "the time-values were hinted at indirectly but not
represented by corresponding symbols directly,"[45] to a period in which the duration-values were directly indicated
by the symbols.

For a survey of the literature up to the death of Dunstable
(d. 1453), see Part III of Reese's *Music in the Middle Ages*.[46]
For additional commentary and bibliographies for this and
the following periods up to the end of the sixteenth century,

---

[42] For further details, see Reese, *op. cit.*, page 252.
[43] *Scriptores ecclesiastici de musica sacra potissimum.*
[44] *Scriptorum de musica medii aevi.*
[45] Reese, *op. cit.*, page 273.
[46] Pages 249–424 (bibliographies, pages 451–463).

consult, for example, Riemann,[47] Schiedermair,[48] Kretzschmar,[49] and Nef.[50]

THE SEVENTEENTH TO TWENTIETH CENTURIES

From the seventeenth century on, the sources of musical
history expand rapidly in range and variety. The great
Denkmäler collections, the sets of complete works of composers, the biographical works, the special bibliographical
publications, the technical journals, the musical cyclopedias,
the general histories of music, and the innumerable special
studies in musical history — all these, and their like, are elo-
quent evidence of the expanding resources of musical historical investigation.

The bibliographies in Nef's *An Outline of the History of
Music* provide an easily accessible, systematic guide to the
chief sources. Further commentary and references are given
in Riemann,[51] Schiedermair,[52] and Kretzschmar.[53] For additional materials, see the reference works, histories of music,
and so forth, listed in the general bibliography at the end
of the book.

[47] *Op. cit.*, pages 136–145.
[48] *Op. cit.*, pages 23–31.
[49] *Op. cit.*, pages 43–50, 52–57, 65–69 *et passim*.
[50] *Op. cit.*, pages 53–145.
[51] *Op. cit.*, pages 145–157.
[52] *Op. cit.*, pages 31–88. Schiedermair includes lists of the volumes in the
complete editions of the works of the more important composers and in the
chief *Denkmäler* publications.
[53] *Op. cit.*, page 51 *et passim*.

CHAPTER X

PROBLEMS AND METHODS OF HISTORICAL
RESEARCH IN MUSIC

A LTHOUGH IT IS DIFFICULT TO STATE A METHOD FOR
solving all problems of musical history, the following
observations concerning methodology will be significant in
typical situations. The method pursued in any particular
research will necessarily be determined by the problem. It
is of first importance, therefore, to formulate a clear and un-
ambiguous statement of the problem. When the statement
of the problem is clear, one will usually find the methodology
implied in, or suggested by, that statement. In fact, it
seems likely that the researcher is often not conscious of the
method he is employing. His chief concern is the validity
of his findings, and he uses any and all methods, scientific
or critical, inductive or deductive, statistical or comparative.
And yet, some consideration of method is needed to insure
the validity of one's work, and to avoid errors, whether in
mistaking the date of a document or in holding an untenable
metaphysical assumption.

In the field of history, the researcher must be able to meet
three general requirements: first, he must be conscious of his
problem; second, he must be able to define his problem; and
third, he must seek the integration of his particular problem
with more general problems. The beginner in research
would do well to bear in mind the three key phrases — *prob-*

lem-consciousness, problem-definition, and *problem-integra-
tion* — to guide him in his work. One of the first products
of the inquiring mind is awareness of the existence of problems that arise in the attempt to answer the questions, *What?,
How?, Why?,* and *Whither?*

BEING CONSCIOUS OF THE PROBLEM

In almost every musical manifestation, problems invite investigation. Take, for example, a fugue of Bach. After
we have felt its musical effectiveness through repeated hearings, questions may arise. Why does this *subject* lend itself
so well to fugal treatment? Can we, by examining a number of fugue subjects, discover some of the principles involved in writing a good subject? Why should the *answer*
be in the interval of a fifth? Did Bach invent the form?
What happened to the fugue form after Bach? The answers
to these and other questions arising from the composition
will entail many kinds of investigations, both historical and
systematic. Similar problems are to be found in practically
every musical activity, whether in composition, performance,
or listening to music. To have an inquiring mind is one of
the first requisites of a researcher.

DEFINING THE PROBLEM

After becoming conscious of problems, the next step is to
define a particular problem. This means, in general, that
the topic for investigation must be so stated as to be susceptible of solution. Complex questions must be broken down
into simpler but significant parts. When the answers to the
simpler problems have been obtained, a synthesis may be attempted. In following such a methodology one must guard
against the dangers of assuming that the whole is equal to
the sum of the parts. To point out "that the whole is greater
than the sum of the parts" is not to say that investigation of

the parts is futile. By searching out the available facts in detail, by amassing the evidence afforded by particular instances, we may lay the foundations for sound generalization. Of course, the reverse procedure may well be pursued. The generalization may be set up as a hypothesis which later investigation of particulars may either establish or discredit, but the two methods are not as different as one might at first think. For, just as the original hypothesis is ordinarily based upon observation of particulars, so the detailed problem is usually formulated in the light of a generalization expressed or implied.

In seeking the definition of a problem, one should remember that one can begin at almost any point and work toward the most universal concepts of art. As we live in a contextual world — a world of relations — in order to attain a comprehensive statement of any particular feature, we must first organize in our thinking a large part of the remainder of the world. We cannot say what a six-four chord is, completely and satisfactorily, without an analysis of very nearly the entire realm of musical phenomena. Similarly, no comprehensive notion of the significance of a cadence, a scale, a sonata, a folk tune, a pianoforte, a school of music, a jazz hit, or any other element of musical experience can be obtained without thorough consideration of the relation of the particular part to other parts and to the whole.

It is not that every special study should be prefaced by a dissertation on the theory of knowledge, but a given research is more significant if the investigator has thought through the fundamental implications of his problem, and the reader can more effectively evaluate the work if the writer makes these implications clear. Only if he attempts to orient the vital points in his research, may his findings prove significant.

Though the particular detail under investigation may seem

insignificant, it may furnish the key to the solution of tremendously important problems. Legends say it was Newton's falling apple that led to the statement of the law of gravity, and Watt's boiling teakettle that led to the invention of the steam engine. Beginning with a treatise on the nature of vision, Bishop Berkeley worked out his most involved metaphysical theories. Starting with some dusty records in an old courthouse in western Texas, Professor Bolton developed his history of American colonization. A history of music might well originate in the treatment of the dissonance, or in a study of the development of musical instruments. Bekker's book on the opera organizes a long strand of musical history in terms of the inherent nature of the human voice.

First of all, the researcher should select a problem sufficiently limited with respect to his personal equipment and capacities for working in the chosen field, with respect to the availability of necessary materials, and with respect to the time available for the completion of the work. For example, a student would be unwise to undertake a highly specialized study of Greek music without a working knowledge of the Greek language; he would be unwise to attempt a study of the works of Costanzo Festa without first making sure of access to the necessary documents. And, finally, if he is planning a master's thesis, he should not attempt a history of music in America, because, not to mention other difficulties, the preliminary investigations would require much more time than he is likely to have at his disposal. This matter is of such importance that it will be well to consider a few examples.

Suppose the student proposes "Johannes Brahms: His Life and Works" for a master's thesis. Students often seem attracted by such a subject! But, obviously, the field is too broad. A young graduate student could hope only to work over the existing works on Brahms. A narrower subject would be much more promising. In view of the frequent complaint that there is little opportunity for original research in America because of lack of library facilities, a thesis entitled "Four Scarlatti Quartets" may be cited as an example of what can be done.[1] The manuscript of these quartets was located in the library of Abbé Santini, which was bought, about 1856, by the See of Münster for a Collegium Gregorianum which was never founded. The location of this manuscript may have been discovered through Dent's biography of Scarlatti.[2] At any rate, within a few weeks of the time a letter was sent to the library at Münster, the photostatic copies of the complete manuscript arrived. Based upon this material, the thesis developed into the following form.

   I. Alessandro Scarlatti: The Historical Approach.
  II. The String Quartets.
     a. Relation to Scarlatti's work as a whole.
     b. Chronological position.
     c. The violin and the early violin sonata.
     d. Some aesthetic considerations.
 III. The Manuscript.
     a. Analytical notes.
       1. Notation.
       2. Part-writing.
       3. Harmony.
       4. Form.
     b. The score.
Bibliography.

This thesis has several essentials for satisfactory research: (*a*) the topic is narrow enough for adequate treatment; (*b*) it

---

[1] Margaret Prall, master's thesis submitted at Mills College, 1932. See also Margaret Prall, "The String Quartets of A. Scarlatti," *Musical Mercury,* Vol. III (1936), pages 1–6.

[2] Edward J. Dent, *Alessandro Scarlatti: His Life and Works.* London: Edward Arnold & Co., 1905.

is articulated with the main current of musical development; and (c) it contains a first-hand study of the materials — in other words, it exhibits original research, not mere quotation of authorities.

Every master's thesis should probably contain these elements, not only to afford the student opportunity to develop skill in historical method, but also to make a definite contribution to musicological investigation. Such work well done will not need to be done again, and on the basis of many such small researches the general history of music may be adequately written and many more general problems solved. Of course it is possible to select broader subjects, but it is inevitable that the broader the scope, the more superficial the treatment.

A student with a broad background in cultural history might choose such a topic as "A Study of the Cultural Conditions Underlying Certain Great Transition Periods in the History of Music." This is an entirely different type of topic and involves different techniques. The periods chosen might be these:

 I. The Early Seventeenth Century: Monteverdi.
 II. The Early Eighteenth Century: Bach and Handel.
 III. The Early Nineteenth Century: Beethoven.
 IV. The Early Twentieth Century: Debussy.

If the student defines his problem clearly and makes a judicious selection of material, he should be able to exhibit a product of real scholarship.

Whether a work is suitable for a master's or a doctor's thesis depends not so much upon the topic selected as upon the treatment, and the maturity of scholarship. The same subject might be suitable for a weekly report, a term paper, a master's thesis, or a doctor's dissertation. For a weekly report, the student might simply look up one or two references; for a term paper, he might read more extensively without doing any original research. For a master's thesis, he would make a thorough investigation and offer more fundamental treatment, preferably with some original work; and for the doctor's dissertation he should make a real contribution based upon exhaustive investigation of the subject.

PROBLEM INTEGRATION

Highly specialized studies require limitation and concentration, but in them the researcher should not lose sight of the articulation of his work with the general history of music. The writer of a special study can usually formulate his problem and direct his investigations so that his work will integrate into a larger section of musical history. To do this effectively, he must naturally have some insight in the problems of the larger field. The writer of the general history of music is more or less at the mercy of his source material. There are countless situations in which he must take the word of others for the facts.

THE SEARCH FOR MATERIALS

After the student has passed the preliminary stages of becoming conscious of a problem, of defining it, and of checking to see how it is related to the general history of music, the next step is to search for materials.

Of prime importance in finding materials is the development of a comprehensive bibliography. From his preliminary studies the student will already have some bibliographical material. Most of the general histories contain bibliographies on more specialized subjects. An investigation of these special references will usually lead to the discovery of other related material, which, in turn, will yield further clues. Subject catalogues in libraries, dictionaries of music, periodical indexes, and such works as Eitner's *Quellen-Lexikon* should be consulted. The search for documents is called *heuristic* procedure. One of the important activities of libraries and learned societies is the preparation of catalogues of rare materials of all kinds.

Many of these will be found at the reference desk of most important libraries. Thorough work in heuristic and comprehensive bibliographical investigations not only affords the material with which to work, but also protects the researcher against errors in fact, and against duplication of labor.[3] A historical fact can be discovered or established only through indirect methods. Primary sources are the original sources of information concerning historical fact. The testimony nearest the fact is the primary source; the secondary sources are those based upon some prior evidence. Though it is not always possible to distinguish clearly between primary and secondary sources, the rough differentiation of material according to the criteria mentioned is usually possible, and the distinction is generally desirable, sometimes crucial. For example, in musical historical, style-critical studies much of the investigation can be based upon the standard editions of a composer's works, which are, ordinarily, secondary sources. At times, however, problems arise which make it necessary to go back to the first editions or to the original manuscripts. In such a case, the distinction between primary and secondary source material is reasonably clear.

In general, the student's bibliography will grow as he works with his material. How it grows will naturally vary greatly with the topic under investigation. The development of photostatic and film techniques in recent years has greatly simplified the collection of materials scattered in libraries, archives, and other repositories all over the world. As the mass of material gradually accumulates, the researcher studies

---

[3] For further discussion of heuristic, see Ch. V. Langlois and Ch. Seignobos, *Introduction to the Study of History*, pages 17–59.

it in more and more detail. In this work two methodological procedures may be distinguished — the analytic and the synthetic. General critical methodology, involving evaluation and selection, and distinguished from specialized style-critique, is applicable at all stages of the investigation.

ANALYTICAL PROCEDURES

Analytic work would imply, first, the detailed study of the source material — including literary works, musical monuments, and whatever other data may be found. This investigation will take into account direct and indirect knowledge, external and internal evidence in relation to the main thesis. Doubtful textual passages, whether verbal or musical, will be checked; questions of authorship will be investigated; and countless other matters will be treated analytically. Many studies will involve varying amounts of technical musical analysis, to afford the basis for later style-critical discussion. Ordinarily, out of the analytic processes will emerge the most suitable criteria for the classification and organization of the data.

SYNTHETIC OPERATIONS

Analytic treatment of the pertinent details — historical and systematic — will lay the foundation for the research. The synthetic organization of the factual material, and the application of constructive reasoning will lead to drafting of appropriate general formulae. In many investigations the analytic and synthetic operations will culminate in the critique of the musical style or styles involved.

STYLE-CRITIQUE

Style-criticism is the ultimate goal of a very large portion of musicological research. Indirectly at least, perhaps all musical investigations could be interpreted in relation to this objective. Just as the word *style* has many different shades of meaning, so the term *style-criticism* is interpreted in many different ways. However, it may be defined in general as *the attempt to establish the musico-technical and aesthetic differentia of the individual styles of various composers, as well as of the various style-species of the past.*

Consideration of the *musico-technical* features of a given style involves scales, tonality, melody, ornamentation, rhythm and meter, harmony and counterpoint, cadence, dissonance treatment, form, medium (vocal or instrumental), and the like.

Under the heading of *aesthetic differentia* we may list problems of expression, content, or meaning; musical hermeneutics; sociocultural implications, including the relation to the other arts; and other pertinent topics which may be formulated according to the particular style and the aesthetic approach.

The Final Statement

The *final statement* — the presentation or exposition — is, necessarily, the last step in research. But, just as the composer may have his whole composition in mind before he sets his pen to paper, so the researcher may have his exposition clearly thought out before he begins writing. Or he may write certain sections of his work in final form before he has completed all the details of his basic research.

For purposes of analysis and understanding, we have broken up the research process into its several phases, or types of procedure. In actual work, however, the various activities may be entwined in an inextricable complex which may not require disentanglement, at least in detail. For, while it is important that the researcher keep in mind, for example, the essential differences between the objective aspects of his work and the subjective, it would be foolish to apply the outlined procedures pedantically. In the very early stages of his work with his basic materials, he may get a glimpse of a fundamental principle to be tested only through

many hours of tedious investigation. The important point
is that all the steps in a research project may be conditioned
by the idea of the final statement — by the thought of what
will lend itself to effective statement in the last definitive
exposition.

BIBLIOGRAPHY
Adler, Guido, *Methode der Musikgeschichte*. Leipzig: Breit-
kopf & Härtel, 1919. Contains bibliography, pages 200–222,
prepared by Wilhelm Fischer.
————, *Der Stil in der Musik*. Leipzig: Breitkopf & Härtel,
1911.
Cohen, Morris R., and Ernest Nagel, *An Introduction to Logic
and Scientific Method*. New York: Harcourt, Brace & Com-
pany, Inc., 1934.
Hurt, Peyton, *Bibliography and Footnotes: A Style Manual for
College and University Students*. Berkeley: University of
California Press, 1936.
Kretzschmar, H., "Anregungen zur Förderung musikalischer
Hermeneutik," *Jahrbuch der Musikbibliothek Peters*, Vol.
IX (1902), pages 45–66.
Langlois, Ch. V., and Ch. Seignobos, *Introduction to the Study of
History*. Tr. by G. G. Berry. New York: Henry Holt &
Company, Inc., 1898.
Marshall, R. L., *The Historical Criticism of Documents*. Lon-
don and New York: The Macmillan Company, 1920.
Nevins, Allan, *Masters' Essays in History: A Manual of Instruc-
tions and Suggestions*. New York: Columbia University
Press, 1930.
O'Brien, Louis (assisted by Henri Langlard), *The Writing of
History*. Adapted from Paul Harsin's *Comment on écrit
l'histoire*. Berkeley: University of California Press, 1935.
Odum, Howard W., and Katharine Jocher, *An Introduction to
Social Research*. New York: Henry Holt & Company, Inc.,
1929.
Parry, C. Hubert H., *Style in Musical Art*. London: Macmillan
& Co., Ltd., 1911.
Smart, Harold R., *The Logic of Science*. New York: D. Apple-
ton-Century Company, Inc., 1931.
Strunk, W. Oliver, "Sources and Problems for Graduate Study
in Musicology," *Volume of Proceedings of the Music Teachers National Association*, Twenty-Eighth Series (1933), pages
105–116.

GENERAL BIBLIOGRAPHY

Bibliographical Works

Aber, Adolf, *Handbuch der Musikliteratur in systematisch-chronologischer Anordnung.* Leipzig: Breitkopf & Härtel, 1922.

Aubry, Pierre, "Éléments de bibliographie musicale," *La Musicologie médiévale: histoire et méthodes,* pages 125–134. Paris: H. Welter, 1900.

Becker, C. F., *Die Tonwerke des XVI. und XVII. Jahrhunderts.* Leipzig: Ernst Fleischer, 1855.

Besterman, Theodore, *A World Bibliography of Bibliographies.* 2 vols. New York: The H. W. Wilson Company, 1940. See "Music," Vol. II, pages 67–79.

Bibliographie der Musik-Sammelwerke des XVI. und XVII. Jahrhunderts. Edited by Robert Eitner and others. Berlin: Leo Liepmannssohn, 1877.

Bibliographie des Musikschrifttums. Vol. I (1936), in two parts, and Vol. II (1937), edited by Kurt Taut; Vol. III (1938), edited by George Karstädt. Leipzig: Friedrich Hofmeister, 1937–1939.

A Bibliography of Periodical Literature in Musicology and Allied Fields and a Record of Graduate Theses Accepted. No. 1: Oct. 1, 1938 to Sept. 30, 1939. Assembled for the Committee on Musicology of the American Council of Learned Societies by D. H. Daugherty. Washington: American Council of Learned Societies, 1940.

Bibliotheca musico-liturgica: A Descriptive Handlist of the Musical & Latin-Liturgical MSS. of the Middle Ages, Preserved in the Libraries of Great Britain and Ireland. Drawn up by Walter H. Frere. 2 vols. Nashdom Abbey, Burnham, Bucks.: The Plainsong and Mediaeval Music Society, 1901.

Blom, Eric, *A General Index to Modern Musical Literature in the English Language.* Philadelphia: Curwen, Inc., 1927.

Catalogue of the Allen A. Brown Collection of Music in the Public Library of the City of Boston. 4 vols. Boston: Published by the Trustees, 1910–1916.

The Edwin A. Fleisher Music Collection in the Free Library of Philadelphia. Philadelphia: Privately printed, 1933.

Eitner (see "Encyclopedias and Dictionaries").

Engel, Carl, *The Literature of National Music.* London: Novello, Ewer & Co., 1879.

Forkel, Johann Nicolaus, *Allgemeine Litteratur der Musik.* Leipzig: Schwickert, 1792.

The Gramophone Shop Encyclopedia of Recorded Music. Compiled by R. D. Darrell. New York: The Gramophone Shop, Inc., 1936.

Grosbayne, Benjamin, *A Bibliography of Works and Articles on Conductors, Conducting and Related Fields in Various Languages from the Sixteenth Century to the Present Time.* Mimeographed. Brooklyn: Brooklyn College, 1934.

Kinkeldey, Otto, "Music and Music Printing in Incunabula," *The Papers of the Bibliographical Society of America*, Vol. XXVI, pages 89–118. Chicago, 1932.

Kinsky, Georg, *Die Originalausgaben der Werke Johann Sebastian Bachs.* Vienna: Herbert Reichner, 1937.

Kretzschmar, Hermann, *Einführung in die Musikgeschichte.* Leipzig: Breitkopf & Härtel, 1920.

Library of Congress Catalogue of Early Books on Music (before 1800). Edited by Julia Gregory and O. G. Sonneck. Washington: Government Printing Office, 1913.

"List of Books on Music," *The Bulletin of the National Association of Schools of Music*, No. 3 (1935). Supplements: Bulletin No. 6 (1936) and Bulletin No. 11 (1939).

McColvin, Lionel R., and Harold Reeves, *Music Libraries: Their Organization and Contents, with a Bibliography of Music and Musical Literature.* 2 vols. London: Grafton & Co., 1937, 1938.

Matthew, James E., *The Literature of Music.* London: Elliot Stock, 1896.

Miller, Dayton C., *Catalogue of Books and Literary Material Relating to the Flute and Other Musical Instruments.* Cleveland: Privately printed, 1935.

Mudge, Isadore G., *Guide to Reference Books.* Sixth Edition. Chicago: American Library Association, 1936. *Reference Books of 1935–1937: An Informal Supplement*, 1939.

Reis, Claire, *American Composers: A Record of Works Written Between 1912 and 1932.* Second Edition. New York: The

United States Section of the International Society for Contemporary Music, 1932.

——, *Composers in America: Biographical Sketches of Living Composers with a Record of Their Works, 1912–1937.* New York: The Macmillan Company, 1938.

Riemann, Hugo, *Grundriss der Musikwissenschaft.* Fourth Edition, revised by Johannes Wolf. Leipzig: Quelle & Meyer, 1928.

Schiedermair, Ludwig, *Einführung in das Studium der Musikgeschichte.* Third Enlarged Edition. Berlin: Ferd. Dümmler, 1930.

Scholes, Percy A., *A List of Books About Music in the English Language.* London: Oxford University Press, 1940.

Shaw, Charles B., *A List of Books for College Libraries.* Second Preliminary Edition. Chicago: American Library Association, 1931.

——, *A List of Books for College Libraries, 1931–1938.* Chicago: American Library Association, 1940. (Contains selective bibliography on music.)

Smith, Carleton Sprague, "Libraries of Music," *The International Cyclopedia of Music and Musicians,* pages 1003–1009.

Song Index. Edited by Minnie Earl Sears and Phyllis Crawford. New York: The H. W. Wilson Company, 1926. *Supplement,* 1934.

Springer, Hermann, Max Schneider, and Werner Wolffheim, *Miscellanea musicae bio-bibliographica: Musikgeschichtliche Quellennachweise als Nachträge und Verbesserungen zu Eitners Quellen-Lexikon.* 3 vols. Leipzig: Breitkopf & Härtel, 1912–1916.

Squire, W. Barclay, *Catalogue of Printed Music Published between 1487 and 1800 Now in the British Museum.* 2 vols. London: Printed by order of the Trustees, 1912.

——, Carl Engel, and others, "Libraries and Collections of Music," *Grove's Dictionary of Music and Musicians,* Vol. III, pages 152–190, Suppl. Vol., pages 350–367.

"Verzeichnis der . . . Bücher und Schriften über Musik," *Jahrbuch der Musikbibliothek Peters,* Vol. I (1894) to date.

Wallace, Ruth (Editor), *The Care and Treatment of Music in a Library.* Chicago: American Library Association, 1927.

Encyclopedias and Dictionaries

Abert, Hermann, *Illustriertes Musik-Lexikon.* Stuttgart: J. Engelhorns Nachf., 1927.

Angelis, Alberto de, *Dizionario dei musicisti.* Third Edition. Rome: Ausonia, 1928.

Baker, Theodore, *Dictionary of Musical Terms.* Twenty-Fifth Edition. New York: G. Schirmer, Inc., 1939.

Baker's Biographical Dictionary of Musicians. Fourth Edition, Revised and Enlarged. New York: G. Schirmer, Inc., 1940.

Brenet, Michel (Marie Bobillier), *Dictionnaire pratique et historique de la musique.* New Edition. Paris: Armand Colin, 1930.

Cobbett's Cyclopedic Survey of Chamber Music. 2 vols. Compiled and edited by Walter Willson Cobbett. London: Oxford University Press, 1929–1930.

Composers of Today. Compiled and edited by David Ewen. New York: The H. W. Wilson Company, 1934.

Composers of Yesterday. Compiled and edited by David Ewen. New York: The H. W. Wilson Company, 1937.

Corte, Andrea della, and G. M. Gatti, *Dizionario di musica.* Third Edition. Torino: Paravia, 1930.

A Dictionary of Modern Music and Musicians. Edited by A. Eaglefield Hull. New York: E. P. Dutton & Co., Inc., 1924.

Eitner, Robert, *Biographisch-bibliographisches Quellen-Lexikon der Musiker und Musikgelehrten der christlichen Zeitrechnung bis zur Mitte des neunzehnten Jahrhunderts.* 10 vols. Leipzig: Breitkopf & Härtel, 1900–1904.

Encyclopédie de la musique et dictionnaire du conservatoire. 11 vols. Edited by Albert Lavignac and Lionel de la Laurencie. Paris: Delagrave, 1913–1931.

Fétis, F.-J., *Biographie universelle des musiciens et bibliographie générale de la musique.* 8 vols. Second Edition. Paris: Firmin-Didot et Cie., 1883–1884. *Supplément et complément.* 2 vols. Edited by Arthur Pougin, 1881.

Gerber, Ernst L., *Neues historisch-bibliographisches Lexikon der Tonkünstler.* 4 vols. Leipzig: A Kühnel, 1812–1814.

Grove's Dictionary of Music and Musicians. 5 vols. Third Edition. Edited by H. C. Colles. New York: The Macmillan Company, 1927–1928. *American Supplement.* New Edition with New Material. Edited by Waldo S. Pratt and Charles N. Boyd, 1928. Suppl. Vol., 1940.

The International Cyclopedia of Music and Musicians. Edited by Oscar Thompson. New York: Dodd, Mead & Company, Inc., 1939.

The Macmillan Encyclopedia of Music and Musicians. Compiled and edited by Albert E. Wier. New York: The Macmillan Company, 1938.

Moser, Hans J., *Musik-Lexikon.* Berlin: Max Hesse, 1935.

Musikalisches Conversations-Lexikon. 11 vols. Edited by Hermann Mendel and others. Berlin: L. Heimann and Robert Oppenheim, 1870–1879. *Ergänzungsband,* 1883.

Pierre Key's Music Year Book. Sixth Edition. Edited by Pierre v. R. Key and Irene E. Haynes. New York: Pierre Key, Inc., 1938.

Pierre Key's Musical Who's Who. Edited by Pierre v. R. Key. New York: Pierre Key, Inc., 1931.

Pratt, Waldo S., *New Encyclopedia of Music and Musicians.* New and Revised Edition. New York: The Macmillan Company, 1929. First Edition, 1924.

Riemann, Hugo, *Hugo Riemanns Musik-Lexikon.* 2 vols. Eleventh Edition. Edited by Alfred Einstein. Berlin: Max Hesse, 1929.

Ronald, Sir Landon (Editor), *Who's Who in Music.* London: Shaw Publishing Co., Ltd., 1937.

Rousseau, J.-J., *Dictionnaire de musique.* 2 vols. Paris: P. Dupont, 1824. *Œuvres complètes,* Vols. XII–XIII.

Schmidl, Carlo, *Dizionario universale dei musicisti.* 2 vols. Milan: Sonzogno, 1929.

Scholes, Percy A., *The Oxford Companion to Music.* London: Oxford University Press, 1938.

Schulz, Gottfried, "Musikbibliographie und Musikbibliotheken," *Festschrift . . . Adolf Sandberger,* pages 129–134.

Slonimsky, Nicolas, "Concise Biographical Dictionary of Twentieth-Century Musicians," *Music Since 1900,* pages 437–520. (Contains corrections and additions to the dictionaries of Grove, Hull, Riemann, and Moser.)

Vannes, René, *Essai de terminologie: dictionnaire universel.* Copyright by author, 1925.

Who Is Who in Music (1941 Edition). Chicago: Lee Stern Press, 1940.

Histories of Music [1]

Adler, Guido, *Handbuch der Musikgeschichte.* 2 vols. Second Edition. Berlin: Max Hesse, 1930. First Edition, 1924.

Ambros, August W., *Geschichte der Musik.* 5 vols. Second Edition. Leipzig: F. E. C. Leuckart, 1880–1882.

---

[1] *Cf.* Warren D. Allen, *Philosophies of Music History,* pages 343–365.

GENERAL BIBLIOGRAPHY

Barrenechea, Mariano A., *Historia estética de la música.* Buenos Aires: Cooperativa Editorial Limitada, 1918.
Bekker, Paul, *The Story of Music.* (Tr. by M. D. Herter Norton and Alice Kortschak.) New York: W. W. Norton & Company, Inc., 1927.
Burney, Charles, *A General History of Music.* 4 vols. London: Printed for the author, 1776–1789. Two Volume Edition. New York: Harcourt, Brace & Company, Inc., 1935.
Combarieu, Jules, *Histoire de la musique.* 3 vols. Paris: Colin, 1925–1930.
Dumesnil, René, *Histoire de la musique illustrée.* Paris: Plon, 1934.
Einstein, Alfred, *A Short History of Music.* Revised Edition, tr. from the German. New York: Alfred A. Knopf, Inc., 1937.
Fétis, F.-J., *Histoire générale de la musique.* 5 vols. Paris: Firmin Didot Frères, Fils et Cie., 1869–1876.
Finney, Theodore M., *A History of Music.* New York: Harcourt, Brace & Company, Inc., 1935.
Forkel, Johann Nicolaus, *Allgemeine Geschichte der Musik.* 2 vols. Leipzig: Schwickert, 1788–1801.
Gérold, Th., *Histoire de la musique des origines à la fin du XIV⁰ siècle.* Paris: Renouard, 1936.
Glyn, Margaret Henrietta, *Theory of Musical Evolution.* London: J. M. Dent & Sons, Ltd., 1934.
Gray, Cecil, *The History of Music.* Revised Edition. New York: Alfred A. Knopf, 1931.
Hamilton, Clarence G., *Outlines of Music History.* Boston: Oliver Ditson Company, 1936.
Handbuch der Musikwissenschaft. 7 vols. Edited by Ernst Bücken and others. Wildpark-Potsdam: Akademische Verlagsgesellschaft Athenaion, m.b.H., 1927–1931.
Hawkins, Sir John, *A General History of the Science and Practice of Music.* 5 vols. London: T. Payne and Son, 1776.
"Histoire de la musique," edited by Albert Lavignac and Lionel de la Laurencie. *Encyclopédie de la musique et dictionnaire du conservatoire*, Part I, Vols. I–V.
Hogarth, George, *Musical History, Biography, and Criticism.* 2 vols. London: John W. Parker, 1838.
Kinsky, Georg, *A History of Music in Pictures.* New York: E. P. Dutton & Co., Inc., 1930.
Kretzschmar, Hermann, *Einführung in die Musikgeschichte.* Leipzig: Breitkopf & Härtel, 1920.

[306]

Landormy, Paul Charles R., *A History of Music*. (Tr. with additions by Frederick H. Martens.) New York: Charles Scribner's Sons, 1935.

Láng, Paul Henry, *Music in Western Civilization*. New York: W. W. Norton & Company, Inc., 1941.

Leichtentritt, Hugo, *Music, History, and Ideas*. Cambridge: Harvard University Press, 1938.

McKinney, Howard D., and W. R. Anderson, *Music in History: The Evolution of an Art*. New York: American Book Company, 1940.

Martini, Giambattista, *Storia della musica*. 3 vols. Bologna: Lelio dalla Volpe, 1757–1781.

Moser, Hans J., *Lehrbuch der Musikgeschichte*. Berlin-Schöneberg: Max Hesse, 1936.

Naumann, Emil, *The History of Music*. 5 vols. Special Edition. (Tr. by F. Praeger, edited by F. A. G. Ouseley.) London: Cassell & Company, n.d.

Nef, Karl, *An Outline of the History of Music*. (Tr. by Carl F. Pfatteicher.) New York: Columbia University Press, 1935. Third printing with additional bibliographical material, 1939.

The Oxford History of Music. 6 vols. Edited by W. H. Hadow. London: Oxford University Press, 1901–1905. Second Edition edited by Percy C. Buck (general editor, W. H. Hadow) with *Introductory Volume* and Vol. VII (Vol. III, First Edition), 1929–1934.

Parry, Charles H. H., *The Evolution of the Art of Music*. Edited with additional chapters by H. C. Colles. New York: D. Appleton-Century Company, Inc., 1932.

Pratt, Waldo Selden, *The History of Music*. Revised Edition. New York: G. Schirmer, Inc., 1930. First Edition, 1907.

Prosniz, Adolf, *Kompendium der Musikgeschichte*. 3 vols. Vol. I (Third Edition) and Vol. II (Second Edition). Vienna: Universal-Edition A. G., 1920, 1921. Vol. III (First Edition). Vienna: Alfred Hölder, 1915.

Prunières, Henry, *Nouvelle histoire de la musique*. 2 vols. Paris: Rieder, 1934, 1936.

Reese, Gustave, *Music in the Middle Ages*. New York: W. W. Norton & Company, Inc., 1940.

Riemann, Hugo, *Handbuch der Musikgeschichte*. 2 vols., 5 parts. Second Edition. Leipzig: Breitkopf & Härtel, 1919–1922.

Rowbotham, John Frederick, *A History of Music*. 3 vols. London: Trübner & Co., 1885–1887.

Schering, Arnold, *Tabellen zur Musikgeschichte*. Leipzig: Breitkopf & Härtel, 1934.

Scholes, Percy A., *The Columbia History of Music Through Ear and Eye*. 5 vols. London: Oxford University Press, 1930–1938.

Slonimsky, Nicolas, *Music Since 1900*. Second Edition. New York: W. W. Norton & Company, Inc., 1938.

Wolf, Johannes, *Geschichte der Musik*. 3 vols. Leipzig: Quelle & Meyer, 1925–1928.

Periodicals[2]

Acta musicologica. Formerly *Mitteilungen der internationalen Gesellschaft für Musikwissenschaft.* Edited by Knud Jeppesen. Copenhagen: Ejnar Munksgaard, 1928 to date.

Archiv für Musikforschung. Edited by Rudolf Steglich and others. Leipzig: Breitkopf & Härtel, 1936 to date. Supersedes *Zeitschrift für Musikwissenschaft.*

Archiv für Musikwissenschaft. 8 vols. Edited by Max Seiffert and others. Leipzig: Fr. Kistner & C. F. W. Siegel, 1918–1927.

Bulletin de la société "union musicologique." 6 vols. The Hague: Martinus Nijhoff, 1921–1926.

Bulletin of the American Musicological Society. Edited by M. D. Herter Norton. Privately printed by the American Musicological Society, 1936 to date.

Mitteilungen der Schweizerischen Musikforschenden Gesellschaft. 3 vols. Edited by Willi Schuh and Ernst Mohr. Zürich: Hug & Co., 1934–1936.

Modern Music. Edited by Minna Lederman and others. New York: The League of Composers, 1924 to date.

Monatshefte für Musik-Geschichte. 37 vols. Edited by Robert Eitner. Leipzig: Breitkopf & Härtel, 1869–1905. *Beilage*, 37 vols., 1869–1905.

Music and Letters. Founded by A. H. Fox Strangways, edited by Eric Blom. London, 1919 to date.

Music Educators Journal. Formerly *Music Supervisors Journal.* Managing Editor, C. V. Buttelman. Chicago: Music Educators National Conference, 1914 to date.

The Musical Quarterly. Edited by O. G. Sonneck, and Carl Engel. New York: G. Schirmer, Inc., 1915 to date.

---

[2] *Cf.* C. B. Oldman and others, "Periodicals, Musical," *Grove's Dictionary of Music and Musicians*, Vol. IV, pages 110–121, and Suppl. Vol., pages 504–507.

The Musical Times. Founded by J. A. Novello. London: Novello & Co. Ltd., 1844 to date.

Note d'archivio per la storia musicale. Edited by Raffaele Casimiri. Rome: Edizioni "Psalterium," 1924 to date.

Publikationen der internationalen Musikgesellschaft. Beihefte. Leipzig: Breitkopf & Härtel, 1901–1914. Series I, 9 vols., 1901–1902. Series II, 13 vols., 1905–1914.

La Rassegna musicale. Edited by Guido M. Gatti. Torino, 1928 to date.

Revue de musicologie. Publiée par la société française de musicologie. Paris: Libraire Fischbacher, 1917 to date. (Published as *Bulletin de la société française de musicologie,* 1917–1921.)

La Revue musicale. Edited by Henry Prunières. Paris: Editions de la Nouvelle Revue Française, 1920 to date.

Rivista musicale italiana. Edited by Luigi Torchi and others. Milan: Frotelli Bocca Editori, 1894 to date. (Publication suspended 1933–1935.)

Sammelbände der internationalen Musikgesellschaft. 15 vols. Edited by Oskar Fleischer and others. Leipzig: Breitkopf & Härtel, 1899–1914.

Studien zur Musikwissenschaft, Beihefte der Denkmäler der Tonkunst in Österreich. 21 vols. Edited by Guido Adler. Leipzig: Breitkopf & Härtel, 1913–1934.

Vierteljahrsschrift für Musikwissenschaft. 10 vols. Edited by Friedrich Chrysander and others. Leipzig: Breitkopf & Härtel, 1885–1894.

Zeitschrift der internationalen Musikgesellschaft. 15 vols. Edited by Oskar Fleischer and others. Leipzig: Breitkopf & Härtel, 1899–1914.

Zeitschrift für Musikwissenschaft. 17 vols. Edited by Alfred Einstein and others. Superseded by *Archiv für Musikforschung.* Leipzig: Breitkopf & Härtel, 1918–1935.

Zeitschrift für vergleichende Musikwissenschaft. 3 vols. Edited by Robert Lachmann and others. Berlin: Max Hesse, 1933–1935.

Collected Writings

Festschrifts:

Festschrift für Guido Adler. Vienna: Universal-Edition A.G., 1930.

Festschrift Johannes Biehle. Leipzig: Fr. Kistner & C. F. W. Siegel, 1930.

"Festgabe . . . Max Friedlaenders." Issued as Part II of *Jahr-buch der Musikbibliothek Peters*, Vol. XXVIII (1921).
Festschrift Hermann Kretzschmar. Leipzig: C. F. Peters, 1918.
Theodor Kroyer-Festschrift. Regensburg: Gustav Bosse, 1933.
Festschrift . . . R. F. v. Liliencron. Leipzig: Breitkopf & Här-tel, 1910.
Festschrift Karl Nef. Zürich: Hug, 1933.
Riemann-Festschrift. Leipzig: Max Hesse, 1909.
Festschrift . . . Adolf Sandberger. Munich: Ferdinand Zier-fuss, 1918.
Gedenkboek . . . D. F. Scheurleer. The Hague: M. Nijhoff, 1925.
Festschrift Peter Wagner. Leipzig: Breitkopf & Härtel, 1926.
Festschrift für Johannes Wolf. Berlin: M. Breslauer, 1929.

Proceedings:
Atti del primo congresso internazionale di musica. Florence, April 30–May 4, 1933. Florence: Felice le Monnier, 1935.
Bericht über den internationalen Kongress für Schubertforschung, Vienna, 1928. Augsburg: Benno Filser, G.m.b.H., 1929.
International Musical Society Reports (*Berichte*). Second Con-gress, Basel, 1906 – Leipzig: Breitkopf & Härtel, 1907. Third Congress, Vienna, 1909 – Vienna: Artaria & Co., 1909. Fourth Congress, London, 1911 – London: Novello & Co., Ltd., 1912.
International Society for Musical Research. *First Congress Re-port, Liége*. Nashdom Abbey, Burnham, Bucks.: The Plain-song and Mediaeval Music Society, 1930.
Papers Read by Members of the American Musicological Society at the Annual Meeting, Washington, D. C., December 29 and 30, 1938. Privately printed by the Society, 1940.
Proceedings of the Musical Association. London: The Musical Association, 1875 to date.
Proceedings of the Music Teachers National Association. Pub-lished by the Association, 1906 to date.
Yearbook of the Music Educators National Conference (to 1932, *Journal of Proceedings, Music Supervisors National Confer-ence*). Chicago: Music Educators National Conference, 1907 to date (irregular in first years). Beginning with Vol. XXX (1941), to be published biennially.

Yearbooks:
Bach-Jahrbuch. 35 vols. Leipzig: Breitkopf & Härtel, 1904–1938.

Jahrbuch der Musikbibliothek Peters. Edited by Emil Vogel
and others. Leipzig: C. F. Peters, 1894 to date.
Jahrbücher für musikalische Wissenschaft. 2 vols. Edited by
Friedrich Chrysander. Leipzig: Breitkopf & Härtel, 1863,
1867.
Schweizerisches Jahrbuch für Musikwissenschaft. 7 vols. Basel:
Heinrich Majer, 1924–1938.

Complete Works of Important Composers [3]

Bach, Johann Sebastian, *Werke.* 47 vols. Edition of the Bach-
Gesellschaft. Leipzig: Breitkopf & Härtel, 1851–1926.
Beethoven, Ludwig van, *Werke.* 25 series, 33 vols. Edited by
Selmar Bagge and others. Leipzig: Breitkopf & Härtel,
1862–1888.
Berlioz, Hector, *Werke.* 20 vols. Edited by Charles Malherbe
and Felix Weingartner. Leipzig: Breitkopf & Härtel, 1900–
1907.
Brahms, Johannes, *Sämtliche Werke.* 26 vols. Edition of the
Gesellschaft der Musikfreunde in Vienna. Leipzig: Breit-
kopf & Härtel, 1926.
Chopin, Frédéric, *Werke.* 14 vols. with Suppl. and *Revisions-
bericht.* Edited by W. Bargiel and others. Leipzig: Breit-
kopf & Härtel, n.d.
Des Prez, Josquin, *Werke.* In progress. Edited by A. Smijers.
Leipzig: C. F. W. Siegel, 1925 to date.
Haydn, Franz Josef, *Sämtliche Werke.* Incomplete. Edited by
Eusebius Mandyezewski and others. Berlin: Breitkopf &
Härtel, 1907 to date.
Lasso, Orlando di, *Sämtliche Werke.* 21 vols. Incomplete.
Edited by F. S. Haberl and Adolf Sandberger. Leipzig:
Breitkopf & Härtel, 1894–1900.
Liszt, Franz, *Musikalische Werke.* 33 vols. to 1940. Edited by
E. d'Albert and others. Leipzig: Breitkopf & Härtel, 1907
to date.
Mendelssohn, Felix, *Werke.* 36 vols. Edited by Julius Rietz.
Berlin: Breitkopf & Härtel, 1874–1877.
Monteverdi, Claudio, *Tutte le opere.* 14 vols. Incomplete.
Edited by G. F. Malipiero. Vienna: Universal-Edition, 1926–
1932.

---

[3] *Cf.* "Gesamtausgaben," Moser's *Musik-Lexikon,* pages 262–263, *Hugo
Riemanns Musik-Lexikon,* Vol. I, page 591. *Cf.* also McColvin and Reeves,
Music Libraries, Vol. II, pages 204–209.

Mozart, Wolfgang Amadeus, *Werke.* 74 vols. Edited by Johannes Brahms and others. Leipzig: Breitkopf & Härtel, 1877–1905.

Obrecht, Jakob, *Werke.* 30 vols. Edited by Johannes Wolf. Berlin: Breitkopf & Härtel, 1908–1921.

Palestrina, Giovanni Pierluigi, *Werke.* 33 vols. Edited by Th. de Witt and others. Leipzig: Breitkopf & Härtel, 1862–1907.

Purcell, Henry, *The Works.* 26 vols. Edited by W. H. Cummings and others. London: Novello & Company, Ltd., 1878–1928.

Schubert, Franz, *Werke.* 40 vols. Edited by Johannes Brahms and others. Leipzig: Breitkopf & Härtel, 1888–1897.

Schütz, Heinrich, *Werke.* 18 vols. Edited by Philipp Spitta and others. Leipzig: Breitkopf & Härtel, 1885–1927.

Schumann, Robert, *Werke.* 34 vols. Edited by Clara Schumann. Leipzig: Breitkopf & Härtel, 1886–1893.

Victoria, Tomás Luis de, *Opera Omnia.* 8 vols. Edited by Philippo Pedrell. Leipzig: Breitkopf & Härtel, 1902–1913.

Modern Collections of Older Music [4]

Denkmäler der Tonkunst in Österreich. 83 vols. Guido Adler, General Editor. Vienna: Universal-Edition, A.G., 1894 to date.

Denkmäler deutscher Tonkunst, I. Folge. 65 vols. Leipzig: Breitkopf & Härtel, 1892–1931.

Denkmäler deutscher Tonkunst, II. Folge. 36 vols. Augsburg: Benno Filser, G.m.b.H., 1900–1931.

The English Madrigal School. 36 vols. Edited by Edmund Horace Fellowes. London: Stainer & Bell, Ltd., 1913–1924.

The English School of Lutenist Song Writers. 2 series, 16 vols. in each. Edited by Edmund Horace Fellowes. London: Stainer & Bell — Winthrop Rogers, 1920–1932.

Das Erbe deutscher Musik. I. Reihe, Reichsdenkmale deutscher Musik. II. Reihe, Landschaftsdenkmale der Musik Bayern. Edited for the State Institute for German Musical Research by Max Schneider and others. Braunschweig: Henry Litolff, 1935 to date. (Supersedes *Denkmäler deutscher Tonkunst.*)

---

[4] *Cf.* "Denkmäler," Moser's *Musik-Lexikon,* pages 156–164; *Grove's Dictionary of Music and Musicians,* Vol. II, pages 47–48; and *Hugo Riemanns Musik-Lexikon,* Vol. I, pages 387–391. *Cf.* also McColvin and Reeves, *Music Libraries,* Vol. II, pages 202–204.

I Classici della musica Italiana. 36 vols. Edited by Gabrieli d'Annunzio. Milan: Istituto Editoriale Italiano — Società Anonima Notari, 1919–1923.

Istituzione e monumenti dell' arte musicale Italiani. Vols. I–V published. Milan: G. Ricordi, 1931 to date.

Les maîtres musiciens de la renaissance française. 23 vols. Edited by Henry Expert. Paris: Alphonse Leduc, 1894–1908.

Monuments de la musique française au temps de la renaissance. 10 vols. Edited by Henry Expert. Paris: Maurice Senart, 1924–1929.

Paléographie musicale. The collection founded by Dom A. Mocquereau, continued by the Benedictines of Solesmes. First Series, reproduction of MSS. in facsimile, with introductions, 14 vols. actually published; Second Series, documentary, 2 vols. have appeared. Solesmes: Imprimerie St. Pierre, 1889–1931.

Publications de la société française de musicologie. Paris: Droz, 1925 to date.

Publikationen älterer Musik. Veröffentlicht von der Abteilung zur Herausgabe älterer Musik bei der Deutschen Musikgesellschaft. Edited by Theodor Kroyer and others. Leipzig: Breitkopf & Härtel, 1926 to date.

Schering, Arnold, *Geschichte der Musik in Beispielen.* Leipzig: Breitkopf & Härtel, 1931.

Steinitzer, Max, *Musikgeschichtlicher Atlas.* Freiburg i/Br.: C. Ruckmich, 1908.

Torchi, Luigi (Editor), *L'Arte musicale in Italia.* 7 vols. Milan: G. Ricordi & C., 1897.

Tudor Church Music. 10 vols. London: Published for the Carnegie U. K. Trust by the Oxford University Press, 1923–1929.

INDEX

(Figures in boldface refer to entries in bibliographies.)

INDEX

Comparative musicology (*Cont.*)
  instruments in, 233 f.
  melody in, 226 f.
  performance in, 232 f.
  rhythm in, 225 f.
  scales in, 222–225
  sciences auxiliary to, 219
  transcription in, 221 f.
  varied uses of term, 8 f.
Complete editions, 311 f.
Composition:
  and comparative musicology, 239 f.
  as aesthetic type, 150
  in system of Aristides, 5
  melodic, 5
  of poetry, 5
  psychology of, 103–105
  rhythmic, 5
  teaching of, 206 f.
Compositional patterns, 138–140
Compression, 24
Conation, 141
Concepts, development of, 93
Condensation, 24
Conducting, teaching of, 207 f.
Consonance and dissonance:
  physical basis of, 35 f.
  problem of, 22
  psychology of, 90–92
Content:
  as aesthetic problem, 140 f.
  in style-criticism, 298
Cools, Eugène, ix, 183
Corte, Andrea della, 304
Counterpoint:
  and harmony contrasted, 165–168
  dissonant, 177
  in style-criticism, 298
  strict, 175
  teaching of, 204–206
  theory of, 173–177
Coussemaker, E. de, 270, 283, 285, 287
Cowell, Henry, 177, 184, 239
Crandall, I. B., 56
Criticism:
  aesthetic, 151 f.
  musical, 152
Croce, Benedetto, 119, 152, 258, 265
Crusius, Otto, 278
Curriculum:
  musicology in, 7
  studies of, 190–193

Curriculum (*Cont.*)
  theory and history in, 11
Curtis, J., 283
Cycle, 31
Cyclic method in musical history, 256 f.

D

Dance, music and, 126, 148 f.
Dashiell, John F., ix, 61, 68 f., 92–94, 99 f., 110, 133
Daugherty, D. H., 301
Davis, A. H., 56
Decibel, 37, 75 ff.
Del Grande, C., 278
Demiashkevich, Michael, 214
Denéréaz, Alexandre, 110
Dent, Edward, ix, 293
Des Prez, Josquin, 311
Design:
  formal, 122
  principles of, 134–136
Dewey, John, 123, 126, 153, 191, 195, 214
Dickinson, George S., 138–140, 153, 181, 230
Didymus, comma of, 33
Diesis, enharmonic, 33
Diffraction, 27 f.
Dilthey, 258
Diodorus Siculus, 271 f.
Diogenes Laërtius, 271
Diplomatics, 270
Diserens, Charles M., 110
Displacement, 24, 31
Dissonance:
  conceptual, 92
  consonance and, 22, 90–92
  in style-criticism, 298
Drake, 102
Dramatic performance, 5
Duchesne, J., 283
Dumesnil, René, 306
Duncker, 272
Dunstable, 287
Dupont, Wilhelm, 56
Duration:
  and rhythm, 163 f.
  and tone quality, 79
  as intrinsic order of sound, 128, 131
  judgments of, 79

INDEX

INDEX

Hipkins, A. J., 217
Historical pluralism, 261–264
Historical viewpoint:
  in the history of musicology, 6
  in the systematization of musical
    knowledge, 7–11
Histories of music, 305–308
Historiography, theory and practice
  of, 264 f.
History:
  relativism in, 258 f.
  relevance and causality in, 259, 261
History of music:
  and comparative musicology, 234–
    238
  in the curriculum, 13 f.
  methodology in, 250–266
    cyclic, 256 f.
    evolutionary or genetic, 250, 252–
      256
    fluctuation theory of, 258
    pedagogical or pragmatic, 250 f.
    reporting or narrative, 250 f.
  philosophy of, 247–266
  sources of, 267–288
  teaching of, 208–210
Hogarth, George, 306
Hohn, Wilhelm, 183, 204
Homophonic forms, 138
Homophony, 174, 227–229
Hopkins, L. Thomas, 189, 197, 214
Hornbostel, Erich M. von, 217, 221,
  223–229, 233, 240 f., 283
Horne, Herman H., 188, 214
Howell, William H., 110
Hughes, Dom Anselm, ix
Hull, A. Eaglefield, 181, 304
Hunt, Arthur S., 277, 280
Hurt, Peyton, 299
Huyghens' principle, 25, 27

I

Idelsohn, A. Z., 275
Imagination, psychology of, 92–95
Individual instruction, theory of,
  193–196
Indy, Vincent d', 3, 185
Inspiration, psychology of, 92–95
Instrumental music, teaching of,
  201 f.
Instrumental performance, 5

Instrumentation and orchestration:
  teaching of, 206
  theory of, 177–179
Instruments:
  design of, 22, 40–56
  electric, 53 f.
  in comparative musicology, 233 f.
  percussion, 51–53
  stringed, 40–43
  tone quality of, 78 f.
  wind, 43–51
Intelligence, musical, 100 f.
Intensity, 36 f.
Interference, 28
Interpretation as aesthetic type, 150
Intertones, 73
Interval:
  harmonic, 84
  melodic, 84
  psychology of, 82–84
Intervals:
  calculations with, 33
  frequency ratios of, 32
  in history of musicology, 4
  law of equal, 90
Intonation:
  artistic, 34
  as aesthetic type, 150
  just, 34
Intrinsic orders of sound, 127 f.,
  130 f.
Isidore of Seville, 6

J

Jan, Karl von, 270, 277–280, 283
Jastrow, Morris, Jr., 274
Jeans, Sir James, 57
Jeppesen, Knud, ix, 3, 160, 165, 174 f.,
  183, 204
Jevons, W. Stanley, 2
Jocher, Katharine, 299
Jones, Arthur Taber, 57
Jones, Stuart, 277, 280
Jordan, Arthur M., ix, 100, 186, 214

K

Kant, 114
Kelsey, 103
Key, Pierre, 305
Kiesewetter, 254

INDEX

Stringed instruments, 40–43
Stringham, Edwin J., 59
Strunk, W. Oliver, 16, 299
Stumpf, Carl, 112, 242
Style as an aesthetic type, 150
Style-criticism, 207, 297 f.
Subjective factor in music, 123
Subjective tones, 73
Suetonius, 251
Summational tones, 34 f.
Suñol, Dom Grégoire, 286
Symphony, 11
Systematic orientation, 9
Systematic viewpoint, 6, 250
Systems of musical knowledge, 4 ff.

T

Tacitus, 286
Tagore, Rajah, 217
Taste:
　aesthetic, 149–151
　development of, 122
　musical, 11
Teacher training, teaching of, 211
Teaching:
　general theory of, 188–190
　materials and methods, 199–213
　(see also Pedagogy)
Techniques of performance as aesthetic type, 150
Teggart, Frederick J., 266
Temperament, tuning and, 34
Tertullian, 286
Tests and measurements, 101–103
Theme, 138
Theon of Smyrna, 280, 281
Theory of music theory, 155–185
　as branch of applied aesthetics, 10, 152
　as division of systematic musicology, 9, 14
　counterpoint, 173–177
　elementary theory, 157–159
　form, 179 f.
　harmony, 169–172
　harmony and counterpoint contrasted, 165–168
　in graduate field, 14
　instrumentation and orchestration, 177–179
　melody, 159–163

Theory of music theory (Cont.)
　rhythm, 163–165
　theory and practice, 156 f.
Thierfelder, Albert, 279, 284
Thinking, psychology of, 92–95
Third:
　neutral, 225
　pure, 33
　Pythagorean, 33
Thompson, Oscar, 304
Thompson, Randall, 199, 203 f., 207, 215
Thorn, Alice G., 215
Thorndike, 100
Thresholds, sensory, 66–68
Thucydides, 251
Thuille, Ludwig, 92, 182
Tiffin, Joseph, 220, 242
Timbre, 77–79
Time, sense of, 79 f.
Titchener, 95
Tobel, Rudolf von, 185
Tonality and cadence, psychology of, 89 f.
Tonality in style-criticism, 298
Tonbestimmung, 33
Tone:
　analysis of, 37 f.
　brightness of, 80 f.
　density of, 81
　fundamental, 30 f.
　intrinsic orders of, 40
　loudness, 74–77
　masking effect, 81
　noise element in, 30
　physical basis of, 29
　physical characteristics of, 31
　pure, 30
　quality, 43, 77–79
　simple and complex, 30
　vocality or vowel quality, 81
　volume of, 80
Tone quality as aesthetic type, 150
Tonic, law of, 89
Tonometer, 220
Tonoscope, 223
Torchi, Luigi, 313
Torossian, Aram, 108, 117, 119, 123, 125 f., 134, 154
Torr, Cecil, 284
Torrefranca, Fausto, 242
Tovey, Donald Francis, ix, 3

[328]

INDEX

Transmission of sound, 23
Trendelenburg, Ferdinand, 38, 59
Tronnier, Richard, 112
Tune and melody, 161
Tuning, theories of, 34
Tyndall, John, 44, 59
Types:
aesthetic, 133, 150
formation of, 122

U

Uhlemann, 272
Ursprung, Otto, 286

V

Value:
aesthetic, 123 f., 146-149, 249
direct and indirect, 147-149
historical, 249
Van Briessen, 102
Van de Wall, Willem, 215
Vannes, René, 305
Velocity of sound, 25
Vibrato, 73, 79
Victoria, Tomás Luis de, 312
Vidor, Martha, 102, 112
Virolleaud, Ch., 274 f., 276
Vocables, 29
Vocal music, teaching of, 199-201
Vogel, Emil, 311
Volbach, Fritz, 6, 16
Volume, tonal, 80

W

Wagner, Peter, 16, 285
Wagner, Richard, 54, 114, 149, 203
Wallace, Ruth, 303
Wallaschek, Richard, 242
Watson, Floyd R., 25, 59
Watt, Henry J., 64, 80, 84, 91, 112, 181
Watt, James, 292
Waves:
length of, 24
motion of, 23

Waves (*Cont.*)
standing transverse, 41
traveling, 41
Weber, Walter, 56
Weber-Fechner law, 74 ff.
Weil, H., 277 f.
Wellesz, Egon, ix, 3 f., 6, 17, 184, 242
Wellman, 100
Wessely, Carl, 277-279
Westphal, Rudolf, 4, 277, 279, 284
White, Harvey E., 36, 59
Whitney, Frederick Lamson, 215
Wier, Albert E., 305
Wilkinson, 272
Williams, C. F. Abdy, 285
Williams, Harold M., 223, 242
Wind instruments, 43-51
effect of temperature on, 25
Winnington-Ingram, R. P., 278, 285
Witchell, Charles A., 243
Wolf, Johannes, 308
Wolffheim, Werner, 303
Wood, A. B., 59
Wood, Alexander, 59
Woods, Elizabeth Robinson, 154
Wood-wind instruments, 46-48
Woodworth, Robert S., 68 f., 73, 81 f., 92, 95 f., 112, 133, 205
Woollett, Henry, 184
Wundt, 95

X

Xylophone, 30

Y

Yasser, Joseph, 157, 180, 183
Yearbooks, 309 f.

Z

Zahm, John A., 59
Zarlino, 171
Ziehn, Bernhard, 183
Zulauf, Max, 183